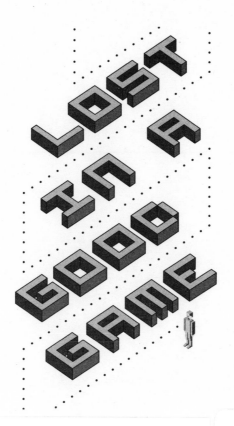

SHANNON STAUB
PUBLIC LIBRARY

4675 CAREER LANE
NORTH PORT, FL 34286

D1160499

31969026969443

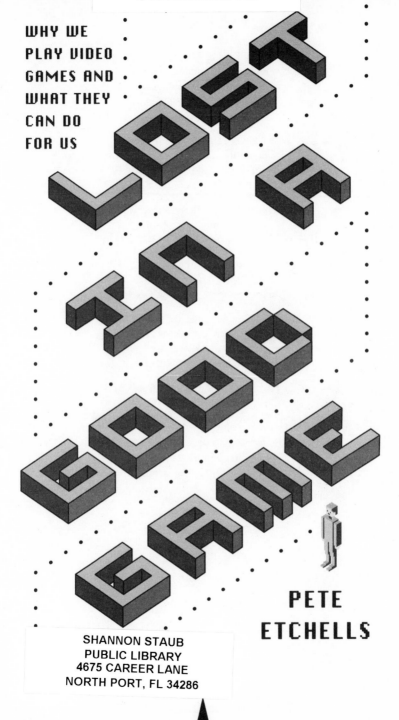

WHY WE
PLAY VIDEO
GAMES AND
WHAT THEY
CAN DO
FOR US

LOST IN A GOOD GAME

PETE ETCHELLS

SHANNON STAUB
PUBLIC LIBRARY
4675 CAREER LANE
NORTH PORT, FL 34286

ICON

Published in the UK in 2019
by Icon Books Ltd, Omnibus Business Centre,
39–41 North Road, London N7 9DP
email: info@iconbooks.com
www.iconbooks.com

Sold in the UK, Europe and Asia
by Faber & Faber Ltd, Bloomsbury House,
74–77 Great Russell Street,
London WC1B 3DA or their agents

Distributed in the UK, Europe and Asia
by Grantham Book Services,
Trent Road, Grantham NG31 7XQ

Distributed in the USA
by Publishers Group West,
1700 Fourth Street, Berkeley, CA 94710

Distributed in Australia and New Zealand
by Allen & Unwin Pty Ltd,
PO Box 8500, 83 Alexander Street,
Crows Nest, NSW 2065

Distributed in South Africa
by Jonathan Ball, Office B4, The District,
41 Sir Lowry Road, Woodstock 7925

Distributed in India by Penguin Books India,
7th Floor, Infinity Tower – C, DLF Cyber City,
Gurgaon 122002, Haryana

Distributed in Canada by Publishers Group Canada,
76 Stafford Street, Unit 300
Toronto, Ontario M6J 2S1

ISBN: 978-178578-481-1

Text copyright © 2019 Pete Etchells

The author has asserted his moral rights.

No part of this book may be reproduced in any form, or by any
means, without prior permission in writing from the publisher.

Typeset in Warnock by Marie Doherty

Printed and bound in Great Britain
by Clays Ltd, Elcograf S.p.A.

For Malcolm

Contents

Prologue

In your pocket, in your bag, on your desk, there is a window onto the entirety of human knowledge and understanding. For the vast majority of us, screens are now an inseparable part of everyday life. They connect us to our friends and family and bring us together with strangers. They are our work, our play – an inspiration and a source of distraction. And yet, despite their ubiquity, despite their familiarity, for many people screens are something to be wary – even scared – of. There are some scientists and intellectuals who will go so far as to say that screens are changing the way our brains work (which is true), and that this is a bad thing (which is false).

Using screens does change the way our brains work, but this is not an interesting point to make, because *everything* that you do changes your brain. Reading these words, right now – whether on a screen or on a page – is modifying the way that neurons connect to each other inside your head. That's what happens every time we learn new things, make new memories, and remember old ones. The interesting question is: *how* do things change your brain? And, as far as the fledgling science of screens is concerned, the answer is complex, nuanced and woefully incomplete.

Nevertheless, spending lots of time parked in front of a computer or smartphone doesn't seem to feel right on an almost instinctual level. This dissonance, between what we feel from past experience, and what we know from current scientific research, might go some way towards explaining the culture war that is currently being waged against screens in general, and video games in particular.

Here's an example of what I mean. If I ask you to think of a stereotypical gamer, who comes to mind? The chances are that you'll conjure up an image of a lone teenage boy with skin so pale it's near-translucent, bathed in the blue-white glow of a computer monitor in a darkened bedroom, playing a shooter game – something like *Call of Duty*, or *Fortnite*, or *Overwatch*. And something about that scenario feels unhealthy and unnatural. If you have that image in mind, and someone comes along and announces that we should be encouraging kids to go and play outside more, mere common sense dictates that it would be silly for us to argue against such a position.

What little scientific evidence is available so far seems to suggest that it isn't a zero-sum game, though – less time spent outdoors doesn't simply correlate with more time spent playing video games. And on top of that, this is a false dichotomy, balanced precariously on a poor understanding of who actually plays video games. It turns out that the demographics of gamers plays counter to our common (mis)conceptions. According to the Interactive Software Federation of Europe, across all age groups there are approximately equal numbers of men and women playing games. And perhaps more surprisingly, adults aged 45 and up are more likely to play than children aged six to fourteen.

There is an unspoken assumption here, of course: that while playing outdoors is a wholesome and healthy activity, playing video games is at best a meaningless waste of time, and at worst an unprecedented health risk. But the reality of the situation is far more complex. Video games are a creative medium, and they offer us unparalleled opportunities for exploring what it means to be human. Certainly, there is potential for them to be misused and abused. But they also offer us new ways to explore the world around us, our thoughts and feelings, our demons and aspirations. And of course, playing outside isn't without its own risk, be it from air pollution, traffic on our roads, or ever-increasing concerns about 'stranger danger'. The rose-tinted view that it is wholesome and healthy often seems to spring from a rather privileged assumption that 'outside' means 'in the countryside'.

There are many different ways to understand video games. One of them is by looking at why we play. What is it that makes some of us want to spend time in those worlds? Different people play different games for different reasons. This is a book that will uncover those reasons and consider the effects that they have on us: as a society, as well as at a personal level.

But I also want to take a grander view of the history of games and look at their relationship with science. Video games were, of course, a product of scientific development; but now they themselves are starting to feed that very development. Science and gaming are locked together in a symbiotic relationship. Through examining that symbiosis I want to uncover a natural history of video games – a sense of where they came from, and how they have changed over the years.

Though I'll try to maintain objectivity – certainly as far as the scientific research into the effects of gaming on the human brain go – I ought to come clean and say that my own engagement in this field began for personal reasons. As far as my own relationship with video games goes, the story is a complicated one.

And, like many things, it starts with an end.

CHAPTER 1

Dragons and demons

There's a landscape, not all that far away from here, that over the years I have come to know in intimate detail. It's a frigid, desolate place where snow-crusted mountaintops give way to ravines scattered with pockets of hardened civilisation. To the east of where I'm camping, the sharp, rocky heads of a mountain range climb towards a purple and stormy sky. Far below, I can just about make out a frozen stretch of water, lined by trees that look, from this distance, like cake decorations dusted with icing sugar. I stare off into the fog. I'm in a dangerous place, but it's one that I have come to associate with a certain serenity. It's peaceful here. Quiet.

I'm waiting for dragons.

Back in my room, I pulled my legs up onto the chair, and reached for a mug of coffee as a lightning storm played out in the distance on the screen in front of me. The mug had been empty for several hours now, and I was left with only a drying brown halo of silt at the bottom. It was late, and I was tired, but I couldn't sleep. I was in the first year of my PhD, but it wasn't work that was bothering me. Today was an anniversary. I blinked as I carefully studied the screen.

No dragons yet.

It wasn't just any dragon I was looking for. This particular one lived up to its epithet. 'The Time-Lost Proto Drake'. What a name! In my mind, it evoked an image of an ancient monstrosity with vast wings of torn and mouldering yellow leather. But the name carried a double meaning – it was also one of the hardest things to find in *World of Warcraft*. You might spend weeks, months – even years, God forbid – tracing a path around the mountains in search of it, and only come across tantalising flecks of evidence reminding you that it's there, but just out of reach; perhaps the old corpse of an instance of the beast that someone else got to first. Or you might be one of the infuriating ones, the lucky bastards who claim that they just 'happened across it' without even trying. A random-number generator masquerading as good fortune, or karma for that rare weapon you didn't receive after killing that dungeon boss* last week. It was somewhere in this snowy landscape, an area called the Storm Peaks, and I was hoping I would be one of the lucky ones. It didn't look like it was going to turn out that way though – this time around I'd been sitting there for over an hour, and so far, nothing.

In a way, I didn't really care whether I actually saw the damn thing or not. This was all about distraction. I was imagining what it would be really like, sheltering on that ledge at the top of this rich fantasy world, watching other players fly by on gryphons, wyverns, and levitating mechanical heads. Trying to imagine what the dramatic storms overhead would actually sound like, feel like. Smell like. Some people get lost in a good book. I get lost in a good game. A message popped up in the chat window in the bottom corner of the screen. It was Dave, the leader of the small guild of which I was a member.

---

* 'Bosses' in video games are usually primary antagonists or significant enemies that the character has to overcome, most often at the end of a particular level or section. They tend to be much more powerful than your average computer-controlled enemy, and often require the player to use a specific strategy to overcome them.

'Seen it yet?'

'Not a chance,' I replied. 'Not really looking though.' His response flashed up after a moment. 'Wanna do a dungeon instead?' An invite to join a group popped up on my screen, and a few minutes later, we were off on an adventure someplace else to take down a monster and grab some loot. The Time-Lost Proto Drake would have to wait for another day.

World of Warcraft is one of the most – if not *the* most – successful 'massively multiplayer online' games, or MMOs, of all time. To the untrained eye, it's an archetypal 'violent video game' – you create a character, grab a weapon, and jaunt off on various quests to smash things, ranging from fairly inno-cent low-level boars to terrifying Lovecraftian monstrosities. But the thing that gets lost in the overly-simplistic narratives you might see in the news about *World of Warcraft* being a violent game is that there's more than one way to play it. Some people like to create an array of different characters, just for the experience: elf druids, human warriors, dwarven hunters, zom-bie warlocks. Or, you can play it as a purely competitive team game – two factions, the Alliance and the Horde, square off in anything from strategic 'capture the flag' style matches to all-out brawls. Or you can play it in true role-playing style, develop a character with a rich and lengthy history, and spend your time acting out a story on the grandest of scales. Sometimes, you find players who approach the game in a completely pacifist way, levelling their characters up solely by harvesting flowers and mining for ore. Other people devote the majority of their time to collecting riding mounts – animals like the Time-Lost Proto Drake that you can use to travel around the world. There are hundreds of them. I once spent three weeks – *three weeks* – wandering around a tiny mine in a distant corner of the game, collecting randomly-spawning eggs, just so that I could claim a Netherwing Drake mount. It became an obsession, and was completely worth the effort. The first time I took to the skies on it, it was beautiful – wings of iridescent purple that spanned the entire width of the screen made it difficult to see where I was flying, but I thought that it was a wonder to behold. It still takes pride of place in the ranking of my zoo's worth of rides. In short, to simply call *World of Warcraft* a violent game is to miss the innumerable experiences that it has to offer.

This sense of freedom probably explains some of *World of Warcraft*'s runaway success. Video games like this provide us with the opportunity to experience the world (as well as other worlds) in a way that no other form of media really comes close to, in part because they are an inherently personal experience. In a 2013 radio essay coinciding with the centenary of Albert Camus' birth, Naomi Alderman, the novelist and games designer, elaborates on why: 'While all art forms can elicit powerful emotions,' she says, 'only games can make their audience feel the emotion of agency. A novel can make you feel sad, but only a game can make you feel guilty for your actions. A play can make you feel joyful, but only a game can make you feel proud of yourself. A movie can make you feel angry with a traitor, but only a game can make you feel personally betrayed.'

Alderman is talking about how games embody the principles of existentialism. Just as philosophers like Camus or Sartre suggested that, in a universe from which God has departed, we define our own meaning in life (that we are nothing but that which we make of ourselves) so too do games force us to define ourselves via a series of choices, to make decisions in order to achieve something; anything. MMOs like *World of Warcraft* encapsulate this idea beautifully. There *is* an overarching storyline, but you're not required to participate in it if you don't want to. It's not a linear game. You're free to do as much or as little as you choose – and from the point of view of the individual player, the possibilities are endless.

There are all sorts of reasons why people play video games, and there are all sorts of people who play them. Over the course of this book, I'll explore these reasons and the scientific research that's gone into understanding them. I should say at this point, though, that the scientific research comes with some heavy caveats. Video games research is only a budding area of science, sitting largely within psychology, which is itself still a relatively young discipline when compared to some of the 'harder' sciences like physics or chemistry. It's made all the more complicated by two facts: firstly, technology develops at a faster rate than research can be conducted, which means that the methods used to study video games are often contentious. The second is that people are messy. Running psychological studies that involve human participants doing anything (let alone playing video games) is *hard*. They do things that you never anticipated: things that can break your experiments. They try to give you the answer they think you want. Some of the more annoying ones try to give you the answer they think you *don't* want. And all of this put together means that there are as yet no universal or conclusive truths about what researchers do or do not know about the effects that video games have on us, or why people play them. Sorry to disappoint you so early on, but I promise that digging deeper into this state of affairs will give you a pretty good understanding of where we're at in terms of the current state of psychological science. And hopefully, along the way, I'll be able to dispel a few myths about the effects of games – and technology in general – that might make you worry less over some of the more hysterical headlines in the news about society as we know it being destroyed by your smartphone, or by Instagram-saturated millennials, or by whichever video game people are taking exception to this particular week.

Anyway, as I say, there is a plethora of reasons why people get into gaming. Some play purely to interact with other people. Some simply enjoy the level of escapism offered by complex and multifaceted digital worlds. Fundamentally, whatever our reasons for playing them, video games afford us a chance to learn something different, to explore somewhere new, and, potentially, find out something about ourselves. Reinforcing this point, Naomi Alderman suggests that 'the game is the only form that actually places the audience on that existentialist stage, where we're all forced to find out who we really are.' In that sense, video game play is one of the most fundamentally important activities we can take part in.

For me though, there was a simpler reason that I was playing *Warcraft* that night, looking for that elusive dragon. I was playing to distract myself from the anniversary of my dad's death.

When I think back to that day, I remember conflicting details. It's like someone has taken an old jigsaw, removed half of the pieces, and thrown some other bits in from another set. The pieces look similar, the sky is the same shade of blue, and they almost fit – but not quite. That day, both of us ended up in hospital for different reasons. In the afternoon, I'd managed to injure my ankle playing football – gamer clichés aside, I've never been a natural athlete. I somehow made it back to my school's main building, which was some walk (or in this case, hobble) from the football pitch, and one of my teachers tried to phone my dad. Someone came to pick me up and take me to hospital – my mum, I think, though my grandad must have been there too because I remember him looking ashen with worry. I remember thinking it odd that he would be so upset about something as trivial as a sprained ankle.

My mum drove me back home after my ankle had been patched up, and I remember my nan calling me on a black-brick-monstrosity of a mobile phone: 'Peter, your father's died.' Sprawled out on the back seat of the car, I started so much that I kicked the door with my duff foot. As it turned out, I'd misheard, but the real news wasn't much better. Not dead. *Dying*. For the past two years, my dad had been slowly succumbing to the tidal onslaught of motor neurone disease. That morning, he'd taken a turn for the worst, and he was on his way to the very hospital I'd just spent the last four hours in. As the phone call ended, I saw an ambulance drive past, and hoped it was a coincidence.

Later, I'm at the hospital. There's a family room; that's where my mum, grandparents, my auntie and my uncle are. They're arguing over silly little things, like who the doctor should be explaining the situation to. My dad's in the next room over, on a ventilator, with strips of white tape covering his eyes. He's not responsive. For the most part, neither am I. I'm just sitting there, in a wheelchair, alone in the corridor, looking and feeling a bit pathetic. As the argument starts, I quietly wheel myself out of the room to get away from the noise. Being lost with my own thoughts out here isn't much better though. Why were they fighting? And what could anyone possibly hope to gain from being told what was going on? It was simple really: my dad's dying, and he shouldn't be. He's only 45. We should be at home, having dinner, or watching a movie, or doing something, *anything* else. Anywhere but here. At some point, the doctor came and spoke to me, but the words didn't really penetrate the cocoon of disbelief I'd wrapped myself in. At another point, he wheeled me into my dad's room, so I could say goodbye.

Death in the virtual reality of a video game is an odd sort of thing. One life might end, but then time rewinds ever so slightly, and another alternative continuity pops up. (Interestingly, some physicists believe that the universe may actually work like this; that for every decision we make, a real alternative history branches away from us, another universe in which we made the opposite decision, or succeeded instead of failed, or got a negative result on that test instead of a positive one.) Each time, a new world opens up: one where you didn't accidentally fall into a massive hole, or trigger a trap, or get shot by a sniper. I think that's part of the reason why I like them so much – you get another chance. In a sense, death is robbed of its terrifying power. It's not the inevitable end that we must all face at some point in our existence; instead, it's a minor inconvenience. It's a way of being told that you screwed up, pressed the wrong button. Ultimately, it's all about failure.

People worry that games are melting our brains, or that they are turning generations of kids into social zombies, incapable of stringing a coherent sentence together in the name of enjoyable conversation. For a time, I wondered, too, if playing games to escape death was a bad thing. I worried that reinforcing this idea – that dying in a video game is, at its core, a commentary on failure – would make it spill over into the real world in some way. That I would start thinking that death is just about some sort of deficiency. Or, that it would somehow interrupt one of the stages of grief. Everyone knows them: denial, anger, bargaining, depression, acceptance. Maybe games override that last one. If you can delude yourself that death doesn't really happen, that there's always another chance, then you can never really accept when someone you love has truly gone forever. That's probably a bad thing, right?

We all know this, deep down, but it doesn't hurt to say it out loud: all that stuff about five universal stages of grief is a load of bollocks. The original idea came about in the 1960s as the brainchild of a Swiss psychiatrist, Elisabeth Kübler-Ross, who developed the model after working with a number of terminally-ill patients. If you look at the scientific research literature, there's not much to back up the idea that people go through some sort of standardised or predictable pattern of dealing with loss. There's never been a study that's shown that these rigid stages of grief actually exist. Our emotions just aren't granular or consistent in that way. Instead, whenever it lurches into our lives, I feel that death has a tendency to throw us into uncertainty: as a way of removing any pretentiousness or psychological veneers with which we might protect ourselves. The heuristics that we use to navigate through day-to-day life fall away, and we must truly and honestly respond to a situation that presents us with what seems like the most terrible of unknowns. In fact, everyone responds to bad news differently. So, rather than vying with the process of grieving for someone lost to the ravages of time, perhaps playing video games instead offers a way to deal with a situation that often seems to escape understanding, that defies any attempt at explanation. They might offer help with other things, too.

'Do you think it helps? Do they draw people in?' I ask.

I'm sitting in a stark, cream-coloured conference room somewhere in the heart of the National Exhibition Centre in Birmingham. On the far side of the room is a table laden with coffee, tea and biscuits, and as I sit on some hastily rearranged blue conference chairs next to Johnny Chiodini, a quiet stream of sleepy passers-by idle past us in search of caffeine.

'I think it doesn't so much draw people in, as it's there for the people who already know', he explains. 'People who use games as a support mechanism do it because they've already been doing it, maybe without realising.'

Johnny Chiodini is the senior video producer for EuroGamer. net, a website which hosts articles and videos covering all aspects of video games journalism, from reviews through to features about games design, industry issues, and more. We began talking to each other on Twitter a couple of years previously, after he started a series of videos for the website, called Low Batteries, where he delivers a spoken essay set to scenes from various video games. Meeting him for the first time in person, I fully expected him to be a hardened, grizzled broadcast veteran with no time for stupid questions. Instead, he couldn't have been more welcoming or amiable – someone with a genuine, infectious enthusiasm for video games, who could speak with equal ease about mental health. Which makes sense, really, because Low Batteries looks specifically at how the two interact with each other, with episodes covering topics such as how PTSD is portrayed in games, how the tired old trope of psychiatric units being a hotbed of horror is perpetuated in them, or how games are used by many as a coping mechanism for dealing with anxiety and depression.

'I was going through a really bad period with depression. I'd been low for a couple of weeks and I was just trying to push through it,' he explains. At the time, the Eurogamer video team were still very much finding their feet. Whereas nowadays they sit down on a Monday, plan out the entire week and have a clear idea what they're producing each day, a few years earlier, Johnny explains, they were flying by the seat of their pants. 'It was about 2pm and I'd done nothing,' he says, 'So I went for a shower to try and clear my head a bit, and I thought to myself "if I'm feeling so shitty and it's all I can focus on, I might as well talk about it".' He came up with the name of the show in the shower, and the script just started falling out of him. The first episode was all done in one draft; it was quickly recorded and edited, and launched online. 'I didn't tell anyone I was doing it. Luckily, the feedback was just lovely. It really resonated with people.'

Talking about mental health online – never mind talking about *your own* mental health – has always been a risky business. It's obviously a sensitive issue and, perhaps because of that, the chances are good that there will always be someone ready to pick a fight with you online, which can hurt even more if you end up getting trolled. So I was surprised to hear that the reception for Low Batteries had apparently been almost universally positive. 'It was really, really overwhelming. Actually, I think it was characterised by an *absence* of people telling us to shut the fuck up,' explains Johnny. For Eurogamer's videos, it's not always this way. 'We could be doing the most innocuous coverage and people will tell us we're awful and that we should die. But [for Low Batteries] there's just been a complete lack of people coming out the woodwork to tell me I'm a dick. Which is refreshing.'

Perhaps one of the reasons that Low Batteries has been so well-received is that it bucks the trend, as far as online video or written content that tries to cross the mental health/video game divide goes. A lot of articles consist of experiential accounts about, for example, how playing *Doom* helped the writer with their depression, or how four weeks of *Skyrim* got them through a particularly difficult point in their lives. Not that I think there's anything wrong with this, but individual accounts dwelling on a specific moment in time can only go so far in helping others. Low Batteries instead tries to take the long view. Rather than a reactive, retrospective account, it is instead proactive – each video provides a starting point for a discussion that can be carried on in the comments section, almost like an open forum. What makes Low Batteries special is that it provides a place where people who share an immediate common interest (that is, video games) can get together and discuss the sort of mental health issues that are both featured in the videos, and which they themselves might be affected by (and a lot of other people besides). It's a nuance that often gets lost in the public narrative about video games, which can end up devolving into an argument about whether or not it's the games that are causing the mental health issues in the first place. Games can help people to process grief, stress – anything that you're going through. And yes, sometimes, they can become an all-consuming obsession – although the scientific evidence behind whether, and to what extent, we can become addicted to video games really isn't all that convincing. I'll talk about this in more detail later, but for the present purposes, the point is this: the discussion about video games shouldn't be black or white, all or none. It shouldn't be a debate where the only two positions we're able to take is either that they're perfectly fine and don't have any effect on us in any way, or that they're literally melting our brains. There is a vast grey area in between these two positions, and that's where the true effects of games lie. In embracing that idea, it's worth considering both the positive and negative experiences that games can afford us. Because in the end, games are imperfect things, made by (and for) imperfect beings. They are able to mirror and amplify both our foibles and virtues in ways that no other entertainment medium can possibly hope to emulate.

In *World of Warcraft*, in an area called Mulgore, there is a small village inhabited by 'Tauren', which are humanoid, cow-like characters. The village is surrounded by a grassy open plain, bordered on three sides by a narrow river. Sometimes, when the sun is setting over the hills in the distance, it's pleasant just to sit there and watch the world go by. A bridge spans the water, and as you enter the village, you might be greeted by an old rancher called Ahab Wheathoof, pinning a notice to the totemic archway that signals dry land. If you talk to the character, you'll be greeted with a simple quest – help him to find his beloved dog, Kyle. It doesn't take long to complete, and it isn't particularly taxing. When you finish it, nothing momentous happens. Ahab thanks you; you receive a token reward and carry on your way.

There's more to that story than a simple quest, though. Ahab, along with the mission to find his lost dog, was designed by an eleven-year-old boy called Ezra Phoenix Chatterton. Ezra was an avid *World of Warcraft* player who had the chance to visit the game developer Blizzard Entertainment's offices through the Make-A-Wish Foundation in 2007. During the visit, he recorded voiceover material for Ahab, and Kyle the missing pup was named after Ezra's own dog. He also got to design a new crossbow for the game, and his character became the world's first rider of a unique phoenix mount – a fitting touch, given his middle name.

Ezra died from a form of brain cancer in October 2008. After he had gone, droves of players made a pilgrimage to Mulgore to complete the quest that he'd designed. It was a simple homage, a way of dealing with a death that didn't make any sense. Afterwards, Blizzard renamed another character in the game after him – Ezra Wheathoof – a timeless memorial for players to find, talk to, and reflect on. We might have a finite amount of time on this earth, but video games allow us to live multiple lives in a countless number of ways. A decade after he died, this virtual backwater still contains an echo of the things that Ezra had thought about and loved, and that mattered to him. And in some ways our digital lives grant us a certain type of immortality – we might go, but the characters we play never really die. At least, not until the servers are switched off. Even then they remain latent, digital possibilities.

As in the everyday world, death in video games is something multifaceted, complex and uncertain. In the most basic, mechanistic sense, it serves as a learning tool; when our characters die, it's because we did something wrong. But we can fix that – we get another chance. There are no second chances in reality but, like games, perhaps death still acts as an opportunity for us to learn something about ourselves. Maybe death gives us a chance to find out who we really are. After all, the way we act in the face of oblivion is something that we can't prepare for; it's something that can only be experienced in that fleeting, indelible moment.

When the doctor closed the door to leave me alone with my dad, I didn't know what to say. I felt *embarrassed*, of all things. Like I was in some ridiculous TV show, and that if I dared to say anything out loud to this wonderful person, comatose in front of me, the walls would give way to reveal an audience in the throes of laughter: *What an idiot! He actually said something!* So I sat there, for a while, silently holding his hand. Eventually, I managed to croak out a few words. I told him I loved him, and that I didn't want him to go. He didn't respond. At some point later – seconds? Minutes? – I wheeled myself out of the room and into the empty corridor, sobbing silently. I never saw him again.

It's a memory that plays over and over in my mind, especially on the anniversary of his death. Time doesn't dampen it; it just seems to bring all of these feelings more acutely into focus. So sometimes, I play games to try to forget. It doesn't always work, though. A couple of hours after finishing the dungeon with Dave, I returned to the Storm Peaks, half-searching for the Time-Lost Proto Drake again. All those years later, I'd had more than enough time to think about what I should have actually said to my dad that night. All those years later, and I still had no understanding as to why I had felt so embarrassed. As I sat there, staring at the screen, I started to develop an increasingly grandiose script in my mind – all the things I should have said, and the way I should have said them to actually mean something. And maybe, if I'd said the right thing …

I thought I caught a flash of yellow flapping out in the distance: *That's the drake.* Leaning forward in my chair, I forced my character on to get a closer look, forgetting the precarious position that he was in on the mountaintop. He dropped off the ledge, flailing, unable to stop me from directing him towards a rocky death. The screen turned to shades of grey as I respawned in a nearby graveyard. *Fuck.* Pulled out of the increasingly hysterical re-run of that night in my mind, I revived my hapless digital self, logged out, and tried to get some sleep.

You never truly die in a video game, you know. You always get a second chance.

CHAPTER 2

A brief history of early video games

When I first booked an appointment to rifle through the Science Museum's collection of video games memorabilia, I fully expected to be deposited in a dusty old attic somewhere in South Kensington where I could get lost among ancient cardboard boxes and leather trunks. And while I'm sure that every museum must have an area like this, I instead find myself in the Dana Research Centre and Library, a state-of-the-art home for viewing the museum's archival collections. Clean, quiet and uncluttered, the library is what you would realistically expect somewhere you can examine rare and expensive scientific artefacts to look like. A window running the full left-hand side of the library looks out onto a grassy courtyard. Row upon row of wood-on-black-metal shelving houses decades of scientific ephemera. A student desperately clatters away at his keyboard on a communal desk, surrounded by dog-eared notebooks. I sit down at a workstation and glance over at the researcher opposite me. He's studying a rather old-looking, leather-bound handwritten book. To save it from being handled too much, it is nestled in a miniature desktop beanbag. It is, I suspect, the comfiest book in London. The reason for my being here, though, sits rather more unceremoniously in a beige envelope on the desk in front of me. The museum curator carefully takes the document out, places it on top of the envelope, and quietly leaves me to my own devices for the next couple of hours.

The document is a pale blue handbook that, despite the odd grubby-looking fingerprint on the spine and leading edge, is in remarkably good condition for paper that is nearly 70 years old. Emblazoned on the top half of the cover are the words FASTER THAN THOUGHT, followed by the title: THE FERRANTI NIMROD DIGITAL COMPUTER. On the bottom half, the price is displayed – one shilling and sixpence – along with the logo for the 1951 Festival of Britain. Nimrod is thought to be one of the earliest-known prototypes of a computer that could play games, and this document is all that remains of it. Built by the British electrical engineering firm Ferranti, Nimrod was designed to allow attendees of the Festival (a national exhibition that was an attempt to instil Britain with a sense of revitalisation and progress in the aftermath of the Second World War) a chance to play the mathematical game 'Nim', against a rudimentary artificial intelligence. Nim is an ancient strategy game and one, I think it is fair to say, that's fairly tedious. In the standard, real-world version of the game, two players start with a number of distinct heaps of objects – usually matches. On each turn, a player must remove a number of matches (it can be any number, but has to be at least one) from a single heap, and the aim of the game is to avoid being the player who has to take the last match. Nim is a game of some mathematical importance, but as an experience, well … Let's just say that I don't think it has much in terms of replayability value.

Nimrod used a bank of lights and a set of 32 buttons to represent the matches from the original game. Each button would switch an adjacent light off (the equivalent of removing a match from a heap), and the display was arranged into four evenly distributed rows, each corresponding to a heap of matches. In this version of the game, each 'heap' could contain a maximum of seven lights, with the eighth button giving players the option to remove the entire row. At the start of each game, a player (or demonstrator) first specified how many lights there were in each starting row by selecting between one and seven lights to be switched on. Once the display was set up, a player could then either battle a computer-controlled opponent, or watch as Nimrod simulated a game between two players. The computer was basically an advertisement: its entire purpose was to demonstrate the principles and possibilities that so-called 'automatic digital computers' could afford.

The machine itself was huge: twelve feet wide by five feet tall, with a depth of nine feet. As I read about it, my mind wanders a little and I try to imagine what it might have been like to be in the presence of something so new and alien. The accompanying handbook details how it worked and lays out the mathematical principles behind Nim, and it's an interesting example of early written science communication for the public. It does get a little dense in places: the latter half is devoted to explaining the mathematical principles behind the algorithms used by Nimrod, as well as the mathematically correct way to play the game in order to win. Nevertheless, while the aim of Nimrod was to showcase the potential power of computing to an audience who could not yet conceive of the reach that such machines would eventually have, the computer also did something else: it demonstrated that even at these early beginnings, science and video games enjoyed a certain kind of symbiosis, with each growing from the other. The first computer games – depending on your definition of what that means – were not created by commercial games studios. Instead they can, in part, trace their roots back to the computational advances that emerged during and just after the Second World War. Tucked away in the middle of the handbook is a brief section on why, when Nimrod was created, the engineers involved decided to make it play a simple game:

'It may appear that, in trying to make machines play games, we are wasting our time. This is not true, as the theory of games is extremely complex and a machine that can play a complex game can also be programmed to carry out very complex practical problems. It is interesting to note for example that the computation necessary to play Nim is very similar to that required to examine the economies of a country in which neither a state of monopoly nor of free trade exists.'

Nimrod's creators, it would seem, were taking great pains to stave off the view that they were developing something frivolous or inconsequential. Yes, at face value this was a simple game. But game theory – which, in a basic sense, involves using mathematical models to describe and predict how decision-making agents interact with each other – has important applications in fields such as economics, political science and biology. By implementing this type of mathematics (albeit in a rudimentary form), the broader aim of Nimrod was to show that the computational processes that powered the machine had practical value beyond its being a mere plaything. Nimrod was not the first iteration of a machine that could play a game; nor was it even the first iteration of a machine that could play Nim – although it was likely the first computerised version. A patent had been placed for an earlier, electromechanical 'Machine To Play Game Of Nim' on 26 April 1940 by a nuclear physicist, Edward Condon, and his colleagues Gereld Tawney and Willard Derr of the Westinghouse Electric Company. That machine was demonstrated to crowds at the New York World's Fair, which ran from April 1939 to October 1940. Throughout the 1940s, the first digital computers began to be developed, but the evolution of computers that could play games remained largely stagnant – other, darker things were preoccupying the idle hands of men. As part of an unpublished manifesto on artificial intelligence written in 1948, Alan Turing mused that games such as bridge, chess, poker and noughts and crosses would be ideal 'branches of thought for the machine to exercise its powers in'. He would go on to develop a chess simulation called *Turochamp* but this was never actually executed on a computer – instead Turing would resort to demonstrating in lectures how the programme would operate using pen and paper.

There are perhaps two other significant milestones that were reached in the history of video games in the late 1940s. The first was known as the 'cathode-ray tube amusement device' (CRTAD), and while not the most inspiring name for a gaming machine, it was arguably the first that incorporated the use of a real-time moving display to simulate a game. The device was patented on 14 December 1948 by Thomas Goldsmith Jr and Estle Ray Mann of Du Mont Laboratories, and where Nimrod can best be thought of as a computer game without a proper visual display, the CRTAD was really a game display without a computer – players could mechanically control a dot simulating an artillery shell to 'attack' targets represented by a piece of transparent plastic overlaid on the screen. The second milestone came in the form of a machine called Bertie the Brain, which debuted at the Canadian National Exhibition at the turn of the next decade, in August 1950. Built by the Canadian engineer Josef Kates of the company then known as Rogers Majestic, Bertie the Brain was a huge computer that allowed people to play a game of noughts and crosses on a static light display. While it didn't incorporate any of the types of moving visual units that would probably allow it to be defined as a true video game, it nevertheless provided the first recorded implementation of a computerised game, the sort that Turing and others had only previously theorised about.

This is an admittedly jolted history of the early days of computerised games, but it shows that it's quite difficult to hone in on an exact starting point. All of the machines I've talked about so far actualised a game in some way, but to call them 'video games' seems to be a little stretch of the terminology and imagination. All of these devices were produced, by and large, in isolation, for a specific (almost single-use) purpose, and they probably didn't have much influence on each other. Moreover, it is likely that the true 'last universal common ancestor', to borrow a phrase from evolutionary biology, was developed quietly in an unassuming university laboratory somewhere, discarded out of hand, and ultimately lost to the ravages of time. Nevertheless, the concepts behind these early machines would each, in their own little way, eventually pave a way through to what we would consider to be modern video games consoles.

After a couple of hours in the company of the Nimrod handbook, I make my way over to the Science Museum itself, dropping in through a back entrance. It's just after Easter, and the place is overrun with hordes of children, either on school trips, or under the watchful eye of parents looking for a way to spend the last few exhausting days remaining of the spring holiday. I head up to the second floor, push open a giant set of doors and descend into a scene of organised chaos. For the past three years, the Science Museum has hosted Power Up, a temporary exhibit of the last half-century of video games. Sprawled across a giant hallway is pretty much every popular games console that you can think of. Towards the centre of the room are sixteen Xboxes arranged in a circle and a group of children huddle around as a spectacular *Halo 3* multiplayer battle gets under way. A sign next to the area states that the game is recommended for children aged sixteen and over; none of these children meet that criterion, but all are apparently fine, all are having a brilliant time. Computers running *Minecraft* sit happily alongside a parent and child playing the original *Secret of Monkey Island*. Along the wall to my right is a living chronological timeline of consoles. It starts with a 1977 Binatone TV Master playing a cloned version of *Pong*, alongside a 1978 Atari VCS running a rather disjointed-looking imitation of *Pac-Man*. At the far end is the latest in gaming rigs – an Xbox One running *Burnout: Paradise*. As I wander along the line through the digital ages, I pause. A volunteer is patiently explaining to a small child how to load a game up on a 1982 ZX Spectrum, a console I had fleeting possession of in my younger years. I look on as the old, familiar multicoloured loading frame dances around a blank rectangle on the screen, while information is slowly drawn from the cassette tape. After what feels like an eternity, *Chequered Flag* by Psion Software – one of the first racing car simulators – finally appears, much to the disappointment of most of the onlookers. While it was a brilliant game of its time, the graphics now look horribly dated, with an uninviting dashboard showing a complex array of gauges and dials taking up the bottom half of the screen. Deep in the room, amid a sea of Mega Drives, Super Nintendos, BBC Micros and PlayStations, there's a VR area where people are getting the chance to play the latest version of *Battlezone*, the original of which is often considered to be one of the first virtual reality games (and one that I will come back to later).

I make my way back to the start of the timeline, sit down at the Binatone TV Master and try my hand at the version of *Pong* on offer. The on-screen paddle is controlled by a small orange box wired up to the main console, the joystick loosened by decades' worth of use. Moving the stick even slightly causes the paddle to dance frantically across the screen, making anything that resembles fine control of the game a distant possibility. It is an infuriating experience. But something else doesn't sit right with the prominence that the console has been given in this chronology. The TV Master originally launched in 1976, and it was by no means the first mass-produced games console to penetrate the home market – that honour belongs to the 1972 Magnavox Odyssey, conspicuous by its absence here. After a couple of attempts at the game, I give up, idly musing about why this console – one that I hadn't really come across before – was placed first in line, in this version of the history of video games. Despite this frustration, I left the Power Up exhibition with a sense of optimism about how games could bring people of all ages together, and a desire to see the original 1972 Odyssey in the flesh.

About a week or so after my trip to the Science Museum, I find myself in the middle of Nottingham's bustling city centre. The National Videogame Arcade* blends in so well with the rest of the shops and cafes in the centre that I almost walk straight past it. Arcades, for me at least, are fortresses of neon and noise, defiantly standing against the onslaught of decay in crumbling British seaside resorts. In other times and other places, they are something different – the mega-arcades of Japan and South Korea are worlds unto their own; digital theme parks built within acres of concrete and colour. But the National Videogame Arcade, or NVA, is something different. The outward-facing

---

* Some months after my visit, the National Videogame Arcade shut down operations in Nottingham and moved to a new home in Sheffield.

facade is quietly serious, almost museum-like in appearance. This is not accidental.

As I walk in, I immediately get a warm, welcoming feeling in the pit of my stomach. It takes me a few moments to consciously realise why. Tucked in next to the entrance is a lone, matte-black arcade cabinet, playing the familiar bit-tone *wakka-wakka* sounds of *Pac-Man*. Billed as 'the first permanent cultural centre for video games' in the UK, the NVA is an idea that arose out of the GameCity Festival, which has been held annually in October since 2006. The NVA itself consists of four floors of interactive exhibits and video game displays, as well as hosting coding workshops, gaming competitions and tournaments, and talks throughout each month. The second floor is a maze of rooms housing every sort of game you can think of – from graphical adventures like 1983's *The Dark Crystal* through to *Rock Band* and one of my own childhood favourites, the *Teenage Mutant Ninja Turtles* arcade game. I have very happy memories of spending endless summers playing it on the north coast of Wales, in an unassuming little village near the surfing centre of Abersoch. My grandparents had an old holiday home there that I would visit with my parents for a few days at a time, but the slow crawl of youthful days felt like months. When the sun started to set on our days at the beach, we would retreat back to a tired little pub at the top of a nearby hill. In the beer garden was a miniature arcade – nothing more spectacular than a small, grey Portakabin, but one crammed full of the best arcade machines of the time. As my parents sat with a drink, I would alternate between playing a few rounds of *Turtles* or *Final Fight* and messing around in a makeshift adventure play area that would likely be a modern-day health and safety nightmare. Returning to things that you once loved in your childhood can be a precarious business – happy memories of games you played when you were young can often be tarnished when viewed again through the jaded eyes of an adult. Happily, this does not happen with *Turtles*. As I stand there playing it in the NVA, I still get the familiar excitement that I did when I was seven years old. I don't remember having seen the game through to completion at the time, which strikes me as odd now, since the entire experience only takes about twenty minutes from start to finish – although it probably helps that it's free to play in the NVA, and that this time I can burn through about 50 lives in the process. As I finish off the last boss, the leaderboard appears on the screen, and with a secret sense of pride – my score is top of the rankings – I enter my initials. I check my watch. I still have a bit of free time. I start playing again, but this time I don't pay so much attention to the game. The background noise of the arcade behind gives way and I become enshrouded in memories, like I've been transported to that Portakabin again, from all those years ago. For a second, I imagine hearing my dad calling for me to come and join everyone for a spot of dinner. Playing that game, feeling the joystick and the buttons under my hands, is a visceral experience – much like when a long-forgotten aroma hits your nose and triggers the memory of your first love, or your favourite holiday. Pulling myself away from my thoughts, and the game, I check my watch and head up to the third floor to find the real reason I'm here today.

In a glass case in a quiet room upstairs at the NVA, above the revelry of the arcade, sits an original, pristine Magnavox Odyssey. It was developed in the 1970s by the inventor Ralph Baer, one of many people who lay claim to the accolade: 'father of video games' (and perhaps the one who has the most right to the title). Born in Germany in 1922, Baer left the country just before the onset of the Second World War to join the United States' war effort. Later on, he would join the defence contractor Sanders Associates as an electronic engineer, where he remained from 1956 until 1987. It was during this time that he started to develop the idea of a home games console, coming up with a series of prototypes in the late 1960s that would culminate in the first mass-market console in May 1972.

Baer was meticulous in his design efforts. In his 2005 book *Videogames: In the Beginning*, he outlines the series of incremental experiments that he conducted in the late 1960s, complete with handwritten schematics, which build up a picture of how the Odyssey was created. The first experiment had the simple (!) goal of developing a system to display a vertical line on-screen that could be manually controlled to move both horizontally and vertically. Progressive experiments added the ability for two players to control on-screen objects at the same time, right up to more complex paddle-and-ball games, colour displays, and even a schematic for a rudimentary light-gun game ('Objective: Point gun at spot displayed on TV set and develop logic-level output if trigger is pulled at same moment').* Admittedly, the final, commercial console – the Odyssey – appeared to roll back some of these more ambitious elements to deliver a relatively simple gaming experience (although the 'shooting gallery' game did come bundled with a light-gun peripheral controller, the first of its kind). The Odyssey couldn't display colour or transmit sound, and had only enough processing power to generate four objects on the television screen: a vertical line that could denote a boundary to split the screen into two halves, and three square dots. Two of the dots could be manipulated by brick-like wired

---

* Page 230, *Videogames: In the Beginning*

controllers, while the third was controlled by the machine. No power was left over to be able to generate the basic quality-of-life information that seems to be second-nature in games nowadays. There was no score counter or countdown timer, nor was there anything in the way of background graphics. Instead, the Odyssey shipped with dice and pencil and paper for keeping score and deciding who would go first, as well as a series of plastic overlays. These were colour transparencies that could be attached to a television screen in order to turn the scene into, say, a hockey pitch or a football field. It was almost as if the Odyssey served as a bridge between more traditional tabletop board games, and a new emerging breed of digital games consoles.

While seemingly simplistic, Baer's creation was revolutionary. It marked the first time that people could actually control the action on a television screen, compared to the more passive experience of watching a broadcast programme. I stare at the Odyssey, sitting almost majestically in its glass trophy cabinet. This is a masterpiece, the very reason that we have an Xbox, PlayStation or Nintendo sitting in our homes right now. And yet, I can't help but feel as though I haven't quite found the first video game machine yet. Clearly it took Baer years to develop, but that still leaves a substantial period of time between Nimrod (in the early 1950s) and the first home games system (in the early 1970s). In order to trace what happened in those intervening years, it's necessary to look back again at the symbiotic relationship between video games and science.

After the Festival of Britain in 1951, Nimrod was transported to the Berlin Industrial Show for the final three weeks of October that same year (although some accounts mention that it appeared at an event of the Society of Engineers in Toronto after Berlin). As with a number of machines of its time, the real purpose of Nimrod was never to function as a gaming device – it was created simply to demonstrate the principles behind computer science. And so the machine was eventually dismantled, and Ferranti moved on to other projects, never to return to the idea. But elsewhere in the UK and US throughout the early 1950s, other scientists were tinkering with the idea of games machines. In 1951 the mathematician and computer scientist Christopher Strachey, then a schoolmaster at Harrow, was introduced to a pilot version of the Automatic Computing Engine (ACE) – a computer based on Alan Turing's designs – at the National Physics Laboratory. To familiarise himself with the computer he wrote a software programme that could play a game of draughts – thought to be one of the first instances of a computer game to run on a machine that wasn't dedicated to that specific purpose. After a number of programming issues and problems with the hardware running at maximum capacity, Strachey finalised the game in 1952, on the encouragement of Turing himself. According to the video game historian Alexander Smith, talks given by Strachey inspired other scientists, such as IBM electrical engineer Arthur Samuel, to write similar programmes.

Another significant moment in gaming history came again in 1952, this time at the University of Cambridge. During the process of working towards a PhD in theoretical physics, a student called Alexander Shafto Douglas wrote software to run games of noughts and crosses on the university's landmark Electronic Delay Storage Automatic Calculator, or EDSAC computer. The programme was notable because it was the first time a computer game had included graphical output to a CRT display. But it wasn't until 1958 that a more complete first prototype of what could be considered to be a video game was made. That game was called *Tennis for Two*, and its creator was William Higinbotham.

Higinbotham is a well-known name in science, but not for his contribution to video games. A physicist by trade, in 1943 he began working at the Los Alamos National Laboratory, where he would eventually lead a team of electronic engineers who would develop the electronics systems for the first nuclear bomb. Later, and more importantly, he would become a founding and prominent member of the nuclear nonproliferation group, the Federation of Atomic Scientists. In 1947, he took up a job at the Brookhaven National Laboratory, where he was eventually promoted to Head of Instrumentation in the early 1950s. It was in this role that Higinbotham would inadvertently develop the first true video game prototype. Every autumn, the Brookhaven Laboratory would host a series of open days for the public. Guests would be invited to take a tour of the facilities, and staff would showcase some of the work that was going on via displays and exhibits. By most accounts, these were generally dry affairs: featuring static displays, but with some attempts here and there by the staff to make them more engaging. In 1958, in one such endeavour to make the visitor days a little more exciting, Higinbotham drew up plans to link up a computer to an oscilloscope: to showcase a simple game of tennis. Working alongside his colleague Robert Dvorak, the entire project took them just under a month from start to finish. *Tennis for Two* used a black oscilloscope screen to display an image of a tennis court viewed side-on – a long horizontal green line represented the court, with a short vertical line halfway to act as the net. The ball's movement was based on a system that had originally been designed to model missile trajectories, and players could direct the action with a controller consisting of a dial and button. The dial was used to select the angle at which to hit the ball, and the button started the volley. Modern recreations of the game show it to be remarkably realistic in terms of the physics used – much more so than later tennis-style games like *Pong*. The game was such a resounding success that Higinbotham brought it back again in 1959, this time with the ability to simulate different types of gravity: high-gravity tennis on Jupiter, or a low-gravity game on the Moon.

Although the idea never went any further, *Tennis for Two* was, in essence, a forerunner to multiplayer games arcade machines. Higinbotham wasn't particularly interested in laying claim to the title of 'father of modern video games' – by his own admission, he wanted to instead be remembered for his lifelong work in fighting the tide of nuclear armament that he himself, regrettably, had had a hand in. However, Ralph Baer was disparaging in his estimation of Higinbotham's contribution, and to be honest, I think he would be pretty pissed off with me for including *Tennis for Two* in any discussion of early video games. In his recounting of a series of lawsuits in the early 1980s concerning patent infringements on games based on the Odyssey's tennis-style games, Baer had this to say:

'Nintendo brought Willy Higginbotham's [sic] existence to the attention of the world by having him testify on their behalf during a lawsuit they laid on our lawyers and me, in an effort to void our patents and avoid having to pay up. If they hadn't trotted Mr. Higginbotham before Judge Sands in Federal District Court in New York in 1982, the myths of Higginbotham's game having been the "first video game" would never have gotten a start. A whole lot of negative nabobs would not now be bleating about Willy Higginbotham having "invented" video games. As it happened, he did nothing of the sort ... Higginbotham had invented a game. No question about that. But it wasn't a video game and it had nothing to do with playing games on the screen of a raster scan device such as a home TV set or monitor.'*

While Baer is perhaps a little heavy-handed in his description of Higinbotham's contribution,** he's probably right in some ways: *Tennis for Two*, like other games of the 1950s, was never intended for the mass market. By and large, they were single-shot demonstrations, which more often than not just served the purpose of demonstrating the technical capabilities of a *machine*, rather than the utility of developing games. Like I've already said, it's difficult to trace a perfect line from one game to another – in most cases, the early games of the 1950s were developed in isolation from each other. It wasn't until the 1960s that games started to move beyond the confines of the laboratories within which they were being created and housed. The game that began that proliferation was called *Space War!*

Space War! was created in 1962 by three members of the so-called 'Hingham Institute' – Wayne Wiitanen, Steve Russell and J. Martin Graetz. Although it sounds rather impressive, the Hingham Institute was simply how Wiitanen and Graetz referred to their apartment, which was located at number 8, Hingham Street. Accounts of the time differ slightly in terms of the jobs that the three had, but all were in some way affiliated with either Harvard University or its neighbouring institution, MIT. At that time, the Electrical Engineering Department at MIT had recently installed an early but important computer known as the PDP-1, and a number of student and researcher groups were itching to get stuck into programming on it.

---

*   Page 16/17, *Videogames: In the Beginning*
**   And of people like me. I've never been called a negative nabob before.

According to the video game historian Alexander Smith, it was over drinks one afternoon at the Hingham Institute (or to put it more simply, in their flat) that the idea for *SpaceWar!* was born, out of a simple passion for science fiction coupled with the general desire to do something fun with the PDP-1. After a few months of tinkering and developing code, the game itself was unveiled in May 1962 at MIT's Science Open House, an event held each year at the university for the public. *SpaceWar!* is a space combat game, in which players take control of two spaceships called 'the wedge' and 'the needle' (named, unsurprisingly, after their shapes). In the centre of the screen is a star, and the object of the game is to manoeuvre around the star's gravity well, so as not to collide with it, while simultaneously trying to shoot the other player's ship. The controls were relatively complex; players could rotate their ship in either direction, provide thrust, and shoot torpedoes. In later iterations, the ship could also jump to 'hyperspace', appearing randomly at a different point on the screen. It was a unique and innovative idea: whereas earlier games such as *Tennis for Two* and *Nimrod* had fairly obvious origins and inspirations, *SpaceWar!* instead was something new, spawned from the unconstrained imaginations of a group of sci-fi geeks. The game was a huge success, and the group would carry on developing it for a number of months after its initial public outing, generating a final version in September that same year. In May though, the same month that *SpaceWar!* was initially demonstrated, its co-creator Graetz presented the game at a conference of the Digital Equipment Computer Users' Society. It was here that copies of the game were provided to other computer programmers, and so began to spread across the country. Accounts vary about how quickly this happened, but certainly by the time that computers with CRT monitors started to become more commonplace towards the end of the decade, so too did *SpaceWar!* become more prolific. The concept of a transferable video game was born.

Running parallel to the developments in the world of computing, the late 1960s saw a rise in popularity of electro-mechanical, coin-operated arcade machines across the world. Based in part on the appeal of the more basic, pinball-style machines found in amusement parks in the 1920s and 30s, one of the key turning points was the release of the Sega (short for Service Games) arcade shooter *Periscope*, in 1966. Players would track cardboard cut-outs of ships set against a static ocean background. Their view was limited through a realistic-looking periscope housed at the front of the machine, and the aim of the game was to sink the ships by timing well-placed torpedoes, represented by a series of flashing lights placed on the surface between the player and the backdrop. Twenty-five cents would get you ten torpedoes (plus bonus shots if you got a perfect score). *Periscope* was an instant hit in Japan, and it was rolled out worldwide a year later.

In the latter half of the 1960s, little headway was made combining the concept of profit-making arcade machines with video games, because the costs of the computer hardware at the time were prohibitively expensive. The original PDP-1 (on which *SpaceWar!* was made) cost about $120,000, or close to $1 million in today's money, which left it strictly in the territory of academic labs. However towards the end of the decade, costs started to drop, and the idea of a monetisable video game arcade machine started to enter the realms of possibility. Inspired by games such as *Periscope*, and the proliferation of *SpaceWar!* during those years, a man called Nolan Bushnell started to develop an idea for a similar game that could be produced for a wider public audience. In 1971 he joined arcade game manufacturer Nutting Associates, who had previously tinkered with coin-operated games like *Computer Quiz* (an early forerunner of the pub quiz machines seen around the UK nowadays) in the late 1960s. The game that resulted from this partnership was called *Computer Space*, which while not a direct copy of *SpaceWar!* (likely due to the computational power needed), borrowed many of the elements of the game. Players control a spaceship as they try to shoot down two UFOs, while at the same time avoiding enemy fire. The arcade cabinet itself, which was designed by Bushnell, was fantastical in concept – promotional flyers for it at the time show an organic-looking thumb-shaped yellow box with a futuristic control unit protruding from the front. While *Computer Space* was a commercial success, Bushnell was disappointed with the number of units sold – allegedly only around 1,500 to 2,000 machines were shipped to distributors, and while they would end up in bars, airports and hotels around the country, the game didn't capture the imagination of punters as much as Bushnell would have liked. Nevertheless, the idea that video games could reasonably be developed into marketable arcade machines took hold, and in 1972 Bushnell left Nutting Associates to form his own company with his colleague Ted Daubney: Atari Incorporated.

It was around this time that Bushnell attended an early demonstration of Baer's Magnavox Odyssey. Inspired by the potential of the console, Bushnell tasked the team at Atari with creating a similar gaming experience – but based on coin-operated arcade machines. Coin-operated mechanical arcade games had been popular since the 1930s, but they had relatively limited mass-market appeal – partly because pinball machines were illegal in many US cities until well into the 1970s (spurred on by a belief that they involved no skill and were largely games of chance, and were thus a form of gambling). Games such as *Periscope* revived the arcade industry in the 1960s, but the idea of a *digital* arcade game was revolutionary. In 1972, the project led to the birth of the iconic *Pong*. Fundamentally a table tennis simulator, *Pong* was similar in concept to the game that had been released with the Magnavox Odyssey: a two-dimensional display showed two white paddles on either side of the screen, with a dotted line denoting the 'net' in the centre. Players could move the paddles up or down to hit a ball, represented by a small dot, back and forth. The first player to reach eleven points was the winner. *Pong* wasn't initially intended as a fully commercial product – by most accounts, Bushnell had simply tasked engineers with creating a tennis-like game (as seen on the Odyssey) as a training exercise. However, early prototypes of the game placed alongside pinball machines in bars in California proved to be a tremendous success with punters, likely due to their having an easier control system and more immediate playability than their predecessor, *Computer Space*. The official launch of *Pong* was in late 1972, and it started shipping worldwide a year later. In its wake, a number of clones would also start to appear from companies such as Midway and Allied Leisure.

Ralph Baer was not happy. Based on the fact that he had patents for the Odyssey's tennis-style game (which had predated the launch of *Pong*), as well as the fact that Bushnell was known to have seen the Odyssey in action prior to working on the game, Magnavox launched a successful lawsuit against Atari in 1974. Two years later, it would be settled out of court: Atari were given a licence to sell *Pong* in exchange for $1.5 million, with Magnavox gaining the rights to any technologies produced by Atari for a year afterwards. Magnavox would pursue further lawsuits against other companies, most notably Nintendo, which would continue into the 1980s. Baer was fairly bitter about both the affair and the settlement, arguing in *Videogames: In the Beginning* that Bushnell's apparently natural flair for publicity and promotion, coupled with Baer's own reluctance to engage in self-promotion, led him to feel as though his contribution to the birth of video games had been erased from the period – 'my reputation as the original inventor of video games was a no-show', as he put it.

Baer's rancorous focus on the idea that he was the sole originator of modern video games is understandable, but it denies a rich history of important developments prior to the creation of the Odyssey. It's true that both Baer and Bushnell made important contributions – if not *the most* important contributions, to their genesis, but they did so in different ways, and off the back of countless incremental developments in computational technology. Baer's landmark achievements came within the realm of home games consoles, whereas Bushnell was more concerned, initially, with the coin-operated arcade market. Both would have lasting impacts on video games still visible to this day, although in Bushnell's case not all of these were positive. In 2018, he was due to receive a lifetime achievement award at the annual Games Developers Conference, but this was cancelled after numerous people came forward to say that he pushed and promoted a particularly unsavoury sexist culture in his time at Atari. In terms of the technology though, both Baer and Bushnell's creations were necessarily based on the scientific advancements in computing in the 1940s and 50s. No single scientific study exists in isolation, and the early development of video games mirrors the progress of science. Each experiment is incremental, based on countless earlier studies that each provide a small piece of a larger, always incomplete puzzle. It's often the case that seemingly disparate strands of research can, eventually, come together in serendipitous ways to generate completely novel lines of inquiry, just as with video games. And while it's true that the early 1970s (and 1972 in particular) were a watershed time in terms of the birth of modern video gaming, the era also saw the release of something else that would shape the future landscape of video games. In 1974, the tabletop role-playing game *Dungeons & Dragons* was launched.

In both the UK and US, the two post-war decades saw a rise in popularity in a new type of hobby, known as 'wargaming'. Using carefully-crafted miniature figurines to represent different classes of troops, players would engage in a form of real-time strategising: commanding large armies in grandiose battles on tabletops adorned with fields, hills and lush forests. The hobby itself finds a deeper history arising out of more ancient strategy games: like chess and the Indian game Chaturanga, with a design for a more complex chess-like game called *Kriegsspiel* being developed in Prussia in the 1800s. These games fascinated a young American called Gary Gygax, who in the 1960s would form the International Federation of Wargamers: a consolidation of several pre-existing gaming clubs in the American Midwest, which for the next few years held annual conventions as well as publishing a magazine, *International Wargamer*, for players to share ideas and tactics. After losing his job as an insurance underwriter in 1970, Gygax would turn his attentions more fully to his passion for wargames, initially creating a medieval tactical combat game called *Chainmail*. In collaboration with fellow wargamer Dave Arneson, Gygax would eventually develop what became known as *Dungeons & Dragons* – a fantasy-based tabletop role-playing game where, instead of controlling entire armies, players would control individual characters.

Dungeons & Dragons combined the rule-based combat of wargaming with improvisational character-based role playing. Players begin by creating a player character, or PC, with as much or as little back history as they wish. A character sheet is used to record the PC's vital statistics – things like strength, intelligence, charisma and dexterity – as well as their occupation (say, a wizard or a thief), species, and alignment (in other words, their moral outlook). A dungeon master, or DM, controls proceedings by concocting an elaborate storyline, explaining the setting to players, guiding them on an adventure, and playing the role of any incidental characters (non-player characters, or NPCs) they might encounter along the way. Players act out their own characters, with the choices they make having an impact on the story progression. Monsters or obstacles that the party comes across are tackled with the use of the character skills developed at the start of the game. The DM might allow trivial encounters (such as opening an unlocked door) to succeed automatically, whereas the outcome of more complex situations (for example, having one party member pick the lock to a gate while another player fends off an advancing horde of monsters) are resolved by the DM taking into account the PC's attributes and the difficulty of the situation, with an element of chance added by the roll of any number of polyhedral dice. Game sessions can last for hours, and are often returned to over multiple days or weeks, during which time PCs slowly accrue experience points and become more powerful.

Dungeons & Dragons was a sensational hit. While successive editions of the game added increasingly complex sets of rules, one of the major advantages that the game had over earlier, more traditional tabletop wargaming was that there was little need to invest in (or paint) a vast army of figurines if you wanted to play – all you needed was the rulebook, a few pieces of paper, some dice and a big imagination. Its popularity would have many influences on the course of video game development, and also gave rise to one of the first game-based moral panics of the 20th century. In the mid-1980s, fundamentalist conservative Christian groups in the US campaigned against the hobby, which they saw as promoting satanic worship, witchcraft and murder. This was spurred in part by events such as the 1980 suicide of seventeen-year-old James Dallas Egbert III, highlighted by (incorrect) media speculation that it was his involvement in playing *Dungeons & Dragons*, and in particular acting out game sessions in the steam tunnels beneath his school, that had caused him to lose touch with reality.* Similar moral panics would revolve around video games in the decades to come, and still show no signs of abating.

While I have my own reasons for arguing that the rise of tabletop RPGs led to a separate lineage in the history of video game development, I'm not the first to suggest the link. In *The Video Game Debate*, the gaming effects scholar Jimmy Ivory notes that the rise in popularity of *Dungeons & Dragons* in the first half of the 1970s directly inspired a new type of text-based computer game, starting with 1975's *Colossal Cave Adventure* which led to the very similar and seminal *Zork*, originally written in

---

* The reality of Egbert's death is much less sensational and much more heartbreaking. In his 1984 book *The Dungeon Master: The Disappearance of James Dallas Egbert III*, the private investigator William Dear instead cited problems with depression, drug abuse, loneliness (Egbert was a child prodigy who entered university at the age of sixteen) and struggles in coming to terms with his sexuality.

1977. Completely devoid of graphics, *Zork* (like *Colossal Cave Adventure* before it) instead had players exploring the game world by inputting commands such as 'look', 'examine', 'take', or 'hit'. The beauty of the game was not so much in the gameplay itself, but in the rich storytelling that took you, an unnamed explorer, on a grand adventure into the 'Great Underground Empire'. But the critical starting point for this parallel lineage in gaming history would come a year later. That year, in 1978, Roy Trubishaw and Richard Bartle, computer science students at the University of Essex in the UK, began to develop a game called *Multi-User Dungeon*, or *MUD* for short. *MUD* was utterly groundbreaking in concept – players could interact with each other at the same time, in the same text-based game world. They would begin by creating a character, in much the same way as a character sheet would be filled out at the start of a *Dungeons & Dragons* session. As they moved around the virtual world (for example, by using text commands such as 'North' or 'In' to enter rooms), typing commands to the MS-DOS-style screen such as 'who', would give you a list of who was playing at that particular time in that particular room. Players could then send each other messages that would either be visible only to a specific person (for example, typing 'Alice hello!' would result in a hello message just appearing for Alice), or to the entire room, or even to the entire game world. Combat, for example, could be initiated with commands such as 'Kill Bob with sword', with the fight being resolved in a similar manner to *Dungeons & Dragons* – via calculations based on a character's strength score, and other variables. Players could form groups to pool their respective powers and take on quests. Players, in fact, could largely do whatever they wanted to do, and completing quests allowed characters to develop and increase in power, with new weapons or new skills. Initially, the game was playable only over Essex University's internal intranet, but when that was connected to ARPANET (an early predecessor to what we now know as the internet) in 1980, *MUD* became the first multiplayer online role-playing game.

The idea exploded in popularity over the course of the next decade, and MUD would become a catch-all term for the new genre. As the number of games in this genre grew, so too did the number of variations, eventually, as Ivory notes, leading to a number of different acronyms. MUSHs, or Multi-User Shared Hallucinations, referred to games that concentrated most heavily on role playing with other users, whereas MOOs (MUD, Object-Oriented) were games that concentrated instead on manipulating the game environment in order to, say, create new rooms or objects for other players to use. Eventually, as computing and graphic processing power became cheaper and more prolific, later games based on the basic concept of *MUD* would incorporate graphical elements and increasingly complex ways in which players could interact with each other. In essence, a lineage can be traced from those early text-based games right up to modern-day massively multiplayer online RPGs such as *World of Warcraft* and *Runescape*, that sits largely in parallel with the evolution of the more action- and sport-orientated focus of home video games consoles throughout the 1980s, 90s and 2000s.

All of this is to say that the history of video games, and particularly the *early* history, is a tangle of multiple stories, developments and dead-ends of ideas. It's difficult, if not impossible, to trace one straight line from a single birth point right through to today's latest releases. In part, this is because 'video games' were never really clearly defined as a stable concept

– and this is still true today. In essence the term is meaningless, or at least it means whatever you want it to mean. My own definition would probably include *Tennis for Two* as one, whereas for Ralph Baer this was very definitively not the case. Your definition will probably be different again, and that's okay. But I think that it's important to understand that for as long as there have been video games, there have been attempts to define them, and so far it has been a fruitless endeavour. This has not come without consequences – the way video games are described has had important implications, both for how the effects that they can have on us is researched, as well as for the tone of public discourse about them. And perhaps just as important as understanding what video games are, is understanding why it is that we play them in the first place.

CHAPTER 3

Why do we play video games?

In September every year, tens of thousands of people descend on the National Exhibition Centre in Birmingham, UK, with a single common purpose. EGX is the UK's biggest annual trade fair for video games, giving people the chance to do anything from trying out the latest consoles, to playing some of the oldest games still around, to listening to talks from some of the industry's best-known developers about the future of gaming. It's an exhilarating and overwhelming experience.

I arrive early on the first day of the 2017 event, a Thursday. Already, hundreds of people are queuing up to play on the latest PlayStation consoles, or trying their hand at blockbuster games like *Call of Duty* or *Star Wars: Battlefront*, which isn't due for release for a few months to come. Over at one games stand, volunteers are firing t-shirts out into hungry crowds. In the middle, in a near-sea of quiet, is a retro gaming area, with the full swathe of historical games consoles attached to old cathode-ray tube monitors and televisions, sitting majestically in the dim light. I go straight to the very first computer I ever owned, an Atari ST, and sit for a while reminiscing in a game of *Treasure Island Dizzy*. It was always an infuriating game to play. You control 'Dizzy', an anthropomorphic egg, in a standard save-the-princess, collect-the-gold sort of scenario. The gameplay involved scouring the world for important objects and using them to solve puzzles that often required precisely-timed jumps to avoid traps, monsters or falls – or, if you played like me, expertly hitting everything you weren't supposed to.

As a young gamer, I didn't have a particularly successful relationship with games. I had a superb track record in *not* completing them: because I got to levels that I found too hard, or didn't understand the game mechanics, or in some cases, simply got scared. I suspect that it was a mentality that came from my life beyond games. By the time I was ten, I had, at various points, briefly tried to learn playing football, hockey, the piano, trombone, tenor horn, cornet, saxophone and the recorder, all with very limited success. I wasn't good at seeing things through to completion, which was something that some of my early teachers took great delight in telling me. I did see games as a pastime though, and looking back I find it strange that I similarly copped out of finishing them.

You might think it a little odd that I didn't complete some games because I got too scared. Let me explain that a little more with a tale concerning a sequence of events that happened sometime around the dying days of 1993. It's dark, and the only source of illumination in my room is the soft glow from my computer monitor, bathing me in light and throwing a shadowy apparition on the far wall behind me. I'm sitting at a Pentium computer, with a 75 MHz processor – grindingly slow by today's standards, but as far as I was concerned, for that brief moment some twenty years ago, state of the art – and I'm playing a game called *Blake Stone: Aliens of Gold*.

And I'm stuck.

There's a good chance that you've never heard of *Blake Stone*, which is a shame, because it was actually a pretty fun game. It was a first-person shooter, a predecessor to modern-day hits like *Halo* and *Call of Duty*. The reason you might never have heard of it is because it was released about a week before *Doom* came out, and although *Blake Stone* got rave reviews, it simply couldn't stand up to the monumental success that id Software's now-iconic game enjoyed. I've always thought that this was a minor tragedy, because although it was fairly derivative, the storyline to *Blake Stone* was nonetheless equal parts brilliant and ludicrous. You played the eponymous hero, a British Intelligence officer somewhat akin to a sci-fi, futuristic version of James Bond. And in typical Bond fashion, the basic premise is that you're on a top-secret mission to foil the world-domination plans of one Dr Pyrus Goldfire, a brilliant but ethically flawed biologist in command of an army of genetically modified aliens, mutants and run-of-the-mill human soldiers. The invasion only seems to be happening inside one particular building that you find yourself stuck in, and each level takes place on successive floors of the tower block. If you get to the top floor and kill the boss, you win. A simple idea, but it sort of makes you think that engineers have ended up making a lot of poor decisions in this future. The backstory tells you that humans have created a new planet on the edge of an asteroid belt in the solar system, yet despite these technological advances, we've not developed teleporters or any other means to traverse vertically through a building. Lifts are still very much in vogue. Come to think of it, it's never really explained why we lost the ability to use things like helicopters, which would be a much more efficient way to get to the boss. Or why we can't just use a gunship to shoot the top floor.

My memory is hazy, but I remember that on one of the levels, there was a room that acted like a gauntlet run. The door slides open, and there you are, greeted by a welcoming party of aliens, monsters and pink-suited space soldiers, making a beeline straight for you, laser guns in hand (or claw). Despite the pixelated, cartoon graphics, it was a pretty scary experience

– monstrous guards stalking towards you, growling 'YOU'RE DEAD!' in a far too matter-of-fact way. I was eleven years old, and I found it terrifying. So just as soon as I opened the door, I closed it again. I'd wander around the rest of the level, occasionally coming across the odd enemy straggler, and periodically go back to the door. A quick peek inside, and another brief moment of unbridled fear. I just couldn't go in there. So I became stuck, left to wander around the rest of the now-empty level, unable to take the next step. In a sense I was fine with that – I knew that there weren't going to be any nasty surprises around the next corner, because I'd already cleared everything up. It was safe. Boring, but safe. Going through the corridor seemed like a monumental challenge; too scary, and too difficult, and even though I really wanted to see what the next level was like, I just couldn't do it. Stuck at this impasse, I flicked off the monitor and went to bed. I told myself that something would change – tomorrow, or the day after, or the one after that – and I'd be able to finish the level.

Some days later, I was idly milling around my home on a pair of roller blades. I'd acquired a pair for my last birthday, and as with video games, I had a fear of failing in them. I'd happily stutter around the house wearing them, leaving tracks in the carpet, as if an intrepid-yet-incompetent arctic explorer had somehow lost his way in the front room of a north Derbyshire bungalow. But I only ever ventured outside in them once, and briefly. The banal danger of falling over on tarmac took some of the interest in using them away from me.*

---

* I also remember regularly wearing them when I was playing on the computer. It's probably fair to say that I didn't have many friends when I was a child.

My dad called me into the kitchen, and he used that tone that parents use when you're about to get told off. You know the one. For me, it's whenever someone calls me 'Peter' instead of 'Pete'. That's when I know I'm in trouble.

I sheepishly glided into the room (I use the term 'glide'; but the friction afforded by a deep pile carpet doesn't really lend itself to making roller-blading look effortless). I see my dad, leaning against the countertop, watching me with a sad smile.

'I need to talk to you about something,' he said. 'I've been having some tests done at the hospital.'

He explained why he was having the tests, that they had come back positive, and that he'd been diagnosed with a disease called motor neurone disease. A specific form of it, called progressive muscular atrophy. There was no cure.

Motor neurone disease (MND) is paradoxical in a way. On the one hand it's quite rare (only about two in 100,000 people get it), but on the other hand, loads of people know about it. High-profile celebrity figures who have had it, like Stephen Hawking, or Lou Gehrig, coupled with books like *Tuesdays with Morrie*, and events like the Ice Bucket Challenge, have engrained this curious and devastating disease in the public mind. The causes of MND aren't all that clear-cut; there seem to be some subtle genetic factors, and various studies have shown that prior exposure to a huge variety of environmental factors might possibly, maybe, contribute to the development of the disease (for example, smoking, or exposure to lead or pesticides have all been suggested). But there is no one single factor, and no convincing evidence that there is a consistent and definitive trigger. I could tell you lots more facts and numbers about MND, which are very interesting and object-ive and all that, but all that would do is to detract from the fact that it is a complete and utter shit of a disease.

Generally, it starts with problems like reduced dexterity in your hands or your feet. Thinking back, I remember very clearly some of the warning signs in my dad – although at the time, they were nothing really – just a bit of tiredness, that's all. If we played football outside, he'd get out of breath far too easily, and generally felt quite weak when he was kicking the ball. After the diagnosis, it very quickly meant that he couldn't run very far, and then he couldn't walk very far, and then he couldn't walk any more. That also meant that he could no longer drive his car and, given that his job required him to drive all over the place to survey houses, the disease very quickly put an end to his career. Later on, he found it tremendously difficult to move his arms. He loved to paint – watercolour landscapes, in particular – so there went that hobby. The heartbreaking thing about MND is that it takes away everything you love doing, but for about 50 per cent of people with it, cognitive functioning isn't affected. So, as it was with my dad, you can be just as bright, alert, interesting and interested on the last day as you are on the first.

I stared at him, not quite taking in the enormity of what he was telling me. I can't remember what my first thoughts or feelings were, but I don't think that they were much of anything really – it was such a huge, awful piece of news, it couldn't possibly have been true. The rest of the conversation is a blur, but I remember at some point it ended – it could have been five minutes or five hours later, and I went back to my room. I took off my roller blades, and sat there for a while, numb. At some point, I booted up *Blake Stone* again.

With almost zen-like effortlessness, I breezed through the level, and stopped by the door to the gauntlet room. It's not that I was ignoring the conversation that I'd just had with my dad, it's just that I couldn't really process it. Our brains are amazing, vastly complex organs, but sometimes they just need a bit of time to crunch through the data we're presented with. So we activate defence mechanisms that manifest themselves in all sorts of seemingly bizarre ways. For me, all of a sudden, I knew I had to finish that level. If I got overwhelmed by genetically-modified monster soldiers, I would pick myself up and try again. Nothing was going to stop me now. I would get through this. I opened the door and, guns blazing, ploughed through the room to the end of the level. Pixelated monsters on a computer screen? Suddenly they weren't so much of a problem any more. And as I made it to the end, a wave of excitement washed over me; I'd done it! Finally, after all this time, I was going to see the next level. I reach the lift, press the button, and ...

Nothing.

All of this time, I'd been playing a shareware version of *Blake Stone*. The level that I'd been stuck on for so long ... that was *it*. The only level I had left. I'd been wasting my time worrying over something that, really, didn't need worrying about at all – there were no more monsters to get scared of later down the line, because this *was* the end of the line. In that cold moment when that brief catharsis subsided, the enormity of what was really happening to me came crashing in. I guess, in a way, the relief of getting through the game forced a trickle of emotion that allowed me to start processing the important things that were going on around me. I spun around on my chair, and did the only thing that I could think of doing, the only thing that made sense. I went to find my dad, and I gave him a hug, and we cried for a while.

I don't get scared of games any more. I've gone from giving up on them too easily to becoming a completionist. The triumphant joy of seeing through a great story to the end – one in which you aren't simply a passive audience member, but where *you* are the centre of the story – is something that I find uniquely wonderful about video games. But, obviously, there are many reasons why people play them, and throughout the course of my travels for this book, it has always been the first question I ask when I talk to people. If you ask it enough, patterns start to emerge in the responses they give. Some play to escape, to switch off from a stressful day. Some play to enjoy the company of other people with a common interest. Some play for the love of competition. Most play because of a combination of these things, and more. Perhaps that's why games are so appealing – because they are able to offer something enticing and interesting to a wide range of people, all with very different internal desires or external motivations for wanting to play. But before I get into the actual scientific research that looks at why people play them, it's worth looking at the games from the perspective of the people who make them.

Perhaps more than any other group of people, developers have a rich insight into what motivates players to get lost in a good game. They are the creators, but they are also players themselves, and this dual outlook often allows them a richer understanding of which specific aspects of games make them so enticing. A couple of weeks after EGX, I sit down with Bill Roper, Chief Creative Officer at Improbable Games, former VP of Disney Interactive Studios, and a former senior developer at Blizzard Entertainment. For him, the reason that games draw us in is simple: they bring people together. Having worked on titles throughout the *Warcraft*, *StarCraft* and *Diablo* series, along with Disney's sandbox game* *Infinity*, Bill's work at Improbable now centres on building gaming systems and computational platforms that the next generation of online games will take advantage of. He bubbles over with enthusiasm when we start talking about what motivates gamers. 'There's a point in the development of every game where something happens, and it's that quintessential moment where suddenly everyone on the team goes: "Oh! That's it! This is the magic, the kernel of truth in the product we're making,"' he says. 'I remember this happening very clearly when we were working on the very first *Warcraft* games at Blizzard. It was simple, really – it was when two of our developers had our first game that was actually connected, so they were playing against each other.'

This happened around 1994, in a time before it was commonplace for people to link up to each other and play over the internet. Two Blizzard developers were sitting in their respective offices, their computers connected to each other over a local area network. 'They finished the match, they both came out of their offices, and they were both like "that was amazing!"' Bill recalls. 'They were both beating their chests, getting all worked up and super-excited over what had just happened.' Probably part of the reason they were so happy was that they both thought they had won – due to a synchronisation problem in the game, the match had finished with both sides erroneously claiming victory. But the underlying truth behind their excitement was that they knew there was another person on the other

---

* A sandbox game is one in which players aren't given a linear set of goals to progress through; instead they are provided with an open world that allows them free reign to explore, create things, or interact with other players in a largely unrestricted way.

end of the game, not just a computer AI. It was the social aspect, the connected experience that added real depth and meaning to the game. 'That's what people crave,' says Bill. 'You're putting them in incredibly rich and deep worlds, and making that time that they're investing less trivial to themselves and other people.'

It might seem like an obvious avenue for scientific enquiry, but a surprisingly small amount of research has been done on why it is that people play video games. Part of the reason is that, despite video games covering a near-infinite range of genres, themes and play styles, the vast majority of scientific research into them has fixated on whether *violent* video games have any impact on our behaviour in terms of things like aggression and depression. It is, in many ways, a missed opportunity, and a discussion that I'll come back to later in the book. Still, when it comes to the little research that has been done so far on player motivations, much of what *does* exist focusses on trying to categorise styles of gameplay or player attitudes. The vast majority of scientific papers on player style and attitudes find their origins in a seminal 1996 treatise by Richard Bartle. Bartle is credited as being one of the pioneers of the massively multiplayer online game genre, and the co-creator of one of the earliest virtual gaming worlds, the groundbreaking text-based game *MUD*, which was published in the late 1970s when he was at Essex University. Based on nearly twenty years of experience with *MUD* and its successors, Bartle argued that there were four types of *MUD* players – 'Achievers', 'Explorers', 'Socialisers' and 'Killers'. According to his classification, the main goal that 'Achievers' have in-game is to accumulate points, collect treasures, or level up their characters. 'Explorers' are more interested in simply finding out more about their virtual world. 'Socialisers' play to communicate with people they share a common interest with, and 'Killers' get their kicks from fighting other players and generally causing them a load of grief. The rest of Bartle's article is devoted to thinking about how these different play styles interact with each other, and critically, how developers might best balance each group within a given player population. It's a good read, but as Bartle himself is happy to point out, it's not a particularly scientific paper. The categorisations came out of online discussions with *MUD* players, but aren't otherwise based on any objective data. Nevertheless, Bartle's ideas were so influential that they formed the basis of further attempts to understand the nature of people who play games for years to come.

Perhaps the largest study of gamer archetypes was conducted by the social scientist Nick Yee in 2006. Building on Bartle's earlier work, Yee collected survey data from over 3,000 players of a number of different MMO games popular at the time: *EverQuest*, *Dark Age of Camelot*, *Ultima Online* and *Star Wars Galaxies*. Although simply a study looking at how players identified themselves within those games, Yee's work nevertheless developed a richer categorisation system. He argued there were three main categories of player motivation: 'achievement', 'socialisation' and 'immersion' – and that each had a number of subcomponents. The achievement category comprised further motivations to do with levelling up or acquiring in-game power and resources, as well as a drive for players to understand the underlying system mechanics that make a game work. It also comprised a subcategory revolving around competition – some gamers, according to Yee, are motivated to play games simply because they enjoy the experience of being pitted against other players (an aspect that is perhaps closest to the 'Killer' archetype that Bartle earlier identified in his classification of player motivations). The socialisation category incorporated subcomponents that relate to the various ways in which players can interact with each other. These include being drawn to games in order to find like-minded people and form either casual acquaintances or deep, meaningful friendships. It also included those who simply find satisfaction in working collaboratively with other players in organised teams. Finally, the immersion category consisted of motivations to do with exploring the virtual environments within games, getting engrossed in a good story through improvised role playing with other players, finding different ways to customise a character, and using games as a form of escape from real-life issues. Critically, where Bartle suggested that player archetypes were to a certain extent mutually exclusive, in Yee's analysis this was not the case. According to him, the reasons why people reported playing MMO games were varied and complex.

There's a problem with Yee's study, though. He used survey questions that were specifically based on Bartle's earlier work on player types, the risk here being that if you ask a particular question in a leading way, you will inadvertently get a biased answer. Here's an example. One of the questions in Yee's study was 'How important is it for you to level up as fast as possible?' The answers to that question will vary from 'a lot' to 'not at all'. The end result is a category of 'player motivation' that basically confirms that some people like levelling up and some don't. To all intents and purposes, this is like Bartle's 'Achiever' archetype, because the question was based solely on that archetype. In other words, it merely confirms the existence of an archetype that's already presumed to exist, rather than allowing for the possibility of hitherto unanticipated archetypes. The problem, then, is that because Bartle's work was *so* influential, everyone else has been using it as a starting point ever since. Pretty much every study, therefore, will come up with nothing more than some slight variation or elaboration on Bartle's original four categories. In 2014, Juho Hamari at the University of Tampere in Finland, and Janne Tuunanen at Aalto University School of Science, also in Finland, suggested just this. Taking a broad look at the research that was available on player types, they argued that work in the field was pretty uniform, with most studies converging on broadly the same motivations (broadly, Bartle's four archetypes, plus a fifth one, concerning immersion). They also noted their surprise that little or no mention was made in the research literature about either basic aesthetic enjoyment, or what they called 'utilitarian' motivations (in other words, playing games in order to earn a living). It is perhaps unsurprising that there has been no mention of this latter type of motivation in particular, as it has only been relatively recently that competitive gaming has become a legitimate form of earning, and scientific research tends to move at a glacial pace. At any rate, it's important to get this sort of research right. If not, there's a risk that this concept of a small number of basic gamer archetypes will become a self-perpetuating phenomenon. For example: say that a games developer hears about research claiming that there are X number of motivation factors as to why people play games. They might then use those findings to steer the content and mechanics of a games they're working on ('some gamers are "Explorers", so let's make sure we reward exploration!'), which in turn reinforces the fact that these archetypes exist. The risk, then, is for games to become too narrow in their scope, and for other motivations for playing them that are just as important to get crowded out.

In a sense, there's an argument here for a greater amount of interaction between researchers and developers. It's not simply enough for a scientist to run a study arguing that there are a certain amount of player types, and to then casually hand this information on to someone who is creating a game. Both scientist and developer might miss some of the motivations that actually enrich the play experience within a game's life cycle. Video game players are an intensely curious breed, often capable of coming up with their own creative methods of playing a game that might not be anticipated or even appreciated by those who originate them. When I spoke to the Improbable Games' Chief Creative Officer and industry veteran Bill Roper about this problem, he agreed, providing a practical example about why the relationship between games researchers and developers shouldn't end at the point at which a game is first conceived. 'I believe there's a strong case to have, at least in an advisory position, if not on staff, a psychologist or behavioural scientist,' he explains. 'Because you really are dealing with an awful lot of issues linked very strongly to those disciplines. The ways that, as game developers, you are forced to find solutions to problems you have in a game, or even in understanding your player population, can be fascinating.' In focussing on a narrow range of player archetypes, other sorts of motivations that actually enrich the game experience might get missed. Bill illustrates this with an interesting story stemming from his work on the 2000 action role-playing game *Diablo 2*, back when he worked at Blizzard. Taking on the role of one of five different character classes, *Diablo 2* pits you on an epic quest to contain and slay the game's namesake, the ruler of Hell. At one point in the game's life cycle, players could obtain a rare and powerful piece of equipment, a ring called the Stone of Jordan (SoJ). But at some stage an enterprising hacker figured out how to make multiple copies of the ring. Normally the game's servers would be able to monitor and detect this sort of cheating, but the player had also found a way to trick them into thinking that the copies were legitimate items. 'And so now we had a massive quantity of what was supposed to be a rare item in the [game] world, to the point that it became the default economy,' he explains. 'You would see people in chats saying stuff like "looking to sell 'Platemail of the Godly Whale' for three SoJs." It was a huge problem.'

The trouble was that the developers clearly had long-term intentions for the game. They had been creating new content that would be rolled out in the future, but some of that content was reliant on the gold-based economy built into the game, which was now totally debased. At the same time, though, players were doing something that developers really love to see: they were coming up with new and previously unanticipated ways to play the game and interact with each other. So the question was: how could the *Diablo* team get rid of this flood of new, but effectively fraudulent, currency without ruining the gaming experience (and its new iterations) for their players?

'There were numerous ways to do it, but unfortunately all of them would have ended up being punitive' explains Bill. 'We could generate a "rust storm" and have all these items disappear. Or we could roll the servers back to a previous time. We even got really clever and figured out how to do that for a specific item, instead of an entire character.' But doing something along those lines would create a whole host of new problems. What would happen for players who had legitimately earned their SoJs by playing the game as intended? What if a player had traded something very valuable to them for an SoJ, and hadn't realise that they'd received a counterfeit, hacked version? Punitive measures would inevitably end up impacting not just delinquent players, but the *Diablo 2* community as a whole, most of whom may have had no idea that something was going wrong. The possibility, therefore, of the developers angering a significant portion of their player base was very real. Ultimately, they concocted an ingenious solution. 'We started to create new items that followed different rulesets in how you could use them and how many you could have,' says Bill. These were very powerful items, immune to duplication. 'We also wrote some code that allowed us to spawn an enhanced version of the main villain in the game, Diablo.' He adds, with a chuckle, 'He was very creatively called "uber-Diablo" and we could spawn him in places in the world where Diablo would never have appeared – shocking places, like "Oh my God! What is he doing in this level?!"' After this, Bill's team primed the pump: they would start sending out in-game messages to everyone playing, saying something like: 'Two Stones of Jordan sold to merchants' (merchants being computer-controlled non-player characters). When the amount sold got to some arbitrary number in a defined range, the message would change: 'Thirty-seven Stones of Jordan sold to merchants. Diablo walks the earth.' 'We didn't tell anyone it was going to happen, we just did it. So people were like, "what the heck *is this*?" And now suddenly uber-Diablo is popping up in places no one's expecting, and players are getting their butts kicked because he's really hard [to beat],' Bill elaborates.

Eventually, a few players started to beat him, and their reward was new, more powerful equipment. 'It started spreading organically,' Bill says. 'Players were now figuring out that if they started to get rid of these [counterfeit] SoJs, it would summon this new version of Diablo, who drops items that are way better.' It took a few weeks, but eventually the development team got the in-game economy back to where they wanted it. Critically, they did it in a way that enriched the gaming experience for their player base, and didn't simply punish them for using a game mechanic in a way that the developers hadn't originally expected or intended.

It's a fascinating story, but one that points to a deeper tension underlying the way developers can come up with innovative ideas to provide meaningful gaming experiences. They often find themselves pulling all kinds of interesting psychological strings to motivate players without having any actual formal training in behavioural science. The example from *Diablo 2* is a situation where this is done in a positive way, which has a beneficial impact on both the game and the playing community. But at the same time, it isn't without risk – if a basic or uninformed knowledge of what drives people to play games is applied cynically or haphazardly, developers might end up doing more harm than good. Nevertheless, as games become bigger, more complex experiences in which players are more deeply immersed, I get the clear sense from Bill that he believes games developers very much have to take a leaf out of Spider-Man's book, and understand that with great power, comes great responsibility. 'If you're able to start building things that become so immersive and really meaningful to people, then we need to be able to understand and react properly to elements that occur between players, and between players and the game,' he adds. This, to my mind, highlights the problem created by scientific research that segments different types of players based on somewhat arbitrary, broad-strokes categories. Games are complex entities. So too are the people who play them. *How* we play games, and the *reasons* we play them, are different things: varying from person to person, game to game. They will even change and evolve as we play the *same* game. Take *Blake Stone* for example. The way I played it changed as other things happened in my life: from wandering around and exploring levels to trying to complete as much of it as I could. Within the context of the archetypes I mentioned earlier, perhaps I shifted from being an 'explorer' to an 'achiever'. But the reason I was playing was different, and that too changed over time. Perhaps I was initially playing it for the storyline – I loved science fiction stories when I was younger (I still do, to be honest), and so the idea of fighting aliens and monsters with laser guns would obviously be appealing. Later on, I played to escape, to distract myself from the news of my dad's illness. It gave me a sense of control over at least one small thing in my life, when everything else had become too obstreperous. So perhaps then, to understand why people play games, it's necessary to look at the deeper psychological drives that motivate us to do anything in life.

One particularly influential account of the origins of human motivation is something known as 'Self-Determination Theory', developed by the psychologists Edward Deci and Richard Ryan in the mid-1980s. The general idea is that some behaviours are driven by 'intrinsic motivation' – in other words, that you do a thing simply because you like it, or enjoy doing it (as opposed to 'extrinsic motivation', which involves doing a thing for external rewards such as money or praise). According to Self-Determination Theory, underpinning intrinsic motivation are three basic human needs: competence, autonomy and relatedness. Competence, in this sense, means having a desire to take part in activities that allow you to feel capable or effective – you want to be good at things, so that you can exert some control over them. Autonomy refers to the need to experience choice or freedom of action during that activity, and relatedness refers to the need to interact with, or connect with, other people. According to this theory, intrinsic motivation is the fundamental type of motivation that underpins most forms of sport and play (as well as pretty much anything from education to religion). It also makes sense, then, in terms of playing video games – for the most part, you play games simply because you enjoy them, not because you're getting some sort of external reward for playing them (with the notable exception of professional e-sports players). One of the reasons why games likes *World of Warcraft* are popular, and why the *Diablo 2* Stones of Jordan fix was so successful, is that these games (and the solutions to situations that come up as they are being played) are crafted to meet these three basic needs – in particular the idea of autonomy. The more competent you feel you are at something, and the greater the freedom you have to make choices about it – particularly when coupled with the possibility of interacting with other people while doing it – the more likely you are to enjoy doing that thing. The best games tick all of those boxes: if it's an easy game to pick up, and one where you can do whatever you like in it, and if you're able to interact with other players from across the world, then the chances are that it will be a popular game.

In 2006, a research team based at the University of Rochester and led by Richard Ryan applied Self-Determination Theory to video games in a series of empirical studies. Across four experiments, their aims were to try to understand some of the motivations that people exhibited for playing different types of games, and to see what the effects of playing games were on their well-being. They focussed on a subcomponent of the original classification of Self-Determination Theory, known as Cognitive Evaluation Theory. This theory concerns itself with the factors that either facilitate or frustrate intrinsic motivation – if a person is put in a situation where their sense of autonomy and competence are enhanced, then intrinsic motivation (doing something because you enjoy it) will be reinforced. On the other hand, any factors that dampen that sense of autonomy or competence will hamper intrinsic motivation. The idea here is that if specific types of video games, or specific features within games, can increase your perceptions of autonomy and competency, then you will get more enjoyment out of that game, which in turn will have a positive impact on your well-being – or vice versa. More broadly, the aims of the 2006 study were to see whether the principles of Self-Determination Theory were of any use in predicting the amount of value that players get out of games. Within the framework of the theory, factors such as autonomy and competence are quantifiable phenomena. They are measured using well-established and validated questionnaires – whereas accounting for something as seemingly esoteric as 'fun' is much more difficult.* If the core factors of Self-Determination Theory could be shown to map consistently on to other, more general measures of enjoyment (such as whether a game sells well, or whether it receives good reviews), then the study could be used as a basis for further research into understanding precisely why people play games.

The first of the four experiments had participants playing the classic N64 game *Mario 64*. As a linear platform game, *Mario 64* has a fairly intuitive control system. However, it gives players relatively little control over where and how they can explore the game environment. As a result, this experiment didn't focus so much on the autonomy and relatedness aspects of Self-Determination Theory, but instead paid particular attention

---

* Fun is an ambiguous concept, and the interpretation of what it means will vary from person to person. As such, it's near impossible to develop a scientific questionnaire to measure it in a consistent way.

to competency. Unsurprisingly, not everyone who played the game enjoyed doing so, but those who did say they enjoyed themselves also reported increased levels of self-perceived competence as they played, which in turn seemed to improve their score on the questionnaires they were given after playing, measuring their mood and self-esteem. The second experiment expanded on the first by comparing player experiences of two different games, *The Legend of Zelda: Ocarina of Time* and *A Bug's Life*. These two were picked because *Zelda* was (and still is) one of the most highly-regarded games of all time, and *A Bug's Life* … well, it isn't. Moreover, one of the major differences between the two is that *A Bug's Life* is broadly linear in terms of gameplay, whereas *Zelda* allows players much more freedom to explore the in-game environment. Unsurprisingly, Ryan's team found that participants were more positive about the better game, *Zelda* – they enjoyed it more, found it more immersive, and were generally more motivated to play it. As would be predicted by Cognitive Evaluation Theory, it was the extent to which players felt they possessed in-game autonomy and competency that seemed to account for these positive experiences.

The third experiment further expanded on the number of games made available to participants, and again found similar results. However, in this case Ryan's team also found specific variations in the experiences participants reported. Participants who experienced greater competency when playing a game also reported increased self-esteem and an immediate positive emotional experience, as well as feeling more energised. The participants who generally reported that they were able to be more autonomous in their gameplay experience tended to also report an overall higher sense of self-esteem and positive mood, and that the game felt more valuable to them. Finally, the team looked at the impact of playing MMO games. Again, they found that autonomy and competency were important factors for motivation and enjoyment. In addition, though, they found that a third aspect, relatedness, also came through as an important factor. This makes sense, given that the whole point of MMOs is to bring people from across the world together so that they can interact with each other in a real-time game world.

The study wasn't perfect – no study ever is – but to my mind it provided an incredibly useful experimentally-based starting point for thinking about the specific factors underlying why people find different sorts of game enjoyable, as well as what motivates them to start, or continue playing them. Following this and a number of other studies along similar lines, Ryan and his colleague Scott Rigby developed a more formal framework for understanding the factors that allow gaming to become an enjoyable experience, which they called the Player Experience of Need Satisfaction, or PENS model. In a White Paper published in 2007, Rigby and Ryan argued that the PENS model was useful because it went beyond simply assessing enjoyment (what they saw as an *outcome* of playing video games, as opposed to an underlying reason) and instead argued that those core components of Self-Determination Theory – autonomy, competence and relatedness – are the causal elements that contribute to a fun experience. If those needs are met, they argue, then games become more enjoyable and positive experiences.

This idea makes intuitive sense. We are more likely to enjoy playing video games if they make us feel we are good at something. Because we have an in-built drive to communicate with people (particularly those with whom we share a common interest) we are more likely to enjoy games that incorporate social elements. The games we love the most are the ones that allow us to experience, in a safe environment, the freedom of making choices that have a profound impact. Those core ideas from motivational theory can also be found underlying some of the other reasons why we play games. When we are sad, playing games can make us feel better, or at least give us a chance to connect with our friends in the online world. If we are playing the right game, it can help us to process and understand things going on in the offline world, empowering us in the choices that we make. Games might not fix anything, and there are definitely questions to be asked about what happens if we distract ourselves too deeply with them. But maybe sometimes, if we need to escape, getting lost in a good game can offer us temporary respite from our troubles by giving us something we feel we have control over.

CHAPTER 4

Control and imagination

Tracy King looks at me from across the table with a wry smile. 'You know when you go camping, and you fool yourself a little bit that you're at one with nature and you're Bear Grylls? Like, because you've made a fire from scratch? *Minecraft* is like that but you don't have to go outside. It's horrible outside, anyway.'

I'm sitting in the basement of a coffee shop on Carnaby Street, deep in London's bustling West End. It's not the best place to interview someone – it's cramped and noisy, and the air feels thick with caffeine and the warm breath of a dozen discussions all happening at the same time. The coffee is good though, as is the company. Tracy is a video and animation producer, writes a regular column on gaming for *Custom PC* magazine, and is an avid gamer. Among many things, we've been chatting about what makes for a good video game, and the conversation has turned to one of the most important titles of the past decade. *Minecraft* was released in 2009, and to my mind it now encapsulates pretty much every discussion about video games, including why we find it so hard to talk about them in the first place. It is a 'sandbox game' – when you first start it, you're deposited into a serene woodland, with no aim or goal. There's no particular narrative, nor are there any quests or missions for you to complete. There are two modes you can play it in: in *survival mode*, the main impetus is the need to construct some sort of rudimentary shelter or build weapons, before it goes dark. If you want some wood, you need to go and break down a tree – with your bare hands at first, but once you have gathered enough resources you can make an axe, which makes things a little easier. As you gather more materials, you can make increasingly complex items. A pickaxe to help you gather stone, a crafting table, armour, a sword. At night, all manner of monsters rise up, and if you're in the vicinity, they will head straight for you. If you want to survive, you need to be prepared, but once you have established a safe haven for yourself, the world is yours to do with as you please. *Creative mode* takes this latter concept and runs with it – from the start, you have every type of material and item at your disposal, in limitless quantities. You're a godlike figure, and the world is yours to shape as you please. *Minecraft*, then, is a game that offers you a multitude of experiences. If you want the complete freedom to see where your imagination might take you, *creative mode* offers you the digital equivalent of a box of LEGO, a way to construct anything you wish. If you prefer more structured play, *survival mode* puts you in the role of a gritty adventurer, relying on your wits to explore, forage and fight all manner of monsters and beasts.

I'm a firm believer in the idea that the best video games have strong stories. Part of the reason I love playing them is that I adore getting swept up in a compelling plot line; one in which you're not just a passive bystander, but in which the actions *you* control can have profound effects on your surrounding digital world. To put this in the terms used in Self-Determination Theory, I value the autonomy that games provide, but I also get a kick out of competency – the feeling that I have a worthy role to play in directing the course of history within whatever game I'm playing. But that's just personal preference, and it's clear from the runaway success of *Minecraft* that it's not the only thing that makes for a good game. I'll admit that I struggled when I first started playing it. I don't consider myself to be a particularly artistic or creative person. Give me a box of LEGO and no instructions, and I'll most likely build you a fairly banal-looking house: a two-up, two-down box with a door placed disappointingly in the centre of the front wall. And so it was when I first picked up *Minecraft* – actually, it was worse than that. My first shelter (playing in survival mode) was, chiefly, a glorified coffin: three blocks of dirt wide on each side, and just high enough that I could fit into it. I generously allowed myself an opening at head height, so that I could idly watch a skeleton with a bow and arrow stare at me from the other side. I'm sure it was as disappointed as I was with the situation. Still, I survived the night, and after digging myself out of the world's most boring abode, I set to work on making something bigger, grander. In my head, I imagined that it would be a mansion worthy of Andrea Palladio. It would be sprawling, resplendent, surrounded by lush gardens. It would be *amazing* …

… After an hour at my screen, I sat back and stared at my creation. A square box, with a rudimentary triangular roof. Two windows on the first floor, two on the ground floor, with a door placed firmly, disappointingly, right in the middle. I logged off, frustrated and mildly embarrassed. Tracy is somewhat sympathetic. 'I got my mum onto *Minecraft* when it first came out on the PlayStation. She dug a one-block square straight down and fell into a mineshaft,' she remembers. 'So I jumped in after her to save her, and she hacked me to death with her pickaxe. Not on purpose I should say! She was just trying to hack her way out.'

As for myself, I did get better. Well, as much as you can get 'better' at something like *Minecraft*. Some people have used the game to create works of sheer wonder: a full replica of Minas Tirith, the fortress-like capital city of Gondor from Tolkien's

The Lord of the Rings series; a scale replica of King's Landing from *Game of Thrones*; galleons; space shuttles. In collaboration with the Royal Society of Chemistry, undergraduates at the University of Hull led by the chemist Professor Mark Lorch developed a *Minecraft* world called MolCraft, full of intricate replicas of various types of molecules and proteins, which they intended as a learning tool for school science classes to explore basic biochemistry. Some players have even constructed fully-working computers, complete with actual hard drives and working screens, within the game itself. All of these things are amazing, but they are feats of creativity, not skill – just because you can make a full-scale replica of the USS Enterprise doesn't make you any better at placing a block than anyone else. And in a sense, that's the beauty of *Minecraft*. There is no learning curve. The only limit is your imagination. When I say I got better, then, I don't mean to say that I ever reached the lofty heights of anything like MolCraft. I once built a giant pyramid, complete with internal tombs and maze-like gloomy corridors sprawling through its bowels, which I thought was pretty nifty. But my crowning achievement, the one that I'm still proudest of to this day, is a log cabin.

There's nothing particularly special about this log cabin. It sits nestled within a gentle, snowy ravine, with a small stream running next to it. There's a woodshed propped up against one of the outside walls. On the ground floor sits a cosy snug, full of books, and at the far end is an open-plan dining and living area. Upstairs are two fairly basic bedrooms: in my mind, one was for me, and the other was for my dad. He loved being outdoors, and I have very happy memories of spending a few short days with him in Yosemite National Park when I was younger. We spent our time there in a log cabin that looked nothing like the one I recreated in *Minecraft*, but that didn't matter – I think he would have liked this one anyway. The whole thing, in its gentle simplicity, took me a few hours to make, over the course of two or three days. I could have made it more quickly, but the end goal wasn't what was important here. It was the journey, a digital memorial to someone I had loved and lost, and a few hours to myself to remember who he was, what we shared, and what he meant to me.

So herein lies some of the complexity, and uniqueness, of what it means to play a video game. In building my log cabin, *Minecraft* was, to me, a way to process loss and deal with grief in a personal and solitary way. When Tracy introduced her mum to the game, *Minecraft* effectively took on the role of a social platform, a way of allowing two people to communicate and bond with each other. Keith Stuart's bestselling 2016 novel *A Boy Made of Blocks* tells the story (based on Keith's own experience) of how a father's relationship with his autistic son was transformed by sharing the game with each other. Through MolCraft, the game has become a virtual online classroom. Video producers like Joseph Garrett, creator of the *Minecraft* persona 'Stampy Cat', use the game as a vehicle for episodic storytelling. Over the course of hundreds of videos on YouTube, Garrett acts out the exploits of the anthropomorphic orange-and-white cat Stampy as he builds an increasingly elaborate town. Each episode of the series, which is a sort of online television show (with over 6 billion views to date), sees Stampy providing a light-hearted commentary as he gives viewers ideas about how to create spectacular buildings – anything from a casino to a lighthouse, even a sushi restaurant complete with working conveyer belt that characters can fling fresh fish onto from the shoreline nearby. In short, *Minecraft* can be any sort of game you want it to be. No other entertainment medium affords this sort of possibility – of course, you can relate to, and empathise with, characters in a movie. A song can move you to tears or fill you with rage, and you can get lost in a good book, but only in games, like *Minecraft*, can you gain a sense of pride or of achievement for having truly participated. You are in control, and the only thing stopping you is your imagination.

Why, then, are games vilified? Why is it so difficult to talk about them? *Minecraft* encapsulates this problem beautifully. On the one hand, I've just explained the manifold ways in which it can be a fascinating experience. On the other, a move to ban it was considered in Turkey in 2015 because it was seen as 'too violent'. At the time, it was reported that the Children Services General Directorate believed that *Minecraft* was based on violence, apparently fixating on a small and somewhat tangential aspect of the game – the fact that monsters come out at night and attack you – and the idea that children who play it were in danger of social isolation. To anyone who has taken anything more than a cursory glance at the game, these claims are obviously farcical. To suggest that *Minecraft* is violent is like claiming that Harry Potter encourages Satanism; the two might seem linked in the eyes of the uninitiated and ill-informed, but to consider the experience just through that single, negative lens misses the full beauty and elegance contained within.

'Games are an emergent cultural phenomenon,' explains Tracy. The technology on which games are built is comparatively new, just as television was comparatively new when it first reached a mass audience in the 1950s, and as radio was before that, the telephone, writing letters, the printing press, and so on. 'At each of those points in history there have been moral guardians who are concerned that the proletariat has got their hands on something that is bad for them – sometimes in defined ways, but mostly it's "bad" because the masses like it,' she adds. Tracy's point brings to mind an oft-cited, yet poorly understood, excerpt from one of Plato's classic pieces of writing, *The Phaedrus*. At one point in the dialogue, the character Socrates appears to rail against the dangers of the written word:

> ... they will trust to the external written characters and not remember of themselves. The specific which you have discovered is an aid not to memory, but to reminiscence, and you give your disciples not truth, but only the semblance of truth; they will be hearers of many things and will have learned nothing; they will appear to be omniscient and will generally know nothing; they will be tiresome company, having the show of wisdom without the reality.

It's worth pointing out here that Plato was vehemently *not* against books as a novel technological concept;* if you read further into the dialogue, Socrates elaborates to explain that books are fine if they are used as intended – as part of the process of acquiring knowledge, to be used in conjunction with discourse and other forms of communication. I think there's an interesting parallel here. If you take a narrow view of what a video game is, then you will see something vacuous, intellectually impoverished, and a pointless waste of time. At worst, one

---

* For an excellent overview of the intention of this particular passage from *The Phaedrus*, it's well worth checking out the Sense and Reference blog: https://senseandreference.wordpress.com/2010/10/27/reading-writing-and-what-plato-really-thought/

could take this view and apply an Adornian critique to games – that not only are they a waste of time, but that they are harmful to society.

In work published in the 1940s and 50s, the philosopher Theodor Adorno argued that the effects of popular forms of mass media aren't merely limited to the overt messages that are conveyed in, say, television shows, but that there are various layers of hidden messages within them that don't necessarily reflect the needs or desires of the consumers. Instead, they reflect the beliefs and opinions of the controllers – the producers and creators of those shows. Approaching popular culture in a passive way, he argued, had the potential to rob us of our freedom in two ways. It robs us of our aesthetic freedom – that is, escaping into repetitive and vapid stories prevents us from developing our abilities to interpret, experience and understand art (and by extension the world around us). It also robs us of our moral freedom – by being carried along in a series of predictable story sequences, we are effectively trained in conformity of thinking. As Adorno notes in his 1944 work *Dialectic of Enlightenment*: 'In a film, the outcome can invariably be predicted at the start – who will be rewarded, punished, forgotten – and in light music the prepared ear can always guess the continuation after the first bars of a hit song and is gratified when it actually occurs.' But, as the examples from *Minecraft* illustrate above, once you start to understand the myriad ways in which a game can be used, you can start to appreciate how important a communication medium it can actually be. Perhaps we could even go so far as to say that games that allow the creative freedom to explore and construct virtual worlds, independently and in our own time, would be something Adorno would very much approve of. The problem just seems to lie in the fact that no particularly erudite vocabulary exists when it comes to unpacking this complexity. Even the term 'video games' doesn't really make sense.

Tracy agrees. 'It's a category problem,' she explains. 'Nobody who plays video games calls them video games. But we need to make a distinction. I have a column in a magazine where I talk about games, but I have to say video games because I also sometimes talk about board games.' 'Games' can mean anything: video games, board games, polo, chess, tag, snap. At school, in the UK at least, 'Games' is also a lesson, another term for Physical Education. In that sense the term encompasses swimming, gymnastics, badminton, hockey. 'So you say "video games", but then you've immediately got this category error, because nobody who plays them calls them that. I don't know how you get past that,' says Tracy. And the problem is confounded all the more by a category problem within a category problem. Whenever I give talks about the effects that video games have on our behaviour, the first question I always ask the audience is, 'do you play video games?' Sometimes, only a smattering of hands are meekly raised, as though people have been caught out committing some sort of embarrassing social sin. But then I press further. 'Has anyone played anything like *Candy Crush Saga* or *Football Manager* on their phone recently? *Doodle Jump*? *Homescapes*?' Suddenly, more hands shoot up. Because 'video game' is such a meaningless concept, everyone has their own ideas about what that means. This inability to categorise video games in a culturally meaningful manner creates all sorts of difficulties – can a particular product be categorised as a video game? Can a person be categorised as a video *gamer*, even?

'I get this a lot: I get, "you don't look like a gamer!" And my response is always, "you are saying that I don't look like someone who *enjoys fun*",' explains Tracy. 'Because the reason that you play video games is that they're fun. Why would I not enjoy them?' This sort of comment is really often about gender, because we typically have an image in our minds of gamers as predominantly being male. Chances are that when we think about who a gamer is, it's also someone in their teens, playing something like *Call of Duty* or *Fortnite*, the sort of exemplar many tend to think of when asked what a *real* video game is. But this idea doesn't necessarily reflect the reality of what games are, or who plays them. 'It was in the 90s that games started to skew towards males, and because males tend to have more disposable income, they started to be made for and marketed to guys. So it became a guy thing,' explains Tracy. That shift then – men playing more games, and games increasingly being aimed at men – necessarily resulted in a shift in perceptions and beliefs about what constituted a 'real' video game. Games like *Candy Crush* aren't seen as 'proper' video games because they don't fit that mould – you don't play them on a console or a PC, there isn't much skill involved, and they aren't typically aimed at that archetypal male demographic. 'As someone who understands how video games are built and how code works, I can assure you that *Candy Crush* is orders of magnitude more complex than *Pac-Man* or *Tetris*, and yet those same sorts of gamers will not say that *Tetris* isn't a "real" game,' she adds. In other words, the way that we define a video game doesn't necessarily rely on the actual features of a game, but more on how a particular category of players perceives that game or its fanbase.

An example that highlights this point is the 2009 Facebook game *FarmVille*. Principally a simulator game, *FarmVille* gives you an isometric view of, initially, a small plot of land. You tend to the land: you plant, grow and harvest crops, and raise live-stock. At its peak, even if you were not one of the 80-million-plus players of it, you might have come across it: players can accelerate their progression through the game by sending incessant Facebook notifications to friends and family to 'ask for help' (among many other things, this is a not-so-subtle form of advertising aimed at drawing in more players). You can also pay real money to purchase in-game currency, which you can spend to help grow your farm more quickly. I have mixed feelings about such games, which seem largely devoid of storyline, and instead seem to serve the more cynical purpose of turning a profit for their publishers. Tracy has a different opinion though. 'I played *FarmVille* for a full year, Valentine's Day to Valentine's Day. It's brilliant,' she explains. 'It had that balance of things that I like: which is that it feels a bit like work, but it's also cute, rewarding and fun.'

At around the same time she was also playing *Farming Simulator 2015* – a hyper-realistic virtual farming game. The *Farming Simulator* series of games features real-world equipment and vehicle brands, and uses more realistic-looking visuals. It is, more or less, exactly the same game as *FarmVille*. It's just not 'cute'. 'The psychology of the game is the same,' explains Tracy. 'I nurture the stuff I've planted. I harvest it, sell it, use the profit to buy more equipment and more land, I buy more seed, I repeat. One of these games has a cult following among your archetypal male gamer, and the other is considered a joke.' In other words, *FarmVille* is derided and *Farming Simulator* is lauded, not because of the way in which they are played – they are largely the same game. What differs is the perceptions that different subgroups of gamers hold, not just of the games themselves, but of the people who play them.

Because there's no clear language system for talking about video games in a meaningful and standardised way, we each impose onto them – inadvertently or deliberately – our own set of thoughts and beliefs about what they are. This can result in anything from fairly specific beliefs about what does or does not constitute a 'good' video game, all the way up to general beliefs about whether the video games themselves are 'good' or 'bad'. As the media scholar Henry Jenkins noted in his seminal book *Textual Poachers*: 'To speak as a fan is to accept what has been labelled as a subordinate position within the cultural hierarchy, to accept an identity constantly belittled or criticised by institutionalised authorities.' *Textual Poachers* was first published in 1992, so these issues are now decades old. It takes time to change views. And one of the practical effects of this is that when someone comes along with a different and seemingly incompatible set of beliefs about video games (at whatever level of discourse), a whole raft of protective psychological mechanisms kick in to protect what we hold to be true.

First and foremost among these is a phenomenon known as 'confirmation bias': a term first coined in a series of psychological experiments in the 1960s by the British psychologist Peter Cathcart Wason. Briefly, this is the idea that people will selectively filter information – any information – to fit in with their already-established beliefs. The way they do this can manifest itself in a number of different ways: they might 'cherry pick' evidence that supports their beliefs and disregard evidence that does not. Or, if there's flexibility in the way that a particular bit of information can be interpreted, people will have a tendency to construe it in a manner that fits in with their expectations. Even if information is gathered in a seemingly neutral manner, at a later date people may selectively recall only information reinforcing what they already believe to be correct. Even in situations in which we are faced with incontrovertible evidence that clearly contradicts a belief we hold, a phenomenon known as the 'backfire effect' can arise, wherein that belief not only persists, but becomes stronger, and more deeply embedded within our minds. Exactly why this happens is unclear – some sociologists have argued that humans possess a deeply-ingrained sense and need for continuity. Those sociologists have even likened the process of abandoning a belief to that of going through grief. In the past few years, some neuroscientists have attempted to look for a biological basis for belief persistence: work by Bradley Doll at Brown University has shown that the way prior beliefs are represented in an area at the front of the brain (called the prefrontal cortex) can influence the way that other areas of the brain (those involved in learning from experience) process new information. As a result, the effects of those beliefs are reinforced or overemphasised, regardless of whether they're correct or not. Applying all this to the subject of games, whatever the reasons, the fact remains that our preconceived notions of what a 'gamer' looks like, what a 'good game' looks like – even what a video game is in the first place – are all remarkably resilient to modification on the basis of other people's opinions or evidence. And this can cause tension – an 'us versus them' mentality – on a number of different levels. At the broadest level, it is evident in societal arguments about whether video games are a general force for good, a trivial waste of time, or a potential health hazard. You can see it in arguments between game players themselves, as to whether a particular title is, in fact, a 'real' game. And it can be seen in arguments between parents and children, in the ever-escalating arms race over how much access they can have to consoles, computers and tablets.

A month or so after my chat with Tracy King, I leave the cold and dreary January British weather for warmer climes. Five thousand miles away, on America's sunny west coast, I find myself sitting in a rental car: a forgettable beige Jeep Compass that, for a car so large, feels remarkably claustrophobic and cramped inside. I turn towards the entrance to a sprawling set of buildings that occupies my entire field of view. Blizzard Entertainment's headquarters in Irvine feels more like a university campus than anything else. The complex has its own road, its own restaurant, a gym, a barbecue area, an art gallery. At the entrance to the main building is a towering, twelve-foot-high statue of an angry-looking orc riding a wolf and wielding a battle-axe. Juxtaposed with this seemingly aggressive image are the company's core values, emblazoned on a compass underneath the statue: 'Lead Responsibly. Every Voice Matters. Think Globally. Play Nice, Play Fair. Gameplay First. Commit To Quality. Learn And Grow. Embrace Your Inner Geek'. The company's headquarters also contains quite possibly the greatest library ever conceived for geeks: complete with a dungeon-like wood-and-steel door framed by softly glowing torches. The door opens up onto a room in four sections. Immediately to the right are shelves upon shelves hugging a long wall, bursting with comic books. Directly opposite them are aisles of textbooks on coding and games development. In the centre of the room is a large wooden table, surrounded by a vast, comprehensive array of board games. My guide, Steven Khoo, tells me that people regularly come down to play a game or two over lunch: partly to relax, and partly for inspiration. At the far end of the library, in the largest section, are the video games. Every game you can think of is in there, complete with the relevant consoles and whatever peripherals you might need. Nestled in the far back corner is the librarian's desk, which I was fully expecting to be staffed by a gruff-looking orang-utan and feature a calligraphic set of rules that included 'do not meddle with the nature of causality'.*

Steven lets me steal a look at one of the developer offices, but the thing that catches my eye is the array of steel swords adorning the wall by the entrance. He tells me that Blizzard has a yearly service award ceremony – not unlike a university graduation – where employees are rewarded with different pieces of fantasy gear depending on how long they've been with the company. Two years gets you a beer stein. Five years gets you a custom-made sword. Shields are awarded for ten years' service, a ring for fifteen, and a helmet for twenty. No one yet knows what the reward for 25 years will be. After I admire them for a moment, Steven leads me through a maze of corridors to a conference room called The Maelstrom, named after a location in *World of Warcraft*. I sit down with John Hight and Matt Goss – respectively the production director and lead designer for the game – and we start to discuss why people find it so difficult to talk about video games.

'Some of it is pervasiveness,' explains Matt. He draws a comparison between talking about video games and talking about sports. If you're a football fan, say, talking to friends who aren't interested in the game, the conversation becomes disconnected. You might talk animatedly for hours about a great time you had at a match, but to them it just wouldn't evoke the same level of emotional intensity. I get this a lot with my best friends – I love them to pieces, and we have tons of things in common, but football isn't one of them. Sometimes, that can be an isolating

---

* The librarian was on a break, so I'll never know if I had, in fact, stumbled into a small, blissful pocket of the Discworld universe.

experience: if they have been to a game, or are watching one on television, I can't share that experience in the same way; I don't get the same level of satisfaction out of it as they do. It also means that I don't have the same vocabulary as them when it comes to talking about football: sure, I understand it a bit, and I could probably make some attempt at trying to explain the offside rule, but it would be clear to anyone who actually *knows* the game that I'm massively out of my comfort zone. The difference in attitudes towards sports and video games is, perhaps, just a matter of time and experience.

'My favourite story is that when I graduated from college and I got a job in the games industry, my mom actually apologised to me for not letting me play more video games,' says Matt. 'She was like, "I didn't know there was a future in this."' He explains that he and his mother talked about what video games meant to him: he explained that they always tested the logic part of his brain, helped him to learn about setting goals (and achieving those goals), and that now, they were a part of his career development. 'It was at that moment I think she realised there was more to it than she had thought,' he adds. I think this is a scenario that takes place constantly in households across the world. If you haven't grown up playing video games, and don't have much experience with them, then watching your kids play them can understandably be worrisome. To the outside observer, it can appear to be an immensely isolating and consuming experience: their full attention is on the computer or television or smartphone screen, and they seem utterly disconnected from the world around them. The game is difficult to follow if you're not the one in control of the character, which can make the experience seem even more jarring. And when it's time to put the game down and do something else, arguments ensue.

'Being a parent is really, really hard,' explains John. 'It feels like you're never quite connecting. I think that understanding what kids enjoy doing, and participating in that, being part of their world is what's key and what's important.' There's now a generation of parents who have the unique benefit of having grown up on video games and computers themselves, and this can be immensely helpful in developing healthy conversations with children about playing games. If nothing else, it helps to shape immediate opinions about their effects: decades of research on a phenomenon known as the 'mere exposure effect' attest to this. Made prominent in the 1960s by the psychologist Robert Zajonc, the 'mere exposure effect' is simply the idea that if someone is repeatedly exposed to a particular stimulus, it results in them reacting to it more positively than they would to a novel stimulus. A classic example of how this works is in advertising – say you see an online advert for a new drink. The next time you go to the shops with a thirst, you might be more inclined to pick the more familiar drink from the advert, as opposed to another new drink you've never seen before. Having had prior exposure to one drink tends to make you react more favourably to it. In the context of video games, a 2014 study by Andy Przybylski at the Oxford Internet Institute showed that adults aged 65 and over reported having less experience of playing video games, and were also more likely to believe that playing games contributes to real-world violence. Looking specifically at parents, a 2016 study by Przybylski and Netta Weinstein at Cardiff University showed, across a series of surveys, that parents who had direct experience of playing games were more likely to provide an estimate of the potential positive effects of gaming (based on responses to statements such as '[Games] promote friendship', or '[Games] develop creativity and thinking skills') that was more accurately in line with what the scientific research literature suggests, compared to people who didn't play games. Parents who played video games with their children were three times as likely to show accurate knowledge of gaming effects as caregivers who did not play with their children.

As the father of two sons, the Blizzard production director John Hight's own experience similarly reflects this. 'I would specifically steer them to multiplayer games that we could do together, whether it was *EverQuest*, or whether it was something we would play on a console together, like *Mario Kart*,' he explains. 'It allowed us to have fun together and interact with each other. It was a part of establishing that trust with your child that I think is so critical and important.' Understanding not just what the games that children play are, but *how* they interact with them, can therefore offer a number of benefits. First, a little bit of knowledge can help alleviate potential fears about the nature of the hobby they are engaging in. 'I think it's important that parents don't look at games and say, "Wow, I'm worried my kid is isolated," but rather try to embrace them a little bit,' suggests John. His thoughts echo recent developments in the scientific research literature, particularly those concerning the application of aspects of Self-Determination Theory to parent-child discussions about technology use. Often, conversations about video game use, and using screen-based technology more generally, focus on practicalities such as time restrictions that parents try to impose in the home, perhaps in favour of other hobbies or homework. In particular, work led by Netta Weinstein published in 2018 looked at three different ways in which parents or caregivers try to regulate adolescent behaviour related to their technology use. She identified three particular ways in which rules might be framed: first, 'external control' frames the conversation around the use of threats of punishment, or actual punishment to enforce a rule; 'introjected control' refers to effectively guilting teenagers into following a rule (for example, by a caregiver saying that they will be disappointed if the rule isn't followed, or acting less friendly towards the teenager); finally, 'autonomy support' frames the conversation in a more positive way, with the caregiver listening to, and understanding, the teenager's opinions while clearly explaining the reasons they are trying to impose a rule. Vignettes depicting scenarios in which these motivational frames were played out were presented to a group of 1,000 teenagers. The teenagers were then asked to put themselves in the shoes of the fictitious teenagers from the vignettes, and rate how they would feel according to three measures: how trustworthy they were perceived to be by the caregiver, the extent to which they felt they would want to resist the rules being imposed, and to what extent they would try to hide their technology use from their caregiver.

In general the results showed that 'external control' didn't work particularly well: the participants felt they were perceived to be less trustworthy, were more likely to conceal their technology use, and to resist the rules. 'Introjected control' didn't fare much better – although the participants didn't feel less trusted in this scenario, they were most likely to say that they would hide their technology use, as well as be more likely to feel as though they would want to rebel and resist the rule being imposed. 'Autonomy support' showed the most positive outcomes. In this scenario, while teenagers still felt as though they would want to rebel against the restrictions being imposed, it led to the highest levels of perceived trustworthiness and discouraged them from concealing their behaviour from the caregiver. It's worth bearing in mind that the results were only the outcome of an imagined situation, so further studies would still be needed to test whether the responses that participants gave would actually occur in the same way in their real lives. However, the findings bear a promising message: authoritarian rule imposition is likely to backfire in discussions about video game and technology use, whereas adopting a more constructive and collegiate attitude to teenagers – one in which they are given the opportunity to voice their opinions and explain their wishes – may lead to a situation in which rules can be imposed that are more likely to be adhered to.

This idea sits well with the notion that it's important both to understand the nature of the games that we play, as well as understanding why we play them. 'I get it man, there are challenges,' says John. 'There were times when I had to shut down the internet on my youngest boy, and it literally led to this cold war between him and me where he would try and figure out how to get past the security blocks I'd put on him.' With a chuckle, he adds: 'Today he's studying computer science and his interest is in network security. So one way or another, maybe something came of that.'

In addition, in playing video games with our kids, we can turn it from something we potentially see as harmful or a waste of their time, into a positive, shared family experience. And the quality of the gaming experience is something that the *World of Warcraft* developers are sensitive to. 'We have conversations about this all the time,' explains John. 'What's the age range of our audience? Because *WoW* really is designed for a broad range, and we have a lot of families that play together. So we'll look at specific content, ask "okay, is this appropriate or not?", and we'll make changes.' One example that he gives is to do with the pace of the game. 'We don't talk about it much, but when we release a new expansion, we don't unlock raids* or the end-game content for a few weeks,' he says. 'We want to let the game breathe and allow players to experience the new parts of the world that we've added, to live in that world for a bit.' Practically, this allows developers to keep an eye on bugs or glitches in different parts of the game in a more manageable way. For players, gradually allowing access to content over an extended period of time affords them the chance to take a break before tackling the next stage, rather than being bombarded with all of the new content at once. This wouldn't be a good outcome for anyone – player or developer. For players, it might lead to burnout: in the rush to get everything done as quickly as possible and be the best, they risk losing out on the more social aspects of the game. For the developers, it means that players might be missing the richness and complexity of the stories they've been working so long and so hard to create.

I'm not convinced that all video games developers share the same sense of moral responsibility evident in my discussions with John Hight and Matt Goss (although I will get to the darker side of video games in due course). My conversations with them were far-ranging, collegiate, and enlightening as to some of the decision processes they go through on a day-to-day basis. Two things struck me, both during the course of our discussions, and in the weeks after I left Blizzard headquarters. The first is that theirs – the developers' – is a voice that is conspicuously

---

* Raids are a particularly difficult type of challenge in which a group of players – in *World of Warcraft*, typically either ten or 25 players – work together to take down a series of powerful bosses, often over the course of multiple attempts lasting hours at a time.

missing from the wider public debate about video games. With the odd exception, the people behind the games don't make the news, providing insights into the processes they go through when making decisions about content or playing style. This may be due to a reluctance from developers (or it could simply be that journalists and news production teams aren't asking them), and in part may stem from a fear of the potential backlash that may result. This is particularly true for female games developers – as games journalist Keith Stuart has noted, in the same way that gamers are often depicted as men of a particular restricted age range, so too has the industry, until very recently, projected an image of developers as white, straight young males – in part because this is the demographic that dominated games development for so long. It is a combination that in recent years has repeatedly led to situations where, when developers who don't fit that mould speak up about their profession, they are subject to a torrent of racist or misogynistic abuse. The other thing that struck me is that, while it's all well and good to say that more people should be playing games, or that more parents should be playing them with their children, to do so misses an important point: when it comes to entertainment media, video games have a ridiculously high barrier to entry.

At the National Videogame Arcade, I speak to the director, Iain Simons, who has a more blunt way of putting it. 'Video games are 90 per cent a pretty shitty experience before you get to the point where you are actually playing the damn thing. And then they're amazing,' he explains. In previous years, as part of the GameCity festival that runs every October in Nottingham, Iain and his team would gather a group of six culturally-interesting yet non-video-game-playing celebrities, and over the course of the summer ask them to play six games, supplying them with all of the necessary hardware. The end result would be a dinner party of sorts, where the celebrities would discuss which game they thought was the best. 'We'd disregard genre or anything like that, so it was just preposterous,' says Iain. 'You would get Peter Gabriel animatedly arguing with David Puttnam about whether *Angry Birds* was better than *Call of Duty*.' It was just silly fun, he explains – it's difficult, if not impossible, to compare games that are so different from each other in an objective way, and to get such cultural luminaries to try to do so made for an amazing, if surreal experience. But the hardest thing, Iain tells me – the thing so easily overlooked – was preparing them to actually play the games in the first place. His team would have to send volunteers out to their homes to help them set up the PlayStation or Xbox and just turn the damn things on. Iain laughs: 'You get the fucking thing out of the box, you plug it in, and immediately the first thing that happens is that it will start downloading all of these updates. It looks like it's broken.'

This isn't a trivial problem. In a way, it shows up the fact that games are incredibly fragile things: not just in the physical sense, but in the experiential one. Playing games is in many ways a transient experience; once it has been finished, there can often be little reason to return to it again. Similarly, that first point of contact holds a sense of fragility. 'There's a point where people come into the NVA, and they haven't played a game ever,' explains Iain. This could be the first time that they have ever played a video game. It could therefore be the defining moment; the basis of everything that that person thinks about them in the future could be shaped by this one experience. 'They could pick up a busted controller, and start trying to work out what's happening,' he adds. 'And then they'll think "this isn't for me", put it down, and that's it.' Games, in that sense, aren't like other forms of entertainment media. If the first film you ever watch is rubbish, this doesn't necessarily put you off films for life: all you need to do is sit down and watch another film. The hill that you have to climb to get to the point where you're even experiencing a 'fail' is considerably lower than for playing video games. With games, once you've run the gauntlet of hooking up the hardware, installing software updates, installing the *game itself*, there's then a level of dexterity needed in order to become proficient at the controls, on top of which, you need a general level of systemic knowledge about how the game behaves before you can get to a point where you're actually good at it. Of course, a lot of what motivates people to continue playing games comes from the satisfaction of getting better at them. But those first few encounters play a crucial role in shaping our worldview about games. 'We have a lot of school trips coming here, and the thing that upsets kids most is *Donkey Kong*,' says Iain. 'We show them what games used to be like, and the first time you play *Donkey Kong*, it's a really fucking hard game. Not many people get to level two. They hate it.'

The reasons that make it so difficult to talk about video games, then, are complex and multifaceted. Due to the very nature of their being a personally absorbing, interactive experience, for those of us who play them it is inevitable that we each develop our own strong ideas about what games 'are', and even what they *should* be. For those who don't play games, they can often come across as alien, isolating experiences, and it can be difficult to see the good that comes from them when viewed from afar. Given the high barrier to entry, trying to change the view of the non-gamer by getting them to actually play a video game isn't as simple a solution as it sounds. This, together with a jargon-filled yet inconsistent language for describing and discussing video games, inevitably leads to a sort of tribalism of entrenched ideologies – gamers versus non-gamers, gamers versus each other, parents versus children. Speaking to Helen Lewis for a 2012 New Statesmen article, Naomi Alderman elaborated on this difficulty of accurately describing games: 'You need the vocabulary of an art critic to talk about the graphics, of a novel critic to talk about the storytelling, of a film critic to talk about the performances: not to mention music criticism, and gameplay criticism.' So there needs to be a better way to talk about video games – a new vocabulary, or style, that really focusses on explaining what makes them interesting and enjoyable, how strong the narrative is (if there is any at all), and this needs to be done in a way that is just as accessible to the people who don't play games as to the ones that do. But gaming is a young phenomenon; it is constantly evolving and trying to understand itself. Imposing too strict a language on what does and does not constitute a game, for instance, runs the risk of limiting what future generations of developers are motivated to create.

Just as important is the need to acknowledge the concerns that people on all sides have about video games. There's no doubt in my mind that games can be a force for good: they allow people the freedom to express their creativity and imagination, allow children to develop both technical and social skills, and allow communities to connect with each other in ways that other forms of media simply cannot emulate. Yet the current story of how video games affect us is not one of complete positivity. Acknowledging and understanding how the bad mixes with the good is critical to bridging the gap between gamers and non-gamers. But before looking at what psychological research can tell us about what video games do *to* us, and what they can do *for* us, I first need to take a brief interlude, and show you some of the problems with how that sort of research is done in the first place.

CHAPTER 5

A brief interlude

If you'll bear with me, we're going to take a little break from talking about video games. I'll move onto some of the issues around the 'darker' side of them in the next few chapters – things like whether games are addictive, whether violent games cause aggression, that sort of stuff. But before getting into the research evidence for and against those particular claims, I think it's important to point out that most of the work I'll be talking about sits broadly in the field of psychology, and that things … well, things aren't great in psychology at the moment. In as short a space as possible, I'm going to try to explain the rather signifi- cant mess in which psychological science currently finds itself, and some of the excellent solutions that have been proposed to fix it all. Throughout, though, it's important to remember that both the problems and solutions I'll discuss have a very real effect on what we do or do not know about the effects that video games have on us. With that in mind, let me now turn to a totally-not-farcical discussion about whether psychic abilities are an actual thing.

It all started in 2011, with the publication of a paper in the *Journal of Personality and Social Psychology* (JPSP) led by the eminent Cornell University psychologist Daryl Bem. The aim of the paper was to take a series of well-established techniques from psychological experiments, and use them to test for the existence of precognition – the ability of humans to psychi- cally predict the future. There were nine experiments in total in Bem's paper, but I'll look at one example. For context, in a typical, run-of-the-mill memory experiment, a researcher might present a participant with a number of words (let's say twenty) that would appear in quick succession on a computer screen, and the participant would be asked to try to remember as many of them as possible. The participant would then get a break for a bit – during this time, the researcher might ask them to do some other task, with the aim of trying to interfere with their ability to remember the word list. After the break, the participant is then presented with a longer series of words, some of which they had seen at the start of the experiment, some of which are new. At this point, they simply have to say whether they think each of the words they see is a new one, or one that they were asked to memorise earlier.

Bem and his team took this standard concept and turned it on its head. In their study, they first gave participants a series of 48 words to read, which were presented one at a time. Immediately after the list had been presented, the participants were given a surprise recall test, and asked to type out as many of the words as they could remember, in any order. Next, the computer programme presented them with a random subset of 24 of the words, and the participants were asked to practice and remember them. The results were extraordinary: participants were more likely to 'recall' words that they would be shown later during the 'practice' phase (that is, the second phase of the experiment where they were shown the random subset of 24 words). Put simply, it appeared as if cause had preceded effect. It was almost as if participants were able to reach twenty minutes into the future and accurately predict a series of words that they were going to be shown later.

As far as superhero powers go, being able to sense which of a bunch of random words someone's going to ask you to remember later is fairly rubbish. But if the findings from Bem's study held up, it would pretty much blow everything we knew about human cognition out of the water – time travel might be a real thing, *Minority Report* would be elevated from being a decent sci-fi flick to a full-on documentary, that sort of thing. Understandably, psychologists were critical of both the methods and the findings. Initial scrutiny of the way Bem had conducted the studies seemed to be fine though. These weren't some hokey parapsychology techniques; he had used well-established and verified psychological experiment procedures.

Psychologists therefore faced a dilemma: either there were very deep problems in the way researchers conduct studies, analyse data and publish results, or psychic abilities would be an actual thing, that we would have to accept. Writing about it in his excellent book *The Seven Deadly Sins of Psychology*, Professor Chris Chambers observed that it was a choice between 'on the one hand, accepting an impossible scientific conclusion, and on the other hand, swallowing an unpalatable professional reality.' Bem himself was aware that the findings were extraordinary and required independent verification; but this is where the real problems began.

Researchers at other institutions around the world took up the challenge, and attempted to repeat the study to see if they could find the same effects. This process is known as 'replication', and it's a cornerstone of good scientific practice. The best way to think about scientific research is that it's not a process of trying to find an absolute truth; it's about finding the least wrong answer. Experiments provide us with evidence either for or against a particular hypothesis, but no single study can ever provide definitive proof for that hypothesis. Particularly in the case of psychology, we're always looking for convergent evidence

– parcels of independent information that slot together, support each other, and ultimately combine to explain something in a coherent fashion. Replication is part of that process, and it's why scientific research papers always have a 'methods section'. The idea is that if researcher A runs a study and finds effect X, then researcher B should be able to take their methods and run the study in exactly the same way, in order to see whether they too get effect X. If they do, then that provides a little bit more evidence that effect X actually exists. If they don't, it adds a little more uncertainty to the situation.

The problem was that none of these groups could replicate the original findings from Bem's study. Actually, to be more specific, that was only part of the problem. When the psychologists Stuart Ritchie, Richard Wiseman and Chris French conducted a replication and found no evidence of precognition, they tried to get their study published in the same journal as Bem's original paper. But the *Journal of Personality and Social Psychology* weren't interested – it was journal policy not to publish replication attempts, and the editors didn't even bother to send this study out for review. For a long time, this has, unfortunately, been standard practice in psychology journals – many, if not the majority, are more interested in publishing 'novel', 'exciting' or 'positive' findings than comparatively unexciting things like replications.

The technical term for this phenomenon is 'publication bias', but many refer to it as the 'file-drawer' effect. In short, it means that studies which don't produce statistically significant effects (so-called 'negative findings'), or studies which aren't new and exciting (like replications, which literally involve doing the same thing someone else has already done) are much less likely to get published, and they end up gathering dust in an old cabinet in a darkened corner of the lab. If left unchecked, the file-drawer effect means that the scientific record – that is, the peer reviewed body of research literature that is published in established scientific journals – won't accurately reflect what we truly know. In the case of precognition: on the one hand, a paper had been produced that was a traceable, researchable part of the scientific record – a paper that stated that precognition exists. On the other hand, other papers that were *not* part of the scientific record showed, perhaps more accurately, that it does not exist.

In the wake of the controversy over the precognition study, psychologists began to start questioning whether, and how often, this sort of situation might have happened in the past, and how many seemingly tried-and-tested findings were actually replicable. One of the most concerted efforts to look at this replication problem came about in 2015. It was spearheaded by Brian Nosek, a professor of psychology at the University of Virginia, and co-founder of the Center for Open Science. In one of the biggest collaborations of its kind, some 270 scientists across five continents attempted to replicate the findings from 100 studies that had been published in three high-ranking psychology journals in 2008. The results were bleak – in total, just 36 per cent of the findings could be replicated, and even in situations where the results *were* replicated, the actual size of the effects were about half as big as the ones that had originally been reported in 2008. The results were bad for social psychology in particular – in that subdomain, it wasn't possible to replicate a staggering 75 per cent of studies.

Why was this happening? It's a simple question, but one that requires a complex answer. In part, the 'replication crisis', as it came to be known, threw a spotlight on an ingrained and deep toxicity in the scientific research environment. Academic scientists live very much within a publish-or-perish culture; for a long time, the marker of whether you're a productive scientist or not has been how many papers you have had published, and how many research grants you've been awarded. More research grants lead to more papers, and more papers increase the possibility of your getting research grants in the future, so the two exist in a symbiotic relationship. However, what's good for an academic career isn't necessarily good for the academic record.

To illustrate: say I have a grant to pay for 100 participants to take part in my research. This means I can afford one of two options, which cost the same. Option A: I design ten experiments to answer ten different research questions, with each of those experiments using ten participants. At the end of them all, I'll be able to write up ten research papers – one for each study. This will look great on my CV, but using only ten participants in an experiment isn't *so* great: because I'm using so few, it will mean that the data I obtain will be 'noisy' – that is, subject to quite a wide range of variability and not very representative of the wider population.* Option B is that I instead design one single experiment with a total of 100 participants in it, which answers a single question. At the end of it, I'll only get one paper

---

* One way to understand this is to think about a study in which I'm trying to figure out what the average height of people in the population is. If I only measure ten people, who all happen to be seven feet tall, the 'average' I'll get won't reflect the true height of most other people. Similarly, if I measure ten people who all have a different height from each other, ranging from four feet to seven feet, I might conclude that the 'average' height is somewhere in the middle, but then erroneously assume that extreme heights are just as likely as those around five to six feet – which again, wouldn't be truly representative of actual height in the population.

published, but it will be a better paper: the data I get out will be much less noisy, and the sample of participants I use will be much more representative of the wider population. Option B is good for science, not so good for my CV. But ultimately, I need a job, because I've got a mortgage and family to support. So I go with Option A: the quality of the research that I do will end up suffering, but at least I will end up getting an academic job (which in turn will validate my idea that this was the right thing to do). Over time, then, I'm going to be more and more likely to go with Option A.

Why is Option A such a problem for science though? The answer goes back to that idea of the file-drawer effect I mentioned earlier. Remember that, for some reason, many psychology journals value statistically significant ('positive') results over non-significant ('negative') ones. Work by Daniele Fanelli in 2010 attested to this, showing that around 90 per cent of published research findings in psychology reported positive effects. Let's say that I run one of my small studies (the 'Option A' approach), and I get a negative result. This is going to be a problem for me, because I really need to get this study published: I'm not going to be able to get that new job, or that next big research grant, unless I've got lots of publications on my CV. The negative result is going to make it less likely that I get this accepted for publication in a psychology journal. However: I had originally thought I was going to find a positive result, because similar, published studies that I've seen have all found positive results. So maybe I should drop one of my participants (participant nine messed around during the experiment any-way, the bastard), and rerun the analysis in a slightly different way. *Bingo*! This time I get a positive result, and my publication record is saved.

The scenario I've just described is a dilemma that I'm sure many, if not all, psychologists have faced at some point during their career. And actually, it's fine to exclude data from your analyses or rerun them in different ways – as long as there's a clear justification for doing so and it's honestly reported in the subsequent research paper. Unfortunately, this hasn't happened much. These kinds of behaviour, alongside a number of others, have become known as 'questionable research practices' (or QRPs). These are habits that scientists might inadvertently engage in that, in isolation, wouldn't typically be considered to be fraudulent, or examples of malpractice – indeed, many psychologists might be guilty of engaging in them unwittingly, because that was how they were taught. These QRPs can include behaviours like deciding to collect more data because a significant effect hasn't been found, stopping data collection early because a preliminary analysis *did* find a significant effect, or failing to report all of the measures that were taken during the course of a study (perhaps because they didn't show significant effects, or because it would make the research paper more confusing to write). But the more QRPs a researcher engages in, the more likely they are to end up distorting the findings of a study: for example, apparently finding an effect where there is none. In extreme cases, if scientists are *intentionally* using QRPs in order to deliberately swing the outcome of a study, then this becomes a slippery slope that ends up in full-blown data fabrication and fraud. Enter, at this point, the famed Dutch psychologist Diederik Stapel.

For many years, Stapel was a superstar of Dutch social psychology, with a wealth of quirky and interesting experiments under his belt. One of his studies claimed to show evidence that meat eaters were more selfish and less social than vegetarians. Another, a field-based study carried out at Utrecht train station, showed that public environments filled with rubbish were more likely to bring out racist tendencies in people. Stapel's were the sort of studies that grabbed the media spotlight and the public's imagination. They were also based on non-existent data.

At around the time that the precognition controversy erupted in 2011, three junior researchers at Tilburg University in the Netherlands put their careers on the line to bring Stapel's data fraud to light. The ensuing investigation found evidence of data manipulation and faking as far back as at least 2004. Nineteen PhD theses that Stapel had supervised were called into question – seven of these were eventually cleared, but there were doubts about the remaining twelve (although none were actually retracted). At the time of writing, he had 58 of his own papers retracted from the scientific journals in which they were originally published, had voluntarily surrendered his PhD, and had managed to avoid criminal prosecution only by agreeing to 120 hours of community service.

Stapel's fraud was career-ending, and it damaged an untold number of researchers who had been caught in his wake, but by his own admission it had all started off with some of those seemingly benign QRPs mentioned earlier. In 2012, surprisingly quickly after the case came to light, he penned a memoir entitled *Ontsporing* (Dutch for 'derailment'), where he explained how he would drop entire groups of participants from an experiment if they produced a result he couldn't explain. Or, if he didn't get the results he wanted, he would selectively report data analyses that did show them. While in the cold light of day these are clearly unacceptable practices, as I mentioned earlier, the reasons researchers start to engage in them in the first place can often be unintentional, or because they are seen as common practice across the discipline. 'I would go hunting in the dataset for outliers (strange cases where individual participants have produced unexpected answers or measurements that are wildly different from the average), and look for reasons why it was OK to throw them out,' he wrote. 'If they were a little older, or younger, or slower, or faster, or in whichever way not quite "normal", then maybe it was OK to eliminate them, to bring the results more in line with what I'd been expecting.'*

But as his data manipulation became the norm, Stapel explained, he had to resort to increasingly drastic measures in order to get the findings he wanted and needed. The prizes were too tempting: progressively-greater levels of academic fame via papers published in prestigious journals, keynote talks at conferences, media coverage and promotion. 'I couldn't resist the temptation to go a step further. I wanted it so badly. I wanted to belong, to be part of the action, to score. I really, really wanted to be really, really good,' he wrote. 'I wanted people to hang on my every word as I headed for coffee or lunch after delivering a lecture.'** Eventually, Stapel would end up in a vicious cycle, in which he would devise an exciting new idea for a study, then make up a fictitious data set from scratch, analyse it to find the groundbreaking result he wanted, publish the study in a high-impact journal, and then start all over again. The exercise was no longer about understanding how the world truly works around us. It was about creating a fantasy of a world which was perfect and predictable, the workings of which he could claim that he alone had privileged access to. In a written statement

---

* *Ontsporing* was translated into English by the psychologist Nick Brown in 2014 and renamed *Faking Science: A True Story of Academic Fraud*. This quote appears on page 101/102.
** Ibid, 103.

released after a report came out about his case, he elaborated: 'I have created a world in which almost nothing ever went wrong, and everything was an understandable success. The world was perfect: exactly as expected, predicted, dreamed. In a strange, naïve way I thought I was doing everybody a favour with this. I was helping people.'

It's tempting to kid ourselves that Stapel was an extreme outlier, that his case was so shocking precisely because it was so out of the ordinary. While it's certainly true that his misconduct sits as one of the most severe ever uncovered in science (the website Retraction Watch, which reports on misconduct across the sciences, ranks Stapel at number three on the all-time retraction leaderboard),* fraud is perhaps more common than many might expect.

In a remarkable paper in 2012 by the economists and behavioural scientists Leslie John, George Loewenstein and Drazen Prelec, 2,000 psychologists were surveyed about their involvement in QRPs. The team estimated that as many as 94 per cent of the psychologists they surveyed had admitted to engaging in at least one QRP: for example, failing to report all of the things they had actually measured in a published study. More worryingly, some 40 per cent were estimated to have falsified data at least once in their career. It's a frightening statistic, and one that implies that for every Stapel who *is* uncovered, there are potentially many more scientific fraudsters going undetected. At the very least, the fact that so many psychologists are engaging in behaviours that will have unintended effects on the veracity of

---

* The top two positions, rather worryingly, go to anaesthesiology researchers. Joachim Boldt has 96 retractions to his name, while Yoshitaka Fujii has an eye-watering 183.

their findings helps explain why the replication crisis has come about.

This all makes for grim reading, but my intent in explaining all of this isn't to make you think that psychology is a hocus-pocus discipline full of dubious results and shady researchers. In fact, my intention is much the opposite: the issues in this chapter aren't unique to psychology (at the time of writing, a comparable replication crisis is starting to emerge in the field of artificial intelligence, for example). And, rather than shy away from the difficult task of fixing these problems, in many ways psychologists are leading the way in developing reforms that will hopefully dampen the effects of QRPs in the future and make it much harder for unscrupulous scientists to engage in fraud. I'm just going to concentrate on one such reform here, but it's the one that I think is the most important and that will have an increasingly vital role to play in video games research over the next few years. It's called preregistration.

Let's have a think about how a typical psychological study is run. You first come up with an idea, a testable hypothesis. For example: whether playing *Super Mario Kart* improves your ability to remember things. You then design an experiment that will allow you to collect data that either supports or refutes that hypothesis. Once you've finished the experiment, you gather up all the data and analyse it, hopefully using an appropriate statistical method. Finally, once you've found some sort of result, you start to write up a research paper that provides an overview of the subject area, a breakdown of the methods you used in your experiment, a results section where you explain your data analysis, and finally a discussion section where you explain what you think your results mean, and what sort of research should be done next. The paper is sent to an academic journal, where an editor then passes it to two or three researchers who are knowledgeable in your research area, but haven't been involved in the study. They then review the paper, via a process called peer review. This typically involves the reviewers carefully reading through the paper to assess the quality of the experimental methods, and whether the statistical techniques used are appropriate for the questions being asked. The reviewers will then provide comments to the editor about what they think is strong about the study, what weaknesses they've identified, whether the paper is acceptable for publication, or whether more experiments or different analyses need to be done first. You might go through two or three rounds of review, and eventually, if you're lucky, the paper gets published.

However, there are a number of hidden decisions that researchers have to make throughout this journey, and as we've already seen, errors and questionable practices can creep in at any point. How much data do you collect before you stop testing and start analysing, for example? What *sort* of data do you want to be collecting? Which analysis method should you use? Do you report all of the measures that you collected, or do you selectively report the ones you think are most interesting? Some of these questions are reasonable, others less so, but the point is that very often in psychological research, these sorts of questions are answered on the fly, as the experiment is happening. Given that, it's easy to see how mistakes can be made. If you don't decide how much data you should be collecting until you're actually collecting it, the temptation might creep in to repeatedly run an analysis and then keep collecting data until you find a significant result: in this example, that playing *Mario Kart* improves your memory. But if that happens, it becomes difficult to know whether your significant result happened because playing a video game *really does* affect your memory abilities, or if it is simply a 'ghost' effect that happened because of the statistical error introduced by running multiple analyses.*

Preregistration solves some of these problems by forcing the researcher to declare, before the start of the experiment, how much data they are going to collect, what measures they are going to take, and what analysis method they are going to use. This is all done publicly: a date-stamped preregistration document that includes the above information, plus a rationale and hypothesis for the study, is uploaded to a website such as the Open Science Framework, free for anyone to be able to view. A variant of this idea, called a Registered Report, takes things a step further. Where an academic journal has a system in place to accept Registered Reports, the preregistration document is submitted to the journal and undergoes peer review. This means that other experts in your field have a chance to assess the quality of your methods and your proposed analysis procedures *before you even start collecting data*, which in turn means that any problems with your study can be fixed before it starts. It shifts the nature of the review process from getting feedback along the lines of 'you did this wrong, better luck next time' to a more positive 'if you change this thing, your results might be more reliable'. If a Registered Report passes muster during the review process, you can then go and actually run your experiment, and provided that you do everything exactly as

---

* If you want to get into the nitty gritty of why this is a problem, the psychologist Tal Yarkoni wrote an excellent blog post on the topic in 2010, which you can find here: https://www.talyarkoni.org/blog/2010/05/06/the-capricious-nature-of-p-05-or-why-data-peeking-is-evil/

you specified at the outset, your findings and eventual full study will be published regardless of what you find. The great thing about Registered Reports then, is that it doesn't matter whether you get a positive or negative finding, because your paper has already been accepted. Ultimately, it means that the incentive for a scientist to run an experiment shifts from 'I must get a good result' to 'I must develop a good methodology'. It shifts the goalposts away from the prevalent toxic culture of having to produce positive, novel findings, towards a more utilitarian culture concerned with producing robust, reliable and (hopefully) replicable methods.

Of course, nothing in science (or life) is ever that simple, and while preregistration is gradually gaining more traction in the psychological scientific community, there are still many researchers out there who don't agree with it, and in some cases are actively hostile towards those trying to improve the way experimental research is conducted.* In some sub-disciplines, the message about the replication crisis hasn't really taken hold yet, and QRPs are still rife. As you've probably guessed by now, one of those sub-disciplines is video games research: specifically, the area concerned with figuring out what the effects are on human behaviour of playing different types of video games.

---

* Why some academics are hostile towards reform isn't particularly clear. By and large, it tends to be more senior academics who are resistant. Perhaps, they genuinely don't see the negative issues with research practices that they've spent so long engaging in, and which until recently were the de facto standard. Or perhaps it's because they've unintentionally enjoyed the fruits of a broken system for much of their careers, and calls for reform are seen as an attack on their life's work. Reform isn't about attacking individual researchers though. It's about improving the way that science is done for the benefit of everyone.

So, now that I have demonstrated how psychological research can go badly wrong, and how it can be fixed, let's look at this through the lens of a specific test case – the age-old question of whether playing violent video games causes aggression.

CHAPTER 6

Are violent video games bad for us?

The best holiday that I ever had was a trip to San Francisco with my dad in 1995. We were going to see distant-but-much-loved family who lived out there, partly-funded by a serendipitous scratch-card win courtesy of Woolworths and Polo mints. A few months earlier, in the midst of a Power Rangers craze, I'd bought the 'Dragon Dagger': an ill-advised combination of knife and musical instrument that was used to summon and command a colossal dragon robot in the TV series. My immediate disappointment that the toy version did not, in fact, confer the same sort of power in real life was diluted slightly by the Polo-sponsored scratch card I'd received for spending my pocket money. Still at the till, I scratched the foil off and revealed the words '£500 in £1 coins'. I looked at the cashier. He looked back, ever so slightly enviously, and apparently unbothered by the fact that he had just introduced an eleven year old to scratch cards. Once it sunk in that I'd actually won something, I ran off to inform my dad of this important turn of events – that we should go home, and await the delivery of a gigantic box full of gold pieces, which we could dive into and swim around.* It was enough money to get the ball rolling

---

* Not that I'm complaining at all, but I never did get to re-enact the opening title sequence for *DuckTales*. A few weeks later, and rather unceremoniously, a simple cheque appeared in the post instead.

and organise a holiday to America with my dad that beforehand had been just wishful thinking, ever so slightly out of financial reach.

One of my enduring memories of that trip was a visit to 'Ripley's Believe It Or Not' museum. My memory isn't of the museum itself, nor of any of the exhibits inside. Instead, it's about an illusion located in the entrance lobby. The illusion is a simple one; a tap appears to be suspended in mid-air, with water constantly flowing out of the nozzle. I remember looking at it with a sort of dubious disbelief, not buying the idea that it was actual magic, but not quite getting how it might work either. My dad wasn't a scientist by trade; he was a surveyor for a building society. But he had a very scientific approach to the world around him, one that he was always keen to instil in me. So when I looked to him for an explanation, he suggested that I figure it out for myself. My gaze returned to the tap, and I thought for a moment. Then, with a slight sense of hesitation, I stuck my hand into the stream of water. Instead of passing effortlessly through, my hand struck the clear Perspex pipe that holds the tap up, supplying the apparently constant flow of water, and providing, literally, the backbone of the illusion. The sense of satisfaction I felt about working out a little something about the world completely negated any disappointment that I might have felt about it not really being magic. But then that's why I find science so fascinating. Figuring out how the world actually works, has, in my experience, produced far more inter-esting results than simply accepting that it does so because of an unknowable power.

It was little encounters like the one with the tap illusion that set me on the road to becoming a scientist. I'm reminded of this twenty years later, as I find myself in a streetcar rumbling along the Embarcadero, the roadway that traces the gentle curve of San Francisco's northeastern shoreline, heading towards the city's tourist hotspot, Fisherman's Wharf. A short walk away from Ripley's museum, nestled in a quiet corner of Pier 45, is the 'Musée Mécanique'. When you walk through the door a vast warehouse spreads out before you, stuffed with pinball machines, antique coin-operated games, mutoscopes and mechanical fortune-tellers. Tucked away at the back of the museum is a treasure trove of machines from the golden age of video game arcades. I wander through the narrow corridor of classic cabinets, and get a sense that this is the closest thing that I could ever get to time travel. Then, one game in particular catches my eye.

Battlezone is a wire-frame, vector-based graphics game, first launched in 1980, in which you control a futuristic tank with the aim of blowing up as many other tanks and (for some reason) UFOs, as possible. It's notable for the fact that you see the screen through a periscope-style viewfinder, experiencing the action in first-person perspective: making it one of the first virtual reality games ever. *Battlezone* is intriguing for another reason, though. Shortly after its release in late 1980, the US Army approached the developers, Atari, with a proposition. They wanted a new version of the game – one they could use as a training simulator for gunners on the Bradley Fighting Vehicle, a multipurpose combat tank that would later see heavy use in the first Gulf War. Despite some resistance within Atari's ranks, a modified version called *The Bradley Trainer* was eventually developed, although only two machines were ever built.

Despite playing only a fractionally small role in the US military machine, the story of *Battlezone* highlights a worry that many people have grappled with since video games became a mass-market entertainment medium; namely, whether or not they are 'bad' for us. If games can be modified to train people to drive tanks, then can they also be modified to train people to use guns and kill others? Do they even need to be modified at all? If we play violent video games, do they make us more violent or aggressive in our behaviour? From a scientific point of view, it's a question I've been interested in for some time, and one that I think about as I stand in the arcade after playing a couple of sessions on the tank simulator. It isn't *Battlezone* that's made me think of this violence question, though. As I look behind me, at another row of classic cabinets, it's a different game that I spot that brings the issue to mind: *Centipede*.

A shoot-'em-up very much in the style of *Space Invaders*, 1981's *Centipede* has you shooting ... well, centipedes, as they drop down from the top of the screen. There are spiders and various other bugs as well, but the titular centipede is the important one – as you shoot its segments, they turn into mushrooms, which block the bug's path and force it to step down a level, towards your character. The more mushrooms there are on the screen, the faster the centipede descends. It's a simple game mechanic that requires more strategic thinking than you might first expect. The control system is tricky too: you use a rollerball to control your character, so fine-grained movements in later stages require a steady hand as well as steady nerves. *Centipede* is notable because it was designed by one of the few female games programmers at the time, Dona Bailey, and was also one of the first video games to have a large fanbase of female players (*Pac-Man* being another early example). So why does it remind me of the violent video games debate?

In 2001, researchers from Harvard University attempted to quantify the level of violence in various sorts of 'E-rated' games (in the US, this means games classed as being suitable for ages six and over). They did this by playing games through to completion, or for 90 minutes – whichever came first – and recorded the amount of time taken up by violent acts occurring in the game. Their definition of violence was pretty broad-reaching – violent acts were defined as those '... in which the aggressor causes or attempts to cause physical injury or death to another character'. Critically, 'character' was also rather loosely defined, as it included personified objects. In this analysis, *Donkey Kong 64* came out as 7.4 per cent violent, whereas *Super Mario Bros.* scored 41.3 per cent. For reference they also included some classic arcade games – *Pac-Man* came in at a whopping 61.7 per cent violent. *Centipede* took the top spot though: the Harvard analysis classified it as 92.6 per cent violent.

It's difficult, perhaps impossible, to say in any practical sense what's actually meant by describing something as '93 per cent violent' or '50 per cent violent'. *Centipede*, realistically, isn't a violent video game – the pixelated characters are wholly unrealistic, and bear little resemblance to anything outside of digital games. But what about the modern incarnations of games like *Battlezone*? When it comes to public debates or concerns about game-playing, first-person shooter games like *Call of Duty* or *Battlefield* often take centre stage, especially in the aftermath of mass shootings. Media stories about the link between violent video games and real-world acts of aggression are nothing new. In 1999, twelve students and one teacher were killed at Columbine High School in Colorado. At the time, the killers were alleged to have been obsessed with *Doom*, the archetypal aggression-fuelled first-person shooter from the early 1990s

– and it was further alleged that they were driven to the act *because* they played such games. More recently, the Virginia Tech massacre (in 2007), the Norway massacre (in 2011), the Sandy Hook massacre (in 2012), the murder of the UK school-teacher Ann Maguire (in 2014) and the Parkland shooting (in 2018) have all been linked at some point to allegedly obsessive video game use by the perpetrators – usually involving first-person shooter games.

This is a sensitive issue. When stories of these sorts of shootings make the news, there's an understandable need to try to explain what happened, to try to rationalise an abhorrent act in some way in order to make sense of it and try to prevent it from recurring. Invariably, the media spotlight will turn to the killer's background in an attempt to look for clues as to what might have driven them to murder. And, because video games are one of the most popular pastimes of the 21st century, the story will then turn to the killer's use of them as being a potential cause. This is where scientific research has an important role to play, because it affords us the tools to determine whether there is any existing relationship between playing games and developing behavioural issues (and if that relationship does exist, to deconstruct it). Perhaps there's a definite link, and playing violent video games does cause people to become more aggressive. Or perhaps the link is reversed – that people who are already aggressive are more likely to commit murder, and more likely to play violent video games. Perhaps only a certain subsection of people are at risk of developing aggressive tendencies, and only after playing certain games in certain situations. Or, perhaps the link doesn't actually exist at all, and other factors, such as mental health or the family environment, are the most important ones in driving behaviour.

Unfortunately, the psychological research that focusses on the effects of playing violent video games is beset by a wide variety of issues, making it difficult to come to any definitive conclusions. The 2001 Harvard study I mentioned above – the one that attempted to quantify video game violence in percentages – highlights one of these issues. Often, the research methods that are used don't map very easily onto the reality of playing video games. Let's try to unpack this problem – and others – by thinking about how an experiment that focusses on video games *should* be run.

Before you start running a laboratory-based experiment – any sort of psychological experiment, that is, not just one about video games – standard practice is to first lay out some basic ground rules about what it is that you're going to do. To start with – what is the specific research question your experiment is trying to address? What variables are you going to measure, and how do these relate to your research question? How are you going to analyse the data? For the purpose of example, you could ask a basic research question like: whether playing violent video games makes people more or less likely to be aggressive in other aspects of their life. The most basic type of experiment that could be run to address this question could be conducted as follows. A number of participants would be invited into the lab, and split into two groups. One group is going to play a violent game (the 'violent' group), and the other a non-violent game (the so-called 'control' group). The experiment starts with both sets of participants filling out a questionnaire. This takes the form of a series of statements that the participants have to read and respond to, all of which are relevant to aggression in some way. An example of the sort of questions you might use is below:

How characteristic of you are the following statements, at this moment in time?

	Extremely uncharacteristic				Extremely characteristic
I get angry easily	O	O	O	O	O
I get irritated easily	O	O	O	O	O
I get upset easily	O	O	O	O	O
I am often in a bad mood	O	O	O	O	O
I lose my temper	O	O	O	O	O
I always complain	O	O	O	O	O

Next, the participants play their allotted game for 20–30 minutes. Following the play session, they are tested again by being asked the same questions as at the start of the experiment: to see if their levels of aggression have changed as a result of playing the game. If the scores are added up separately for both questionnaires, then the pre-game score is subtracted from the post-game score, a rudimentary measure of change in self-assessed aggression will result. Finally, the scores of the violent game group are compared with those of the 'control' group, to see if one group shows a larger change in aggression than the other. This process, of systematically changing one thing in the study (in this case, whether a video game is violent or not) in order to see whether it has an effect on some other thing (whether people feel more or less aggressive), forms the standard framework in which most psychological experiments are devised and carried out.

Let's imagine that the results of the study are as follows. Both the violent game group and the control group show the same levels of aggression, as measured by the questionnaire, at the start of the study. This is good, because it means that there aren't any differences between the groups at the outset.

However, the post-game questionnaire scores show a difference. On the one hand, the control group shows no change in aggression as a result of playing a non-violent game. On the other hand, the violent group *does* show a difference – they report being more aggressive after playing the violent game. Is this evidence that playing violent video games causes aggression then? Well, not quite. Using a questionnaire to measure aggression won't necessarily produce a convincing or incontrovertible result here, largely due to the fact that participants can behave in strange ways if they figure out (whether inadvertently or not) what the study is about. The chances are that if you were to actually run this study, your participants would cotton on pretty quickly to the fact that you're trying to see whether playing a video game has any influence on how aggressive they see themselves. As a result, they might modify their responses in order to give you, the experimenter, the answer that they think you want, because they want to be seen as 'good' participants. Alternatively, maybe they don't like the idea that you're trying to show a link between something that they like doing (playing video games) and something bad, like violence, so they might instead give you an answer they think you don't want, in order to undermine your work (the 'screw-you effect'). In other words, because the answers the participants provide might not truly reflect how they were actually feeling at the time, you can no longer be sure that the results you've got are due to the effect of the variable that you've manipulated (in this case, the violent content of the game), or due to other, more random factors.

This is the first big stumbling block with violent video games research: the question of what constitutes an appropriate measure of aggression. Obviously, there are some practical ethical considerations to take into account here. If the aim is to gather scientific evidence to help answer those wider societal questions about whether video games cause actual, real-life aggression (say, in the form of school shootings), then in an ideal scientific world, the laboratory measures of aggression would mimic those as closely as possible. But that's simply not going to happen – no institutional ethics board would ever approve a study that would involve observing how severely the participants beat each other up, for example. Instead, scientists have to use proxy measures of aggression. The questionnaire idea above is one such example. Things like the screw-you effect aside, if you ask people whether they're feeling aggressive, although you aren't measuring actual physical aggression, you're still measuring something that could be considered to be some other form of aggression. In studies that have looked at aggressive behaviour more generally, researchers have used measures such as the amount of verbal aggression that can be observed after a participant has been provoked in some way. But again, linking this to physical aggression isn't straightforward. Alternatively, other studies involve allowing participants to subject others to electric shocks: which is perhaps a more direct measure of physical aggression. Aside from the ethical difficulty of running this sort of experiment (the electric shocks can't be so severe as to cause actual pain, which in turn raises the question of what sort of aggression they are actually representing), widespread awareness of Milgram's*

-- --

* Stanley Milgram was an American social psychologist who gained notoriety in the 1960s following a series of ethically-dubious studies looking at the willingness of people to obey authority figures. Milgram's studies involved participants being led to believe that they were assisting an 'experimenter' in a (fictitious) study to see whether inflicting a punishment could improve a person's ability to remember. Briefly, the participants were asked to administer an electric shock to another person (the 'learner')

famous obedience experiments – especially among university students, who often form the bulk of volunteer psychological participant pools – means that no one ever really thinks they're actually administering a shock.

Taking all this into account, when it comes more specifically to video game studies, two sorts of proxy measure have been used extensively in recent years to establish how much more 'violent' a participant is after playing a video game. The more commonly-used of these proxy measures uses a modified version of an experimental paradigm that was first developed in 1967, called the Competitive Reaction Time Task, or CRTT. Under similar circumstances to the questionnaire-based study above, in these sorts of experiments participants are first asked to play either a violent or non-violent video game. Afterwards, they are seated in a room on their own, in front of a computer, and told that they are going to play a game which will test reaction time, against another, unseen player in another room. This reaction-time game is simple: at some point, some sort of target object will appear on both the participant's and the unseen opponent's screen. As soon as one of the players sees this target object, they are tasked to press a keyboard button as quickly as possible. Whoever 'wins' the encounter will get to 'punish' the other competitor by blasting them with a loud noise.

---

if that person answered a question incorrectly. While in reality no shock was actually delivered, participants were led to believe that the voltage level would increase with each wrong answer. If the participant wanted to stop the experiment, the 'experimenter' would repeatedly instruct them to continue. While there is some debate around the veracity of Milgram's findings, his results suggested that some 65 per cent of participants across his initial experiments would obey the 'experimenter' to such an extent that they were prepared to deliver fatal 450-volt shocks to the 'learner'.

The unseen opponent in the CRTT experimental paradigm doesn't actually exist. The 'opponent' is instead controlled by the same computer programme that presented the reaction-time task to the participant. That means that researchers have very precise control over how often, and in which order, the participant wins or loses rounds. On top of that, the participant is told that if they win a round, it will be up to them to choose how loud the noise blast is, and for how long it lasts. The idea, as far as this research is concerned, is that you can be considered more aggressive if you choose to blast your opponent with a louder noise for a longer period of time.

But let's hold it there for a second. There are actually *two* measures of aggression that could be assessed here: the noise volume, and the noise duration. So which one should be used? Well, there are a number of different options, depending on what the researchers' pet definition of 'aggression' is. Maybe they could just use the average volume that the participant chooses over all of the trials in the experiment, because it could be argued that choosing to inflict a louder noise on their opponent implies that the participant is being overtly aggressive. Or one could just take the average duration and argue the same point – choosing to inflict a noise on an opponent for a longer period of time intuitively seems like a more aggressive thing to do. If it isn't obvious which of the two measures is best, then instead the average volume could be multiplied by the average duration – which will account for both. Perhaps, instead of using the data from all of the trials in the experiment, it would be an idea to take only the trials where the participant 'lost' the preceding trial: which you might call 'retaliatory aggression'. Or, taking it to the extreme, the participants could be made to always win the first trial in the experiment, and then just that data could be measured. You might call that 'unprovoked aggression', because the first trial will be the only time a participant can win, having never lost before. Or maybe one should take the average volume multiplied by the square root of the duration. Or the volume multiplied by the log duration, or …

You get the point. There are a *lot* of ways in which the data could be analysed. And it turns out that the choice of analysis method you use *is* rather important. In 2014, a team led by Malte Elson, then at the University of Münster, took data from three earlier experiments that had used the CRTT to study whether playing video games was a potential cause of aggression, and reanalysed them using a number of different options for combinations of duration, loudness, and trials. It turned out that, depending on which analysis method the team used, they could provide evidence showing that playing violent video games increases aggressive behaviour, that it decreases aggressive behaviour, or that playing violent video games has no effect at all on aggressive behaviour, *using exactly the same data.* In other words, if you want to find out whether violent games cause aggression, you won't find the answer in the data you collect. It will be entirely in what you do with that data.

It gets worse. Elson later set up a website, flexiblemeasures .com, where he systematically catalogued every paper that has ever used the CRTT as a measure of aggression (not just in games research) along with which analysis strategies the papers use. To date, his database contains 130 papers, and they use a total of 156 data analysis strategies – in other words, for every new paper that's published using the CRTT, researchers come up with 1.2 new ways in which to do something with the data. Some papers have more than one experiment in them, and in some of those cases, different experiments *in the same paper* use different data analysis strategies, which explains why there are more strategies than papers.

Hopefully, the little interlude in the previous chapter into preregistration and the replication crisis in psychology will now start to make some sense. Theoretically, it might be perfectly acceptable that there are so many different ways in which to analyse the data: after all, there are some different types of aggression described above that could be studied by looking at the data in different ways. But if that's the case, there absolutely has to be some sort of justification for the analysis strategy that your study uses. And very often this justification is notable by its absence. Preregistration forces you to think about this justification. At the very least, it forces you to pick an analysis strategy and stick with it, rather than fish around using different strategies until you get a statistically significant result. So given that the overwhelming majority of studies using the CRTT haven't, to date, protected against this sort of flexible data analysis risk, it's very difficult not to come to the conclusion that some researchers, either deliberately or inadvertently, choose analytical strategies that will give them either the answer they want, or the one that fits with their particular worldview.

Not every experimental study on violent video games uses the CRTT, but the alternatives don't help out much either. Another framework that's sometimes used is called the 'hot sauce paradigm'. In this sort of experiment, researchers ask their participants to play either a violent or non-violent game. Afterwards, the researchers tell them that they're taking part in a slightly different experiment, this time about food preferences. The participants are given a choice of sauces ranging from fairly mild to blow-your-head-off hot, and are asked to prepare a concoction for another (again, fictional) participant who will be coming along after they've left, and who they're told doesn't like spicy food. If they go for hotter sauce in greater quantities, then they're being more aggressive. Apparently.

Sure, blasting someone with noise or sabotaging their jambalaya with cayenne pepper can make for an attention-grabbing study. And there are plenty of media pundits out there who are perfectly happy to blame acts of real-world violence on video game use, despite their only scientific justification for doing so (if they ever invoke any) coming from experiments of the type just mentioned. But because of the flexibility in the way that data can be analysed in the CRTT, it's very difficult to meaningfully compare the results across all of the different studies that have used it to date. Even if one were to be generous, though, and assume that the entire body of studies using the CRTT and hot sauce paradigms are consistent and comparable, what could they actually tell us about aggression? What are we trying to get a handle on here? A good number of papers in this area preface their literature reviews with commentary on some or all of those high-school shootings that I mentioned earlier. That's the kind of aggression we're worried about and that we want to look into: real-world aggression, where real people can get hurt or killed by others. But it's difficult to see how noise blasts and hot sauce can tell you anything useful about that sort of situation, because it's never clear what sort of 'aggressive' behaviour is being talked about in these studies – it might just be a case of annoyance, for example. Whatever it is, it certainly doesn't say much about real-life instances of aggression, let alone mass murder.

Let's return to the basic, questionnaire-based experiment for a moment, because there's another big stumbling block in laboratory-based research that I haven't considered yet. At the point at which participants are being selected to take part in the experiment, they need to be split into two groups: one that will play a violent game, and one that will play a non-violent game. How is it decided which games they will play? Something like *Call of Duty* might be an intuitive choice for the 'violent' video game group (or to give it its more technical term, the violent 'condition'). Presumably the right sort of game would be one that requires the participants to fight and kill other players or computer-controlled characters. For the non-violent ('control') condition, obviously, the ideal choice would be a game that doesn't embody those sorts of play requirements. Let's say a puzzle game is chosen, like *Candy Crush Saga*. But this creates a new problem, because *Candy Crush Saga* and *Call of Duty* differ in ways other than the amount of violent content in each. *Call of Duty* is a multiplayer, three-dimensional, fast-paced, first-person-perspective shooter game. *Candy Crush Saga* is a two-dimensional, relaxing, cartoon-like experience that you play alone. If a difference is discovered in reported aggression levels between players of these two games, can it be assumed that this is a result of either the presence or absence of violent content? The results might be due to one of those other differences between the two. Consistent with this idea, some researchers have suggested that other factors, such as frustration with the difficulty of the game, can be important. Others, such as the Brock University psychologists Paul Adachi and Teena Willoughby, have shown that factors like the level of competitiveness in games, rather than the level of violence, can actually be what drives apparently aggressive behaviour. Across a series of experiments published in 2011, Adachi and Willoughby asked participants to play one of four games: a competitive violent game (*Mortal Kombat versus DC Universe*), a competitive non-violent game (*Fuel*), a non-competitive violent game (*Left 4*

Dead 2), and a non-competitive non-violent game (*Marble Blast Ultra*). Using the hot-sauce-test measure of aggression I mentioned above, the researchers found that participants showed the highest levels of aggressive behaviour after playing either the competitive violent, or the competitive non-violent games, but that there was no difference in aggression levels between these two conditions. Similarly, for the two non-competitive games, participants showed relatively low levels of aggressive behaviour after playing each, and there was no substantial difference in the levels between the violent and non-violent games.

It's an interesting study, but one that we should nevertheless be wary of reading into too deeply. Perhaps it simply shows that the hot sauce paradigm isn't an adequate measure of aggression. Or it might fall foul of the very problem I've been using it to highlight: the four games used in Adachi and Willoughby's study are very different from each other, and perhaps it was some other, unconsidered difference between them that accounted for their results. The ideal, then, would be to use two games that look, feel and play as similar to each other as possible, with the only difference between the two being the amount of violent content present in each. Unfortunately, this happens exceedingly rarely in the published research literature – instead, it is more often the case that researchers fall into the trap I've outlined above, and use 'violent' and 'non-violent' games that aren't particularly comparable to each other. Here's an example of a study that actually has managed to overcome this problem. In 2016, a team led by Julia Kneer at Erasmus University in Rotterdam asked participants to play one of two modified versions of a first-person shooter game called *Team Fortress 2*. In the 'high violence' condition, the player (along with all of the computer-controlled characters they were fighting) was equipped with a flamethrower, the use of which resulted in some fairly gruesome deaths. In the 'low violence' condition, the player was equipped with a trumpet-like contraption that emitted rainbows when fired. Instead of killing other characters, the weapon incapacitated them by making them drop to the ground in an uncontrollable fit of laughter. In all other respects, the two games were the same. Kneer's team used a version of the CRTT to measure aggression, but didn't find any differences between the high or low violence conditions. In other words (if one accepts the usefulness of the CRTT as a metric) the amount of violent content in the game didn't seem to have any substantial effect on either the gameplay experience or behaviour of the players.

Principally as a result of these two major flaws, the experimental, laboratory-based research that has been conducted into the behavioural effects of playing violent video games has so far largely failed to provide convincing or strong evidence of any real-world effects. Some studies show effects, others don't, but these differences are largely down to peculiarities in the way the studies are conducted and the statistics analysed.

There is a way to overcome some of these problems though. Rather than looking at experimental data, researchers can look at the data obtained through something known as a 'longitudinal study'. This is a type of observational study where lots of people – ideally tens, or even hundreds of thousands – are followed over the course of their lives and assessed at various time periods (perhaps every six months or every year) to collect information on a wealth of topics: everything from what they do in their spare time to how they're performing at school, to what's going on in their home life. As far as the present context goes, the idea is that over the course of their lives some people will play video games and others won't. Similarly, some people will end up becoming aggressive and developing antisocial behaviours, and others won't. With a longitudinal study, the aim is to see whether one thing (playing video games) is correlated with another thing happening later in life (becoming aggressive or antisocial), while also taking into account other factors (for example, socioeconomic status, or parental monitoring) that might also have an effect. These other factors are called 'confounding variables', because they have the potential to affect both of the other factors we're interested in.

As an example, let's take 'parental monitoring': which basically refers to how much attention a parent pays to their child. 'High' parental monitoring tends to result in a situation where children are heavily supervised, where the parents have full knowledge of the friendships and activities that their kids enjoy, and might include things like insisting on a curfew at night. 'Low' parental monitoring is the opposite – it involves a family situation in which parents largely let their children do whatever they want, whenever they want, with minimal adult supervision. If the idea is to conduct a longitudinal study to look at whether playing video games is correlated with antisocial behaviour, this would have to take into account (or to give it a technical term, 'control for') parental monitoring, because both of these things are influenced by parental monitoring. In the case of low monitoring, a child would be more likely to play video games, and particularly those that might not be age-appropriate (because the parent has bought the game without considering the age rating, or because the child has gone to a friend's house to play it, or the parent simply doesn't care). But they are also more likely to engage in delinquent behaviour – if the child is allowed to do what they want, and isn't restricted to a curfew at night, then the likelihood that they may come into contact with delinquent peers, and be influenced by those peers, would increase. So in the analysis, a positive correlation between playing video games and antisocial behaviour might become apparent – one showing that those kids who play more video games will show greater levels of antisocial or aggressive tendencies later in life. But we would need to check whether it's actually the levels of parental monitoring that are driving both factors.

So while longitudinal studies can provide useful population-level data about a given topic, interpreting the results in a causal way is something that should only be done with caution: because different results might be down to which confounding factors are controlled for. A number of these sorts of studies have been published over recent years with video games in mind, but because of this caveat the results aren't particularly clear-cut. Some of these studies argue that violent video games are linked to aggressive behaviour. For example in 2008, a team led by Craig Anderson, a researcher based at Iowa State University in the US, ran three independent longitudinal studies on a total of 1,595 students aged nine to eighteen years old. Anderson argued that kids who played a lot of violent video games early in the school year were more likely to be physically aggressive later on. However, his team only controlled for two things: the sex of the participants, and prior aggressiveness. Other researchers have controlled for other things, and found different results. In 2011 for example, Chris Ferguson, then based at Texas A&M International University, ran a longitudinal study on 165 students which took into account a much wider range of variables – things like depression, evidence of family violence, evidence of antisocial behaviour, and whether the students had friends who smashed stuff up. Ferguson found that after controlling for all of these things, there didn't seem to be any association between playing violent video games and aggressive behaviour. Similarly, a study by Adachi and Willoughby (the Brock University team mentioned above) in 2013, which followed 1,492 students over four years, found that it was competitiveness in games that seemed to be driving the relationship with aggression.

In 2016, together with colleagues at the University of Bristol and University College London, I used data from the Avon Longitudinal Study of Parents and Children (also known as the 'Children of the 90s Study') in an attempt to bring some sort of resolution to the debate. Founded by Professor Jean Golding, this longitudinal study is a treasure trove of information, and I'm firmly of the belief that it is one of the greatest endeavours ever undertaken in UK scientific research. Beginning in the very early 1990s in the Avon area of South West England, some 14,000 pregnant women with an expected delivery date of between April 1991 and December 1992 were recruited for the study. During their pregnancy, and at regular interviews following birth, parents and children were asked to complete questionnaires on pretty much any aspect of life you can think of; everything from their experiences at school, to what home life was like, to religious beliefs, health issues, and beyond. They were also periodically asked to provide various physical measurements and biological samples – saliva, blood, hair, urine, toenails, placentas and more. Over the past 25 years it has become one of the most substantial and richest available databanks for understanding how both genetic and environmental factors affect human health and development. And, luckily for us, they also thought to ask about video game use.

Using this database, my colleagues and I set out to try to answer a relatively simple question: does video game use at an early age (in our study, eight or nine) have any link to problems with aggression and depression in teenage years (specifically, fifteen or sixteen)? Given the richness of the dataset, we tried to identify as many confounding factors as we could reasonably account for – anything that might have an impact on that association. This isn't the complete list, but to give you a flavour, we included things like: family history of mental health problems, maternal education and socioeconomic status, and whether the child at age eight was a victim of bullying or had emotional problems. As a measure of aggression, we used a clinically-validated assessment tool to measure a problem known as 'conduct disorder'. This is a clinically-diagnosable behavioural disorder that encompasses a range of what might be termed socially-unacceptable or 'bad' behaviours: it takes into account things like bullying and fighting, being cruel to animals, vandalising property, stealing, and engaging in risky behaviours.

What did we find? Well, taking into account all of the above potentially-confounding factors, and others, we found a weak association between the type of game that was played at age eight/nine, and the risk of showing some or all of the signs of conduct disorder at age fifteen/sixteen. Plus, the absolute risk of being diagnosed with conduct disorder was small – just 26 out of a total sample of 1,815 children met the full criteria for the disorder. So in other words, while we did find a correlation between playing a certain category of game (shoot-'em-ups) at a young age with later aggressive behaviour, it was so weak as to be negligible.

This goes to show a particular problem with longitudinal studies; the factors that you control (or don't control) for can be really important to your results. No longitudinal study is perfect; it's nigh-on impossible to account for every potential factor that might have an influence on whatever it is that you're interested in. So when you see a study saying that 'an association' has been found, or that X 'has been linked to' Y, what this really means is that a correlation has been found. As violent video game play increases, aggressive behaviour either increases, decreases, or remains unchanged, depending on which study you're talking about. Critically, that doesn't mean that the increase in violent content in a video game is *causing* the increase in aggression. As always, correlation does not imply causation. It also doesn't mean that longitudinal studies are useless – far from it. But it does mean that caution is needed when interpreting the results from them.

So, where does this leave us? I would love to be able to tell you that if we were to take the sum knowledge of everything that we've learned from both experimental and longitudinal scientific research, we would have a definitive answer either way about the effects of playing violent video games. But we don't, because, as you can see from the above, it's all a bit of a mess. That doesn't mean that all the research done in the area is worthless, or that it can't tell us anything of value. I think it's really important to remember that this is a nascent field of study: video games are a relatively new form of technology, and the scientific research looking at the effects of playing them is newer still. In a sense, it's unreasonable to think that an instantaneous and definitive understanding of what they do to us would be immediately available. Science just doesn't work that way. Instead, it's import- ant to look to the future of video games research, and think about how the mistakes of the past might be overcome in order to improve the field.

There are at least two main ways to do this. First off, the way video games are categorised within a research setting needs to be improved. It's not good enough to use divisions like 'violent' and 'non-violent' as comparison conditions, because those terms are so vague as to be meaningless. A slight improvement in this regard would be to focus on genre-based categorisations – for example, to compare the effects of playing first-person-shooter games with sports games, or platform games, or flight simulators, or puzzle games. But this isn't much better, because it doesn't deal with the problem of comparability between the games used. Instead, a more useful approach might be to think about how to modify individual games to become more or less violent, more or less competitive, and to set up comparison categories that use the same game, with tweaks here and there to change the gaming experience. Of course, such an approach could potentially be quite costly, in terms of the amount of both time and money needed to develop bespoke and modifiable games. But there are ways around this, and the example that I gave above of Julia Kneer's research is excellent in this regard. Kneer's work used *Team Fortress 2*, which has a highly active community of players who spend their time developing alterations (called 'mods') for the game. These can range from something simple like changing the font that's used for on-screen information, to novel modes that allow you to play the game in a completely different way. Kneer's team were able to take advantage of the fact that *Team Fortress 2* was developed so that creating mods relevant to their research question was a relatively simple process. Not every game works in this sort of way, of course – *Candy Crush Saga* can't be modified to create an ultra-violent version where instead of switching around sweets, bugs or animals are twisted around and killed in a gruesome manner.* But there are enough games out there with dedicated 'modding' communities to cover a broad spectrum of genres and types of play, and I think researchers should be leveraging this practice, and engaging with those communities more.

Alongside a better way of thinking about how to systematically change and assess the *content* of games, researchers also need to think more carefully about what effects the *context* of play has. People play games for lots of different reasons, which means that they play them in lots of different ways. Some play alone. Some play with friends or family in the same room, and some play with friends and strangers from across the world, in multiplayer online environments. None of these are mutually exclusive from each other. But while it seems like an obvious question to ask, vanishingly little research has considered the different sorts of effects that these sorts of situational types of play might have on behaviour. It's an important question to ask, though, because if it matters who you play with, or how you play the game, then developing a richer understanding of these factors might help to start reframing the questions and worries we have about the effects of playing games – any sort of game, not just 'violent' ones. Rather than thinking of gaming as a cause of aggression, could it be better to think of it as a risk marker? In other words, if someone is starting to play games to the exclusion of anything else, then should this be interpreted as an indication that they are having other problems in their life, and that it is these problems that might drive any aggression

---

* Well, in theory it could be – you'd just have to create a new version of the game, and then tweak that as you wished. But then it wouldn't actually be *Candy Crush*.

issues they have? And, critically, how can we best help them to overcome these problems?

As a final point, to have any hope of improving the state of the research area in the future, there need to be better measures of 'aggression'. To be completely honest with you though, I don't know what these might look like – not yet, at least. In a sense, it doesn't matter what, specifically, this new sort of measure would look like. What's more important is that it's developed in a systematic, open and robust way. There are already too many measures that are susceptible to biases in interpretation or statistical analysis. What is needed, ideally, is something that is agreed on by all scholars in the field as a useful and reasonable representation of aggression, regardless of what those scholars believe about video game effects. There's just one problem here. Over the past couple of decades, a clear warfront has emerged between research groups who show that violent video games do cause aggression, and groups that show no effect. And getting those groups to talk to each other, to work across the battle lines, is harder than doing the research itself.

CHAPTER 7

Moral panics

Nestled in the grandiose surroundings of Balliol College in Oxford University is the Oxford Internet Institute. While the name conjures up an image of a cutting edge, state-of-the-art, technology-saturated building, the institute is much like any other university department – shoehorned into the quirky rooms and hallways of a venerable old edifice. Nevertheless, the Oxford Internet Institute is home to some of the world's best and brightest minds, a few of whom are currently tasked with tackling those seemingly intractable questions about the behavioural effects of video games, and of technology use more generally. Among them is the director of the institute, Professor Andy Przybylski, who I've come to talk to about why video games researchers often find themselves at ideological loggerheads with each other. In this conversation, and the many I have had with him since, I have come to understand two things about Andy. The first is that he is unflinchingly, unequivocally, a family man – he cares deeply about the sort of world that his children are growing up in. The second, I always sense, is that he holds a deep frustration about the way that scientific researchers – particularly those interested in the effects that video games and other media have on us – conduct themselves, coupled with a fundamental belief that practices like open science (preregistering experiments, and sharing data in a collaborative and cooperative way) can do an immense amount of good when it comes to understanding video games.

Nowadays, Andy's research tends to concentrate on questions about the societal-level effects of using screens, and what the relative contributions are to general well-being of social media, gaming, watching movies, and so on. His earlier work concentrated more specifically on video games, though: using motivational theory to study what it is that draws people into playing video games, as well how the structure and content of video games impacts upon aggression. Andy's work shows that the amount of violent content in a game is only weakly related to a person's intrinsic motivation to play it: in other words, their desire to play is not because of a particular interest in the violent content itself. His research (which is grounded in the framework of Self-Determination Theory mentioned earlier) suggests that, despite popular belief, the presence of violence in video games doesn't actually add anything to their appeal.

When I first meet up with him, we sit in the grounds of Balliol, reminiscing about our early video game experiences. I rave about both the time travel mechanic and excellent soundtrack in *Sonic CD*, but Andy dissents. 'I am of the opinion that *Super Mario Bros.* might actually be the perfect game,' he explains to me emphatically. 'Like it might be like the Platonic ideal of a platform video game, and everything else is a variant in my mind.' I can see where he's coming from, but I have other ideas about the perfect game. For me, it's *The Legend of Zelda: Breath of the Wild*. And I'm sure there are many people who would vigorously disagree with both of us. Such is the personal nature of video games.

Andy Przybylski has built a career around using the best possible research methods to interrogate questions about why we play games, and what they do to us. In a sense, it's a dream job – rarely is it the case that someone is able to combine a hobby or personal interest with their day job, and both Andy and I are hugely lucky to be able to do so. More than that though, I believe that having a longstanding relationship with video games is key to developing a richer scientific understanding of their effects. Andy and I might disagree on what the perfect game may be, but in order to have that discussion in the first place, we need to have an understanding of how games work at a mechanistic, motivational and emotional level. But the relationship that games researchers have with video games doesn't necessarily always result in positive attitudes. 'At a conference I went to recently, I had a very strange experience,' Andy says. 'Remember before you took a university exam, sometimes people would tell you "oh, I didn't study at all, I was so drunk last night", and it was almost like a sort of social handicapping strategy? I hear this with video games researchers sometimes – they can be very quick to tell me "oh but I don't *play*, I've never played them". It's such a strange thing to say, almost as if it's a purity check. It would be like studying music, but going around saying "oh, but I don't actually *listen* to any of it".'

So there's a tension here. On the one hand, some researchers – and I include myself in this category – see no problem with both researching video games, and counting them as a hobby. As long as the science is robust, and we remain alert to our potential biases, there's no reason not to play them. On the other hand, there are other researchers who believe that to play video games is to compromise your own ability to conduct appropriate research on them. Perhaps this stems from a deep-seated insecurity or perception that, for some reason, video games research isn't a 'proper' science. Or maybe there are political issues at play between different research groups, so that if you admit to playing games, it's something that others can latch onto as a way of calling your research into some sort of doubt. In extreme cases, this tension has resulted in accusations being thrown around that researchers who claim there are negligible effects from playing video games are either 'apologists' for the games industry or, in one outrageous case, are equivalent to holocaust deniers.* It doesn't take a psychologist to tell you that name-calling isn't the best way to convince someone that your viewpoint is the right one, but this is the situation, as games researchers, that we find ourselves in. Pettiness aside, this divide in research cultures causes problems in terms of how we approach a difficult subject in a scientifically sound way, but also in how the results of our research might be communicated to the public at large. If nothing else, the simple experience of actually playing games gives you a much clearer understanding of how system mechanics work, the types of people you encounter, the motivations for why you have to perform particular actions at particular points, what it's like to play when you're in different moods – everything. Put simply, it exposes you to nuanced effects of different types of content, in different types of games, played in different contexts. Without that insight, it's no small wonder that the public discussion around games similarly misses their multifaceted nature.

---

* I'm not making this up. In a 2014 commentary paper for the journal *Pediatrics*, games scholar Victor Strasburger and colleagues wrote: 'Despite thousands of research studies on media effects, many people simply refuse to believe them. Some academics may contribute to this because they like to "buck the establishment", which is an easy way to promote themselves and their research. Of course, many people still believe that President Obama wasn't born in the United States, President Kennedy wasn't assassinated, men didn't walk on the moon, and the Holocaust didn't occur.'

Given the many problems with the research methods, some
of which I mentioned above, and the often intransigent (sometimes scandalous) opinions that some scholars hold, it should
be no surprise that there is little scientific consensus about the
proposed links between playing violent games and either aggression or violent crime. In 2015 for example, at least four papers
were published that studied academic consensus on the subject.
Depending on the types of researchers, and the nature of the
question asked, the levels of agreement among scholars about
the negative effects of playing video games ranged from 10.1 per
cent (for the statement 'agree the effects of digital games on
aggression are a problem for society') to around 66 per cent
(for the statement 'agree there is a causal relationship between
exposure to violent media and aggression'). That last statistic
was an odd one. It came from a paper published in the journal
Psychology of Popular Media Culture, written by a team led by
Professor Brad Bushman at Ohio State University. The team
solicited opinions from four groups of people interested in video
game effects – media psychologists, communication scientists,
paediatricians and parents. Agreement with the statement was
highest in the paediatrician group (80 per cent), followed by
the group of parents (about 63 per cent). For the two research
groups, agreement with the statement was lower: 61 per cent
for the psychologists, and 56 per cent for the communication
scientists. For another, related statement – 'violent video games
can increase aggressive behaviour in children' – 66 per cent
of researchers agreed, 17 per cent disagreed, and the remaining 17 per cent sat on the fence. But the way these findings
were reported was bizarre – in a press release for the paper,
Brad Bushman is quoted as saying that 'among researchers who
have an opinion, eight out of ten agree that violent video games

increase aggression.' This is a very tendentious interpretation of the data, and it ignores a fair chunk of people who were reasonably undecided about the statement. But unsurprisingly, the narrative that emerged following the publication of the paper was that there was a broad consensus that exposure to violent media increases aggression.

I'm picking on this paper for two reasons. The first is that claiming that there is a consensus among researchers when none exists risks shutting down future academic debate about the issue. Why would anyone bother researching violent media when there's already a 'clear' consensus from scholars in the field? The second reason is that, around the time the paper was published, I ended up writing about it for my column in the *Guardian*, because the problems ran deeper than the somewhat creative interpretations in the results. At the time, my colleague Chris Chambers and I were contacted by an anonymous source who had been very close to the peer review process that the paper had gone through. This source had an interesting story to tell. To put it simply, the version of the paper that was finally published and is now available for all to see, is *not* the one that went through peer review.

According to our source, the research paper, like any other, started off life by going through a standard review process. In one of the reviews that the journal solicited, the reviewer pointed out a fundamental statistical flaw in the analysis of the data the authors had undertaken. Under normal circumstances, this situation would mean either that the paper is rejected, or that the authors are asked to redo their analyses addressing the reviewer's comments; after which they would resubmit their article for another round of reviews. Strangely though, in this instance the editorial team decided to accept the paper, flaws intact, and instead invite the reviewer to write a reply that would be published alongside the article, explaining the statistical issues. This is a weird thing to do, albeit not entirely unheard of, and so the reviewer agreed.

But things then got a little stranger. Once the original authors – Professor Bushman and his colleagues – had seen the reviewer's reply article, they submitted a *new* version of their article to the journal. This version was unsolicited, and included changes to the paper that directly addressed the critical reply, effectively making the reply redundant. As we wrote at the time, this is a highly unusual practice – the editorial team should have rejected the unsolicited article, or at the very least hit the pause button while it was sent out for review again. Not only did this not happen, but the article went through a further *three* revisions (including the addition of a new author) before finally being accepted for publication.

One particular sticking point for me was a footnote that appeared in the final, published version of the paper. This is the only public record of anything substantial having changed in the paper during the review process, and suggested that the authors had actually changed their definition of the word 'consensus' in order to fit their conclusions. The footnote states that one of the reviewers of the earliest draft of the article 'correctly pointed out that these results could not be interpreted as consensus. The editor gave us permission to conduct a new set of analyses using a different operational definition of consensus.' Perhaps I'm being overly conservative about the whole thing, but this seems like a pretty substantial change, and certainly one that would have warranted another round of reviews.

I think it's important to point out here that journal editors do regularly make decisions about an article without going back to the reviewers for further consultation. This is fine, and generally relates to fairly minor changes that aren't really worth bothering reviewers with, like spelling errors, or trivial changes to sentences that improve readability but don't substantially alter the meaning of the research. But as we explained in our *Guardian* article at the time, what had happened with Bushman's consensus paper was different from standard practice in two key ways. First, the article had already been accepted by the journal before the authors made some pretty substantial changes to it. Second, the changes that they did make to it were fundamental to the way that the results were interpreted. The whole debacle left me disappointed, frustrated, and acutely aware of the consequences of allowing unchecked zealotry to creep into the scientific research process. And it made me think again about whether the beliefs that we hold about games, and our experiences with them, affect the way we approach studying them.

Trying to understand the reasons why various types of researchers might hold either positive or negative attitudes towards video games has itself been a topic of research in recent years. In 2017, Professor Christopher Ferguson at Stetson University in Florida surveyed 175 scholars with research interests in the link between games and aggression or violent crime, to try to dissect the reasons for the attitudes that they hold. This research was carried out in the context of something called Moral Panic Theory, or MPT. In its simplest form, MPT argues that societies periodically go through a process of creating 'folk devils' – people, groups or objects depicted in the mass media as being deviant in nature – which are then held up to be the source of any number and variety of social problems. According to the theory, by banning, limiting, or in some other way removing the influence of these folk devils, we feel as though we have some control over the social crisis that we're worried about, and it gives us a (false) hope that whatever the problem is, it is being fixed. In their seminal 1994 book *Moral Panics: The Social Construction of Deviance*, the sociologists Erich Goode and Nachman Ben-Yehuda further define some of the characteristics of a moral panic, and these features go some way to explaining why the panics themselves are problematic. Goode and Ben-Yehuda point out that moral panics are always, and without exception, 'bad' – that is, the folk devil will unequivocally have a negative impact on society. They also argue that there is an element of disproportionality, in that the political or societal response, as well as any action that is taken to remedy the issue, is far more excessive than the actual threat posed to society (although, perhaps, not excessive in relation to the *perceived* threat). Furthermore, moral panics are often volatile, in that they both appear and disappear quickly, as public interest in the issue is first whipped up, and then dissipates either naturally or as concerns move on to another folk devil.

In the past century at least, it is various forms of entertainment and communication media that have routinely taken on the role of the folk devil. The attendant social crises take the form of worries about youth violence, drug-taking, pornography, and anything else generally perceived to be 'unwholesome' and in direct opposition to an idealised concept of a carefree childhood and stable family unit. For example, in his 1954 book *Seduction of the Innocent*, the psychiatrist Fredric Wertham claimed that comic books were the root cause of juvenile delinquency. In an ensuing congressional hearing on the issue that same year, he is quoted as saying 'I think Hitler was a beginner compared to the comic-book industry. They get the children much younger. They teach them race hatred at the age of four before they can read.'

In the 1980s, the spotlight shifted to the tabletop role-playing game *Dungeons & Dragons*. At different time points various religious groups claimed that playing *D&D* was linked to suicide, ritual satanic abuse and murder. Rock music, death metal, horror movies and 'video nasties' have all been held up as examples of folk devils. Even *The Simpsons* found itself on the verge of a moral panic in the early 1990s, when then-president George Bush lamented that American families should be 'a lot more like [the wholesome television family] the Waltons and a lot less like the [much more dysfunctional] Simpsons.' For the last couple of decades, the folk devil has been video games. Increasingly, it is becoming screen time more generally – a topic which I'll get onto soon. In a few years, I surmise, it will be virtual reality that is thought to be the source of all of society's illnesses.

One of the points Ferguson made in his 2017 study into people who have a research interest in violent video games was that the researchers can end up promoting and perpetuating the moral panic themselves. This stems in part from the pressure exerted on scholars to produce research results that have a meaningful impact on society. The starting point for a moral panic typically lies not in objective scientific studies, but in a groundswell of anecdotal or personal experiences. These can proliferate quickly, especially in the age of the internet, and researchers are always in the position of having to play catch-up in order to provide evidence to inform public opinion. Where a research base already exists, evidence that supports the existence of the panic risks being accepted uncritically, whereas studies or scholars who refute the panic risk being treated with distrust – regardless of the actual quality of the research on both sides. A salient example of this comes from the case of the Sandy Hook massacre in 2012, in which a twenty-year-old man called Adam Lanza murdered his mother and then proceeded to shoot and kill 26 children and teachers at an elementary school in Newtown, Connecticut, before killing himself. At the time, a major focus for news stories was the speculation that Lanza was an avid player of violent video games, isolating himself for hours on end to play them. This idea sat neatly with the sort of research I've already looked at, which claimed to show a link between playing violent games and aggression. To suggest that such a link in the Sandy Hook case was tenuous and premature was to court suspicion – here, clearly, was a real-life case showing the horrendous effects video games can have on us, so why would anyone refute that? However, the final investigation report into the killings, which was released nearly a year after the event, painted a very different story. Although Lanza was known to play violent video games, the game with which he had by far the clearest obsession was *Dance Dance Revolution*, a rhythm-based game in which players have to move their feet across a dance platform (which contains pressure sensors) in time with music and video cues on-screen. In the rush to try to explain Lanza's actions, the focus on violent video games was a red herring.

As Ferguson points out, scientists are only human, and as such aren't immune to the incentives that are afforded if they get caught up in this sort of rush. Real-life tragedies aside, it's a really nice feeling when a study you've been working on for a long time gets picked up by a major news outlet and is suddenly read and discussed by many more people. It can make you feel like your research is having a real impact. That's apart from the academic kudos, and even potential future grant funding, which might come in its wake. Given the flexibility in the way that research is done on violent video games at the moment, it's very easy, inadvertently or otherwise, to produce results that suit a particular narrative. It's not difficult to see how games researchers, from a position of apparent expertise, can fuel moral panics by making statements that at first glance seemed to be based on evidence, but are in fact based either on conjecture or personal opinion. So understanding those opinions, and where they come from, is important.

Ferguson and his team surveyed some 175 scholars (mostly criminologists, psychologists and media researchers, as well as a smattering of paediatricians and psychiatrists). Alongside basic demographic data, his team asked them questions relating to their attitudes towards video games, towards youths in general, and what they pleasingly described as 'sanctimonious self-deception' – or the extent to which you see yourself as having a higher level of morality than other people around you. The team tested a number of different hypotheses, and found varying levels of supporting evidence for them. In general, researcher age was a significant predictor of attitudes towards games – older researchers were more likely to be negative about video games than younger researchers. However, once video game experience was taken into account, this relationship disappeared. In other words then, it seems to be that the less time a researcher has spent playing video games, the more negative the attitudes about them they hold, regardless of their age. Moreover, researchers who held youths in more disregard were also more likely to have negative game attitudes. However, sanctimoniousness didn't have any effect – holierthan-thou attitudes didn't seem to have any relationship with game attitudes.

The final hypothesis that Ferguson's team tested was that criminologists (the group of researchers who generally have the

most experience of crime data) would tend to be more sceptical about the supposed links between violent games and youth
aggression than other types of researchers. The team did indeed
find this to be the case, but they also found that media researchers were equally sceptical, and that both were much more
sceptical than psychologists. They tried to unpack this finding
in further exploratory analyses, which showed that although
criminologists played fewer video games, media researchers
tended to play more (which is somewhat counterintuitive, considering that the team also found a relationship between game
experience and negative attitudes earlier on). You might expect
from this that criminologists should actually have the *most*
negative views, but then, this isn't a simple relationship. Video
game experience alone isn't going to wholly explain whether or
not a given individual holds a positive or negative view about
video games. As Ferguson points out, criminologists largely
work with data relating to real-world aggression and violence.
It's not unreasonable, then, to think that they will be sceptical
of the purported conclusions of laboratory-based aggression
studies, particularly in terms of their applicability to the world
beyond university psychology departments. In sum, the findings from Ferguson's work clearly show that a scholar's positive
or negative view of video games is influenced by a number of
factors: research experience, beliefs about younger generations,
and their own experiences with playing games. There's another
important take-home message from this study though. Given
that different types of researchers, at different stages of their
lives, hold different beliefs about games, the findings suggest
that researchers aren't 'special' in any way. They're just as susceptible to generational and attitudinal biases as anyone else.
This means that when it comes to expert pronouncements about

the effects of video games, we shouldn't just take a talking-head researcher's word for it – we need to make sure that what they're saying is based on a good read of the data, and not grounded in their own biases and beliefs. Doing this isn't easy, I know – it requires time, effort and skill. It requires us to go beyond the news headline and search for the studies on which those commentators base their claims. It requires us to read those studies dispassionately, with no agenda, and to figure out whether they fall foul of the sorts of problems with methodology or analysis I've outlined in the past few chapters. Not everyone has the skill to be able to do this, which is why it's all the more imperative that scientists who do have that expertise should talk about both good and bad research in their own areas of interest, so that everyone can benefit. Good science communication, coupled with a sort of constant vigilance when it comes to thinking critically about what we read, is key to keeping scholarly research in check.

I think the issues I have been discussing here – the types of beliefs that video games researchers hold, what might drive those beliefs, and how those beliefs might shape how they conduct research – are important ones to tackle. If nothing else, doing so will help to build up a certain amount of immunity to hyped-up, scaremongering news stories about how video games are literally melting our brains. But I also think it's important not to lose sight of the real issues – the ones that we, as video games researchers, are doing an immeasurably poor job of dealing with right now. Most public discussions about video games are polarising, simplistic, all-good or all-bad dichotomies that completely miss the important questions we should be asking. At the time of writing, the President of the United States has been holding discussions with games industry leaders and a group of people who, as far as I can ascertain, can only be described as random conservative gun nuts, to discuss the link between violent video games and mass shootings in the context of the Parkland massacre of February 2018. No scientists were on hand at these meetings to explain that there is simply no evidence that playing violent games can lead to these sorts of atrocities.

But the conversation shouldn't end there, because there are other sorts of questions that should be being asked: questions, for instance, about the relationships between games developers and the US military-industrial complex. In 2002, the US Army developed a government-funded first-person shooter game called *America's Army*, and by 2005 it claimed that as many as 40 per cent of its new enlistees had played the game. In a column for *Eurogamer* in 2013, the excellent video games journalist Simon Parkin highlighted how the names and visual appearance of real-life guns, like the Barrett M82, are allegedly licensed for use in games like the *Call of Duty* franchise. In that column, a representative of Barrett Rifles is quoted as saying 'video games expose our brand to a young audience who are considered possible future owners.' There are, therefore, important research questions to ask about the ethics of using video games to encourage enlistment, as well as around whether or not games like *America's Army* are used as basic training simulators. There is obviously a precedent here – *Battlezone* variant *The Bradley Trainer* was used in just this way in the 1980s. Whether this is effective is an important question to ask, because if it isn't, soldiers could potentially be put at risk through the use of worthless training programs. And if it is, what does that imply for commercial versions of these products? In a similar vein, there are important research questions to ask about the relative effectiveness of in-game gun advertisements versus more traditional forms of advertising, and what this means for long-term trends in gun ownership.

There are other questions that violent video games research should be targeting. For example, there is very little existing research that looks at the question of whether there are specific groups of at-risk individuals who are likely to become violent or aggressive if they actively immerse themselves in violent media. Identifying the characteristics of such groups would be immeasurably useful not just in preventing downward spirals in the mental states of those sorts of individuals, but also in getting a clearer understanding of how, and to what extent games can exert differing effects on people as a function of individual differences. There is relatively little research on understanding how children process newer forms of video games, or how that interacts with their ability to interpret and understand reality. How does game-playing behaviour develop and change over time? How do video games fit in with other developmental processes at specific ages, and do they hinder, help, or have no effect on those processes? And how does all of that fit in with other influences on development? Even simple questions about rating systems are relatively under-studied – video games have a similar age rating system to movies, both in the US and UK, but they are poorly adhered to. Why is that the case, and how can awareness of such ratings be improved? There are no good answers to these questions at the moment.

I appreciate that I've been painting a pretty negative picture of violent video games research here. There are problems with how aggression is defined in experimental work. There are problems with how *video games* are defined in this line of work. There are problems in how experiments are set up and data is analysed, and there are problems in the way those data are reported in the published scientific literature. On top of all of that, there are problems in the way that researchers interact with the news media, and in the way that the news media goes through cycles of perpetuating the myth that playing violent video games and going out into the real world and killing real people are somehow connected. And because we're stuck in this cycle of overly-simplistic narratives about video games effects, there is the problem that new research, which might ask more insightful questions and generate more helpful answers, simply isn't happening. I think it's important to highlight all of these problems though, because brushing them aside isn't going to fix them. That being said, there are some positives that can be taken away from all this.

The first thing to say is that despite the hysteria around violent video games, things aren't as bad as they seem. In 2015, a team of researchers led by Patrick Markey at Villanova University ran a series of analyses looking at the long-term associations between violent crimes and video games sales. Rather than finding a positive correlation between the two, they found much the opposite. Since 1978, aggravated assaults and murders in the United States have been declining, after reaching a peak in around 1992. On the other hand, sales of video games have been steadily rising over the same period of time. If anything then, it looks like the correlation between the two is negative. They also looked at the incidence of violent crime following the release of three popular, archetypal violent video games – *Grand Theft Auto: San Andreas* (in 2004), *Grand Theft Auto IV* (in 2008), and *Call of Duty: Black Ops* (in 2010). Using an interrupted time-series analysis, Markey's team looked at the trends in violent crimes between one and twelve months after the release of each game. Although the data for aggravated assaults tended to show a slight decrease in the months following each game's release, the effects weren't significant. However, there were statistically significant dips in murder rates approximately three to four months after game release. As with a lot of research in this area, it is necessary to be careful before drawing causal interpretations from these results – there could be countless other factors not tested for in this study that could account for both the trends in video games sales and in the violent crime that is recorded. However, if there was a clear relationship between playing violent video games and violent real-world behaviour, we would see *something* in these data. Markey's team concluded that either the effects that violent video games have on violent crime don't exist, or they are completely dwarfed by other, more important and more salient factors.

The second thing to point out is that video games developers themselves aren't ignorant of these issues. Of course, just as attitudes within researcher populations (and in the wider public) vary, so too do those within the development community. When I spoke to the *World of Warcraft* Production Director John Hight, he had some unique insights to offer on the matter. 'Prior to coming to Blizzard, I certainly worked on one of the more violent games, and I also got to work on one of the least violent games at the same time. Simultaneously I was on *God of War* and on *Flow*,' he explains. *God of War* is a flagship 'hack and slash' game series for Sony's PlayStation consoles that places you as a mythological demigod on a mission of revenge against the higher Greek gods for their wrongdoings. *Flow* couldn't be more different – at its heart it's a 'life simulation': the game puts you in charge of a simple worm-like aquatic creature who evolves by consuming other microorganisms in the surrounding environment. '*God of War* knew its place. It was there to be the most macho character on consoles,' Hight points out. But his experience with the *World of Warcraft* team has been very different. 'With *WoW*, we want this comical feel, we don't want things to feel too serious or too real. We know that people are escaping into a fantasy. The world has bumpers in *WoW*, it's a relatively safe place to be.' Speaking to him, I get a real sense that developers – well, some of them at least – really do care about the sorts of experiences that their games afford. 'Because of my unique position, I've always had tons of games in the house,' Hight points out. 'My kids understood the rules about what's okay to play and what's not okay to play, but they'd often invite their friends over and want to play something. I'd feel obligated to call their parents and check with them, "Hey, your kid wants to play a shooter, your kid wants to play *Call of Duty* and it's not necessarily age-appropriate, how do you feel about that?" I feel like the issues are becoming less severe as the generation of kids that grew up playing video games are now parents themselves.'

In the same way that developers aren't blind to some of the wider debates taking place in the public sphere about the potential negative effects of playing video games, it is also worth being mindful of the fact that some of the big development houses are also actively seeking ways in which to combat what they refer to as 'toxic' behaviour in games. Toxic behaviour might take the form of hurling abuse at other players in-game, or deliberately targeting a single player over and over again with the intent of making them quit, or even just 'AFK-ing'* – deliberately leaving

---

* AFK stands for 'away from keyboard', a shorthand message that gamers often send out to other people they're playing with to let them know they're having a quick break.

your character in a game but not taking part, with the intent of irritating your team mates. All of these behaviours, and others, are at best antisocial, and at worst can lead to people suffering racist, sexist or violent verbal abuse. Ultimately, they make the game a less pleasant experience for everyone, and it is perhaps these sorts of behaviours that researchers are worried will spill over into real-world actions.

In late 2017, Jeff Kaplan – the lead designer of *Overwatch* at Blizzard Entertainment – set out precisely why this was a problem in an online video. 'We want to make new maps, new heroes, new animated shorts – that's where our passion is. But we've been put into this weird position where we're spending a tremendous amount of time and resources punishing people, trying to make people behave better,' he explained. 'Bad behaviour is making the game progress, in terms of development, at a much slower pace.' During my visit to Blizzard HQ, I asked him to elaborate. 'Traditionally in first-person-shooters, you're mostly looking at the scoreboard. There's no real teamwork happening. We tried so hard to create a team-based experience and I think we were super successful with that,' he explains. The downside to this, though, is that when a player is on the losing team, or when things aren't going exactly the way they intended, they tend to lash out. 'They like to go through this cycle of, "Well, it's obviously the game's fault." Then if it's not the game's fault, it's the people who made the game's fault and if it's not the people who made the game's fault, it's their teammate's fault,' he adds.

Let's face it: losing a game isn't always going to be an uplifting experience. And if it's happening for around half the time that you're playing (if a game has been particularly well-balanced by the development team, then there should be a 50–50 win rate*), it can take a lot of self-control to not get frustrated. It's not surprising, then, that players sometimes get angry and end up looking for someone else to blame. It's clearly something that plays on Jeff's mind. 'We could greatly reduce toxicity by doing extreme things that I don't believe in, and that's part of what's frustrating for me,' he explains. 'For example, if we stripped anonymity from the game, people would be far less likely to be toxic. However, I'm not a believer in internet games forcing real-life identity. I think that creates a whole host of new problems.' An alternative approach might be to significantly reduce the ability for players to communicate with each other. But to do so disrupts a fundamental aspect of why people play games in the first place. 'I feel like some of those solutions are cutting off your nose to spite the face' explains Kaplan. 'There are so many great amazing social interactions coming out of online games and when we go to these dramatic measures, it saddens me in some ways. I don't want to get to that point.'

Perhaps he won't have to. In March 2018, a coalition of over 90 gaming professionals and development companies started an initiative known as the Fair Play Alliance. The aim of the alliance

---

* It might seem counterintuitive, but if an online multiplayer game such as *Overwatch* is well-balanced, a player's win rate over hundreds or thousands of games shouldn't be solely reliant on their skill level – it should tend towards a 50–50 rate. This is because you, as a developer, don't want to end up in a situation in which highly skilled players are regularly being matched against poor or novice players, because the game experience would be bad for both groups. The highly skilled players would get bored with winning all of the time, whereas the low-skill players would give up and stop playing the game. Instead, as a player practices and improves at the game, you want to have a system in place whereby they are always matched with other players of the same skill level. That way, every match will be fair, and give players on both teams an equal chance of winning.

is to provide a conduit through which collaborative research can be conducted, and insights and best practices shared between developers, with a view to reducing disruptive behaviour and promoting fair play in online games. It's an incipient initiative, but by sharing the problems that individual companies have experienced, alongside examples of solutions that have or haven't worked, then over time the hope is that the alliance will be able to produce a set of standards and rules that have been shown to reduce toxic player behaviours, and that can be administered across games and gaming platforms.

There might not yet be definitive answers to the question of how best to tackle toxic behaviour in games, but the clear sense I got from talking to both Jeff Kaplan and John Hight was that they aren't turning a blind eye to the worries that people have about video games. Whether it's games causing real-world physical aggression, or simply whether they just make us act like foul-mouthed clods to each other online, these are issues that the developers care deeply about. Probably because they are a part of the more general question that drives most games developers: how do you create the best and most positive gaming experience for your players? More than that though, my brief time talking to the development teams at Blizzard made me think much more carefully about the questions psychologists and media effects researchers should really be asking, and made me wonder why the voices of the developers are not heard more. Those brief conversations I had threw up more interesting ideas and avenues for research than the previous five years I had spent looking at the available video games effects research literature. It made me realise just how immature some of the science we're doing is. We're asking the wrong questions, in the wrong way, using the wrong methods. Until we resolve those problems, research into video games isn't going to be at a level of maturity to answer some of those bigger, more useful questions I suggested earlier. And perhaps the most important of those questions is one that has been bothering me for as long as I've been interested in the science of games: are they addictive?

CHAPTER 8

Are video games addictive?

The day that my dad died started off like any other November morning in the North of England: grey and miserable. The excitement of having nearly made it to the weekend was offset somewhat by the fact that Friday mornings held the dreaded games session – a weekly reminder of how terrible I was at school sports. This week, we were playing football, outside, on the school's all-weather pitch. It doesn't matter what the weather's like; snow, sleet, showers or sunshine, all-weather pitches are always awful to play sports on. It's like someone has found a giant kingdom of moles, and covered the sea of mounds with sandpaper and disappointment.

The pitch was strategically positioned on the exposed side of a hill just on the outskirts of Oldham, Lancashire. On a sunny day you could see as far as Manchester city centre – but we never really used it when the weather was good. Not that you had much time to spend daydreaming and gazing off into the distance. It was freezing cold, and standing still was a slightly less desirable option than half-heartedly chasing a ball meandering along an increasingly sludgy beige surface. At least running around conjured up an illusory moment of warmth. I was playing in my usual, innocuous position as left side full-back, where I could do a minimal amount of damage. Football was not really my sport.

And then, it happened. Someone halfway down the pitch hoofed the ball in my general direction. I ran to get under it, and in a momentary lapse of sanity, decided that this was the perfect moment to try out a bicycle kick. Oh, it would be *glorious*! Time would stand still, the wind would drop, and everyone would see me spin effortlessly though the air, connect with the ball, and dismantle the threat.

I missed.

Terminally off-balance, right leg in the air like some bizarre fourteen-year-old can-can dancer, I slammed my foot back onto the ground to try to stop myself falling over.

I missed again.

Well, technically I didn't miss the ground. I just missed it with the intended part of my foot. I went down at an angle, bringing my full weight down on my ankle. I don't know whether it was the cold or the embarrassment that meant that the pain didn't register straight away. I do know that it was a misplaced sense of pride and stubbornness that led me to attempt the exact same kick a minute or two later. This time, my damaged foot connected with the ball. As it did so, an explosion of pain rippled up my leg. I crumbled to the ground, hands covered in muculent beige grit, and suddenly it didn't seem so cold any more.

A combination of my idiocy-induced ankle injury during the day, and the death of my dad later that evening, meant that I didn't return to school for some time. I moved in to live with my mum and her partner (my parents had divorced some years earlier) and for the next few weeks I was sofa-bound and forlorn. To try to take the edge off the situation, my mum gave me a thoughtful distraction in the form of an early birthday present: a brand-new Nintendo 64, complete with what I have come to consider one of the greatest games ever made. *GoldenEye 007* was hugely important for its time. Launched in 1997 (two years after the Bond film on which it was based), it was considered one of the first ever first-person shooter games for a home games console to demonstrate that the multiplayer genre could actually work in that setting. The Bond branding certainly helped – from the classic opening crawl, I was enthralled. That first day, I completely lost myself in the game. All of my attention was focussed on it, and for those few, blessed hours that I played, the twin pains of my loss and my injury dulled, if only for a little while. Over the next week, the game gradually became an obsession. When I wasn't in the living room playing it, I was upstairs, scouring the rudimentary internet for walkthrough guides, hints and cheats. I didn't want to think about what had happened. I wanted to think about the next level. When I finished the single-player campaign, I went back over it, again and again. When I got bored of playing, I would just wander around multiplayer levels, scouting out every shadowy corner for the best places to attack – not that I ever really played the game with anyone else. I was the archetypal gamer, playing alone, my skin bleaching from the double whammy of the harsh artificial glow of a television screen and the lack of venturing outside into what little sunlight the winter could afford. But was it a problem? Not really. I recently asked my mum whether she was concerned about it at the time. She was worried about me, but not the gaming. To her, it was simply my way of dealing with catastrophic loss.

When I returned to school, nobody really talked to me about my dad, and I didn't really talk to anyone about my brief relationship with *GoldenEye 007*. I had a considerable amount of work to catch up with, and quickly lost interest in playing it. I never really did deal with that initial grief though – rather than face it full on, I packaged it in a flimsy box in the back of my mind, allowing it to periodically spill out and cause me to shut down, physically and emotionally, for a few moments at a time. Eventually, I got another game for my N64 – *The Legend of Zelda: Ocarina of Time* – and once again got lost in a fleeting obsession with it. That cycle, of completely immersing myself in a game for a month or so, followed by casting it aside completely, would go on for a few years.

In discussions on the harmful effects of playing video games, one thing that crops up again and again is that issue of obsession – or, more precisely, the question of whether, and when, obsession can become an addiction. It is, I think, one of the most difficult issues that parents have to grapple with when it comes to games. If games are something you don't understand, then watching a kid play one can be a jarring and sometimes unsettling experience. It seems as if their attention is completely consumed by the events on the screen in front of them, as if nothing else matters, or even exists. And when the time comes to put the game away and have dinner, do homework, or go to bed, vociferous arguments can ensue. So when stories crop up in the media with experts claiming that video games can damage our children, can cause them to become *addicted*, it can often be difficult not to reflect on our own experiences and wonder whether you're witnessing that addiction in the people closest to you. But, as is becoming a common theme now, what you read in the media about gaming addiction and what the actual scientific research says about it are two very different things. That's not to say that we shouldn't worry about games at all – I have real concerns about the way that they are monetised and marketed towards children, for example. It's just that the public discourse about games is far too frequently derailed by facile narratives that seem to argue that because some aspects of gaming are problematic, the entire pastime is problematic. Navigating around this problem is really difficult, and it's no small wonder that parents, bombarded with confusing and often contradictory messages about gaming addiction in the media, are left confused as to what to do, or even as to how much they should really be worried about video games. So it's a good idea to have a look at what the research evidence does show, to see if it can help figure out where our concerns should be directed.

For as long as video games have existed, there have been questions about their addictive properties. In a letter to the *Journal of the American Medical Association* in 1982, researchers at Duke University Medical Centre reported three cases of men aged between 25 and 35 who they claimed had '*Space Invaders* obsession'. The men in question reported a massive increase in the amount of time that they played the game in the weeks leading up to their respective marriages, and that they would often fantasise about the game before going to sleep each night. Some of the claims in the letter were bizarre, and arguably overstepped the mark of reasonable inference from such a limited number of cases. For example, at one point the authors claimed that 'each man's obsession with playing *Space Invaders* was a means of handling his anger over the recent commitment to marriage. The disintegration of invading aliens who were trying to overrun the "home base" took on symbolic significance.'

A pretty bleak indictment of something that's supposed to be a positive life experience in my view, but I guess we all have our own opinions on marriage.

The letter marked the first in a long line of inquiry into the potential personal and interpersonal harm that an obsessive relationship with video games could engender.* Observational research in the 1980s started to coalesce around the idea that video game addiction was a real possibility, which perhaps manifested either like other behavioural disorders (such as gambling addiction), or in a way that resembled substance abuse disorders. Much of the work at this time was observational though: it wasn't until the 1990s and early 2000s that experimental research began in earnest. The majority of this work involved taking questionnaires that had been developed to measure things like gambling or substance addiction, and adapting them to focus instead on video games. This has led to an approach that surmises that some people in the gaming population might exhibit a certain set of symptoms, or meet a certain set of criteria, that can be assumed to be 'gaming addiction' – because they are the same set of symptoms that manifest in other sorts of addictions. Ultimately, research in this vein led to gaming addiction being classified as a fully-fledged mental health disorder in the summer of 2018.

---

* An honourable mention should in particular go to 'Nintendo Enuresis', which isn't the (terrible) name of a new games console, but the title of a 1991 paper published in the *American Journal of Diseases of Children*. The author, Julian Schink, had identified three cases of children who developed enuresis – bed-wetting, basically – after receiving and playing a Nintendo Entertainment System. 'The problem resolved after 1 to 2 weeks,' he explained, 'when the children learned to use the pause button.'

But, just as there have been difficulties in pinning down the definitions and relationships between playing 'violent' video games and aggressive behaviours, so too has the literature on gaming addiction been fraught with controversy and disagreement. By and large, the arguments have boiled down to the question of whether it's appropriate to use the criteria for gambling addiction, or substance addiction, as the criteria for gaming addiction. Many researchers have argued that restricting research in this way potentially misses other types of symptoms that might be unique to, and more representative of, a gaming-related disorder. Moreover, such an approach makes the assumption that video games are harmful in and of themselves – for example the idea that excessive use is a bad thing, just as excessive gambling or excessive substance use is. Games are, by their very nature, hobbies designed to be immersive and interactive – therefore, standard criteria for addiction, such as *being preoccupied with them*, or *playing them instead of engaging in other hobbies*, doesn't really sit well as a benchmark for 'harmful' engagement. Just because a person is immersed in playing a game doesn't necessarily mean that other aspects of their life are suffering. This idea is particularly salient with regard to socialising with friends.

As far as playing games goes, there is often an assumption that socialising through these channels online is somehow less worthwhile, less fulfilling, than doing so offline. However research over the past two decades shows that this is simply not the case – starting with work by the social psychologist Katelyn McKenna at New York University in the early 2000s, various studies have shown that deep and meaningful relationships can be formed with other people over the internet, and that they remain stable over time. Online socialising isn't necessarily better or worse than the offline equivalent, it's just different.* If an individual has started to lose interest in, say, going to the cinema with friends because they have been playing online games, it can't therefore be assumed that this is an indication of a problematic gaming habit. It might be that they are socialising with the same friends, or a wider social group, through whichever game it is that they are playing. To the outside observer, what looks like a situation in which that person has become absorbed in a digital facsimile of real life, is in fact a modern-day equivalent of going down to the pub with another set of your mates.

As I've mentioned, this all came to a head in the summer of 2018, when one of the most important documents that clinicians refer to in classifying and diagnosing mental and physical health problems, the World Health Organisation's International Classification of Diseases (ICD), set its sights on gaming addiction. The ICD contains sets of criteria for an exhaustive list of disorders that can be used to help diagnose and categorise patients for the purposes of, among other things, healthcare, research or insurance. The draft of the 11th version of the manual, 'ICD-11', published that summer, for the first time included 'gaming disorder' as a formal behavioural problem. The decision sparked a furious debate in the academic community. Some scholars argued that the inclusion was a good

---

* Through a series of surveys and lab-based experiments, McKenna's work, for example, showed that because there is an absence of 'gating' features when you first meet someone online (such as their physical appearance, or whether they look anxious or shy), people are more likely to like each other than if they initially met face-to-face. Moreover, relationships are more likely to develop quickly and become more stable online because people are more likely to disclose real information about themselves.

thing – by formally recognising an addictive disorder relating to video games, people who were experiencing genuine harm from excessive play could receive better access to treatment, as well as becoming eligible for insurance or financial support for that treatment. But other scholars argued that there was a lack of scientific research evidence that the disorder, as defined, was accurate or meaningful. Where the pro-inclusion group argued that a formal categorisation would reduce the stigma surrounding excessive gaming, the anti-inclusion group argued the opposite: that because there was no clear distinction being made between people highly engaged in playing games who suffer no harm, and those for whom excessive gaming has negative consequences, stigmatising attitudes about video games being 'bad for us' would increase. It's a debate that still rages on, and it shows no sign of abating any time soon.

At this juncture, I should probably come clean and point out that I'm firmly in the anti-inclusion camp, and that I was a co-author on a commentary paper published earlier in 2018 in the *Journal of Addictive Behaviors* (*JAB*) that outlined some of the reasons the WHO's inclusion of gaming disorder was premature. To my mind, there are very good reasons that it would be prudent to postpone a formal classification of such a disorder. Firstly, the fact that there isn't yet any clear picture of what gaming addiction, or gaming disorder, or whatever you want to call it, actually looks like. This is largely for the reasons I mention above – that the research literature on gaming addiction has become too rigid in how it tries to understand and approach the issue. A good example of this comes from another major diagnostic manual last published in 2013: the American Psychiatric Association's *Diagnostic and Statistical Manual of Mental Disorders* (*DSM-5*), which also included gaming addiction, in the guise of something termed 'Internet Gaming Disorder' (IGD).* Here, it was included in a special section on conditions that require more clinical research and experience before they should be fully included as a formal mental health disorder. The main aim was to try to encourage further research into the phenomenon, so that a decision could be taken at a later date as to whether it is, in fact, an actual disorder. Nine criteria were proposed, which researchers could use as a basis for future research. They were: having a preoccupation with internet games; experiencing withdrawal symptoms when not playing; experiencing tolerance towards them (i.e. feeling the need to spend greater amounts of time playing the games); difficulties in exerting control over playing; loss of interest in other hobbies; continued excessive use despite the problems caused by playing; deceiving family or friends about how much time is spent playing; playing to escape or avoid negative moods; and risk or loss of relationships or jobs as a result of playing. It was a laudable idea, but in the years since the *DSM-5* was published, instead of research being driven by attempts to understand *whether* Internet Gaming Disorder exists, the main focus has ended up being confirmatory in nature. In other words, rather than trying to more accurately define gaming addiction and distinguish it from cases where people play often but don't come to any harm, the research field instead became fixated on the idea that the *DSM-5*'s initial diagnostic criteria were correct. The result is that subsequent research concentrated

---

* Somewhat confusingly, Internet Gaming Disorder covers offline video gaming as well: 'internet' was used as a preface to distinguish it more clearly from gambling disorder, and because a lot of work around gaming addiction in the early 2000s pertained to MMOs.

on providing incremental evidence based on those criteria, and has just reinforced them without confirming whether they were right in the first place.

Another reason I think the WHO's classification of gaming disorder is premature comes down to the issue of prevalence. If we don't get our understanding of the nature of gaming addiction right, then it makes it difficult to get a true sense of how much of a problem it is in the gaming population. And if we can't get an idea of how many people gaming addiction is actually affecting (or what the characteristics of those people are), then this leads to two further interacting issues. The first is that we will be in danger of over-diagnosing, and thus minimising the importance of, what could be a genuine clinical disorder. If the criteria that are used end up defining non-harmful behaviour as harmful or addictive, then a significant proportion of the gaming population will be pathologised (treated as abnormal in some psychological way) and effectively misdiagnosed. The second resultant issue is that those people for whom gaming addiction *is* an actual, debilitating disorder might end up not getting the recognition, understanding, and treatment they need. Or worse, that ill-defined but expensive private treatment programmes will start to pop up, that lack any clear evidence of being effective. This has already happened in China, where military 'bootcamp' style institutions have appeared in recent years to combat an apparent 'epidemic of internet addiction'. As reported in investigations by the *New York Times* and the BBC, camps such as the Internet Addiction Centre in Shandong Province have come under repeated criticism for using brutal methods to 'detox' patients: electroconvulsive therapy and physical beatings appear to be commonplace, and in some of the most harrowing cases it has led to the deaths of young patients.

Understanding the true prevalence rate, alongside the characteristics of addicted gamers, is a problem for the research field – estimates of how widespread the disorder is vary wildly, from as low as 0.2 per cent of the gaming population to as high as 46 per cent. In 2011, a review of the available literature conducted by the games scholar Christopher Ferguson estimated that the true figure could be around 3.1 per cent of the gaming population. But even here, Ferguson specifically cautioned that this figure should be treated with a certain level of scepticism, because many of the studies included in his review didn't make a clear distinction between pathological, harmful gaming and intensive-yet-unharmful gaming. In other words, someone who is highly engaged in playing video games, plays them for many hours per day, and uses them to relax, but shows no problems in other social relationships, health or work, is probably not someone who is being harmed by that activity. Much the opposite; it is likely to be a positive experience for them. It might even be a source of income – people who test, review or professionally play video games will all necessarily be 'highly engaged'. However, if some studies assume that a characteristic of pathological gaming is 'spending large amounts of time doing it each day', then in the examples above, those people would be erroneously categorised as being addicted, and the prevalence rate would be incorrectly inflated. So, getting this prevalence rate right is important, because if it is overestimated, a vast chunk of the gaming population would be misdiagnosed with a disorder that they do not have.

These two issues – the nature of gaming addiction, and how widespread it truly is throughout the gaming population – are important, because if the science is wrong, and the message that gets sent to the public is that video games are unequivocally addictive, a number of unintended consequences could ensue. Games scholars such as Rob Cover, Rune Nielsen and Daniel Kardefelt-Winther have argued that if high engagement in video games is misinterpreted as addiction, it could be used as an excuse to undermine children's rights, by restricting access to something that isn't harmful and may in fact have positive effects. Moreover, those restrictions may simply be ineffective, or even backfire. We made a similar point in our 2018 *JAB* paper: moral panics and attempts at either formalising diagnosis or creating legislation have a tendency to feed off each other, often with unproductive results. A clear example of this can be seen in attempts in South Korea to curb what has been considered to be an epidemic of excessive gaming, particularly at night, among the nation's children. Fuelled by concerns about that epidemic, in late 2011 the Korean government enacted legislation that became known as the 'shutdown policy': children under the age of sixteen were blocked from accessing the internet between the hours of midnight and 6am. Although the policy wasn't based on any research studies explicitly suggesting that it should be levied, at face value it doesn't seem like a heavy-handed approach, and in fact may appear quite sensible. After all, no one *needs* to be playing video games in the early hours of the morning. And given that by some estimates, Korean teenagers don't appear to be sleeping as much as their Japanese or American counterparts (31 per cent of the day versus around 33–37 per cent of the day), then the shutdown policy could be seen as a simple solution to a pervasive problem. The trouble was, it doesn't seem to work very well. In a 2017 analysis, a team led by Changjun Lee of the National University of Singapore showed that the shutdown policy had the effect – for whatever reason (it wasn't stated) – of *increasing* the amount of time that children spent on the internet each day. In terms of the impact on sleep duration, statistical analysis suggested that although the policy worked in terms of getting teens to sleep more at night, this effect was tiny – the policy resulted in an increase of 1.5 minutes of sleep each night for boys, and 2.7 minutes for girls. Arguably, as far as government legislation goes, it hasn't been the most effective, and it's an example that shows, acutely, what happens when policy is created without a clear and consistent scientific evidence base to support it.

While nothing as drastic is known to have happened since the WHO announced the inclusion of gaming disorder in ICD-11, their decision was nevertheless reported uncritically by news outlets around the world, stoking a continued media panic about video games in the summer of 2018. It was the very worry that the *JAB* authors all had concerns about: a policy which didn't have a coherent evidence base was being rolled out without any consideration for how it was likely to be picked up in the news, and without any appreciation of the likely knock-on effects that both the policy and the coverage would have on the public. This came at a time when the latest gaming craze, *Fortnite*, was causing parents many anxieties, resulting in a slew of stories about schools banning the game and parents worrying about whether their kids had developed an addiction that would put them on a course to hard drugs (this notion encouraged in part by the story of one individual who claimed that playing *Fortnite* had resulted in him taking up cocaine). In order to try to provide a calming corrective, in June of that year, I, along with colleagues from the Oxford Internet Institute and the Royal College of Paediatrics and Child Health, held a press briefing at the UK's Science Media Centre, based in the Wellcome Collection building in central London. It was a chance to talk directly to journalists and explain some of the issues we had with the WHO announcement I've mentioned above, and for the most part our concerns were accurately relayed in subsequent news coverage. Not everyone was happy with what we had done though – in the week afterwards, I received a number of aggressive and negative messages from both researchers and members of the public. Experts and non-experts alike, it would appear, have deeply held beliefs about what is clearly an emotive topic.

Let me state, because I think this is worth emphasising: no one is saying that there aren't some cases out there where playing video games is having a demonstrably harmful effect on a person's life. However, as far as the research is concerned, there is no clear picture of how many people are likely to be affected, what the characteristics of those people are, and most critically, whether playing video games is the *causal* reason behind any negative issues in their lives. This makes developing anything that might even vaguely resemble a useful treatment for any potential disorder extremely difficult, if not currently impossible. Moreover, enacting a poorly-thought-out national policy is likely to do more harm than good, and this would be a real disservice for that group of people for whom video game play is evidently not a healthy endeavour.

For the most part, my opinion is that I don't think we should be worrying too much about video games (in a general sense) being 'addictive' in the literal, harmful sense of the word for the vast majority of people who play them. I base that opinion on my reading of the state of the research literature that we have to date, and I should point out here that if further robust and transparent research comes to a different conclusion, I'm more than happy to change my position. Part of the reason I don't think we should worry too much is that some of the best research evidence that's available to us right now seems to suggest that even if gaming addiction were to affect a large chunk of the population, it isn't a chronic problem. For example, pre-registered research conducted by a team led by Netta Weinstein at the University of Cardiff looked at data from almost 6,000 American participants over a six-month period. None of the participants who reported, at the start of the study, meeting the diagnostic threshold for Internet Gaming Disorder (which is defined as meeting five or more of nine possible criteria for the disorder, and experiencing distress as a result) did so at the end of the six months, nor did the disorder being present have any direct, observable effects on health over time. Along similar lines, a review published in 2017 by the United Nations International Children's Emergency Fund concluded that, based on the available research, there was little evidence to suggest that playing video games for extensive periods of time was inherently harmful to childhood well-being.

None of this means that video games shouldn't give us anything to worry about though. Over the past few years, driven in part by the proliferation of smartphones that have enough processing power to function as a gaming device, there has been an observable shift in the way that games are marketed and monetised. With free-to-play games that initially require no outlay, but that encourage players to spend money through in-game micro-transactions (that is, frequently spending small amounts of money to purchase new levels, characters, items or other additions to a game), there is a risk that gaming mechanics that exploit the same sorts of psychological weaknesses that gambling machines do might become more commonplace. This is one of the reasons that makes it all the more imperative that we get the science of gaming addiction right, and we get it right quickly.

Making money from video games has always been a tricky thing to do, and particularly so in the case of mobile games. Whereas a typical console game might retail for around £50 (about $60–65), it simply isn't viable to use the same sort of price point for a mobile game – smartphone apps are typically priced around the 99 pence mark (usually 99 cents in the US). Over the past decade or so, other ways of making money from such games have started to proliferate. Rather than charging players a single, seemingly high price for a game, the 'freemium' model provides the game completely free of charge instead. Or at least, the first few levels free of charge. Once players get to a point where they have some sort of investment in the game – be it the amount of time they've already spent playing, a genuine interest to progress further through it, or some sort of emotional attachment to it – then additional levels or additional game content is suddenly gated, and players are encouraged to spend small but frequent amounts of money if they want to go any further. For example, a typical way of applying this model involves forcing players to wait for content, and there are endless examples of this in the form of 'match-three' puzzle games. In this genre, players are given a grid of objects, with the aim of switching neighbouring items with each other to create a line of three (or more) similar items in a row. Once a match is made, those items are collected, and in order to win a level you might be given the goal of collecting, say, 100 objects in 30 moves. If you don't achieve the goal, you lose a life, of which you're only given a limited number. In many of these types of games, if you run out of lives on a particular level, you're either made to wait for lives to be replenished (perhaps anything between 30 minutes and 24 hours), or you can pay a small amount of money to replenish them immediately. Often, the relationship between your hard-earned cash and the opportunity to have another attempt at a level isn't direct. Instead, games like this tend to get you to purchase a fictitious in-game currency – typically gold coins or gems – which you can then spend on unlocking lives or other features (like special powers that make levels easier to complete). The concept isn't just restricted to puzzle games either; it's very easy to lock any sort of content in any sort of game behind a timer, in such a way as to encourage players to spend a little money, often. It's a spectacularly lucrative model – for example, within a week of *Harry Potter: Hogwarts Mystery* launching in April 2018, it was earning over a million dollars per day through in-app purchases. But because the key to ensuring a successful freemium model lies in encouraging people to repeatedly part with small amounts of cash, it's a system that's wide open to misuse. Unfortunately, the potentially disastrous ramifications of a model that has been growing, by and large, unchecked are only now becoming clear.

I've been playing freemium games, on and off, for as long as I've had a smartphone. For the most part, I've tried to take a sensible approach to spending money on them; I'll play them for free as much as I can, but if there's a particular feature that I really want to have access to, and it's a game that I feel that I'm getting a decent amount of play out of, then I will give myself a limit of around £5 to spend on it. This seems fair – after all, there is a developer out there who has spent time, money and effort crafting a nice gaming experience for me, so it's not unreasonable to reimburse them for that. I would much rather pay an initial fixed cost, though, and know that I'm not going to be coerced into spending much more later on.

I became acutely aware of how much it could be possible to spend in the dying months of 2017. On a whim, I downloaded

Game of Thrones: Conquest, because I was looking for something that would fill the epic fantasy space before the final season was released on television. *Conquest* tasks you with building and improving a castle in the mythic lands of Westeros, and the purpose of the game can be boiled down into two main goals. The first is to gather resources like wood, food and steel, in order to craft and improve buildings within your grounds, build up armies, and forge powerful weapons. The second is to send your armies out to trash other players' castles, and ultimately vie for domination of your surrounding lands. It starts off simply enough. If you want to recruit soldiers, and you have enough resources, like wood and food, you can spend these to train troops. This process takes time, though, and the game is gated: they won't be accessible to you until, say, twenty minutes of real time has passed. In the early parts of the game, actions like these take minutes, so it consistently feels like there's a lot to do. But as things progress, and your castle becomes more power-ful, the amount of time you have to wait until new materials or troops become available starts to increase. Before I stopped playing it, I managed to get my castle to level fifteen, at which point everything was taking 24 hours or more to create. And so, because you've invested all that time in building your little fiefdom, the prospect of spending a bit of money to buy an in-game currency (in the form of gold), which allows you to buy speed-ups, which in turn allows you to carry on playing at a consistent pace, becomes more enticing. The problem was that there was seemingly no end to it – at the time I was playing, the maximum level you could get to was 30, which, at the level I was at, seemed a distant possibility. But games in these sorts of genres regularly add updates wherein the maximum level you can reach increases. The in-app purchases ranged from 99p for a meagre amount of gold and equipment, up to £100 for much more – although even at that higher price point, the virtual currency you received could still take just moments to use up. The amounts seemed all the more ludicrous when you considered that the game itself wasn't really a finished product – glitches, such as randomly losing all of your resources, would happen often, and many of the features that were initially advertised weren't yet available.

Despite being more or less a clone of an earlier game, *Clash of Clans*, *Conquest* felt unique to me among the freemium games I had previously experienced. What made it interesting was that it allowed you to form alliances and teams with other players, and to communicate and coordinate attacks with them. As I got more experienced, I joined a team of players who had set up a text chat group on a gaming communication app called Discord. Some players took a light-touch approach to *Conquest*, content to drift by at low levels without spending any money. Others were happy to admit that they were eagerly waiting for payday so that they could sink some money into the game, with some claiming to have individually spent over £1,000 in the never-ending quest to get their castle to the next level. But it was the story of one player in particular that started to make me think about the path on which in-app purchases were setting the industry. King Aerys (not his real name: although thinking about it, I don't know that for sure – kudos to his parents if it was) was the highest-level player on our server, with a level 30 castle and a terrifying army that would raze any other player's castle to the ground before they even realised they were being attacked. Given the relatively short time span for which the game had been available and the gating process that restricted the speed at which you could improve your keep, there was no question that he had spent a substantial amount of cash in order to reach the top spot. The question was: just how much? By most accounts, from the players who had spoken to him in person, it was somewhere in the region of an eye-watering £13,000.

No game is worth that amount of money. Especially one that has no apparent win condition or end goal. Further conversations with players who had spoken to him revealed that he had, allegedly, complained to the developers about the quality of the game and received his money back – only to reinvest it all to improve his castle further. I will reluctantly admit that I spent more money than I cared to myself on *Conquest*. In a moment of weakness, I spent £100 to get some virtual currency after getting too frustrated with the gating mechanics, an amount which I later managed to claw back after a glitch in the game design rendered my in-game progression fruitless. It was the detachment from the financial cost that worried me the most. It wasn't as if I had gone to an ATM machine, drawn out bank notes, and handed them over in return for something equally tangible, or even useful. In a matter of moments, by typing in a password that linked my bank details to my app store account I transferred money from one to the other, which abruptly became reconfigured into virtual gold speed-up tokens, which just as abruptly were converted into slightly less time on a virtual countdown clock. It was an entirely dissatisfying process, albeit one I worried I might well become more susceptible to if I were to play the game for any longer.

Aerys and the other high-investment players in my team are what are known within the industry as 'whales'. The term is borrowed from a sardonic reference to Vegas-style high roller gamblers – people who invest substantially and consistently in whatever game they are playing. By some accounts, mobile games that employ a freemium model rely heavily on these 'whales'. In an analysis by 'mobile monetisation and engagement company'* Tapjoy in 2016, the top 10 per cent of people who spend money 'in-game' account for around 60 per cent of that game's total revenue, and they spend an average of around £260 (or $335) per month. In a sense, this is a necessary part of the model – developers have to rely on whales to balance out the vast majority of players who will never spend any money, or very little money, on the app they have downloaded. But whales are those at highest risk of developing problematic relationships with the games they play. Not long after I managed to get a refund, I deleted *Conquest* from my phone. I haven't returned to it since. But it's all too worryingly easy to envisage an alternative reality: one in which I didn't remove myself from the game, and lost track of how much I had spent on the unfulfilling pursuit of an end goal that is always just out of reach. This is a problem that largely seems to have gone unnoticed, and increasingly freemium-style games appear to be introducing mechanisms that exploit well-known psychological weaknesses in order to keep players interested in them.

One of the key mechanisms freemium games employ involves a concept known in behavioural psychology as 'variable-ratio schedules of reinforcement'. 'Reinforcement' is a basic concept in psychology that relates to learning, and it describes what happens when an activity is preceded by a

---

* No, I don't know what this means either. I think it's a fancy way of saying that the company runs an advertising platform that's embedded in mobile apps and games. It's hard to tell from their website though, which is mostly just buzzwords and repeatedly uses the term 'maximum impact'. The data here are taken from games that use their advertisement platform, but they don't say which games these are.

specific positive or negative event. Historically, research in this area was conducted on rats, and the simplest example of a case of 'positive' reinforcement occurs if you place a rodent in a box that contains a button and a treat dispenser. If the rat presses the button, it gets a reward in the form of a tasty treat. If the rat continues to press the button, it repeatedly gets a reward, and so the treat serves to positively reinforce the button-pressing behaviour. You can get negative reinforcement too though. Say you start using anti-histamines because you've got itchy skin. If the pills cause the itching to subside, then you might well start using them more regularly; in this case, the itching 'negatively reinforces' the pill-taking behaviour: the absence of something bad, rather than the presence of something good, provides the reinforcement. It might seem intuitive to suggest that the strongest way to reinforce a behaviour is by providing a reward each and every time that behaviour is exhibited. However, a wealth of research suggests that actually, and somewhat bizarrely, behaviours tend to get more strongly reinforced if the reward is presented intermittently – and this is where the above-mentioned 'variable-ratio schedule' comes in. To use a more concrete example: slot machines at casinos use this concept to great effect. Let's say that you're playing on a one-arm bandit slot machine, and you're told that every time you pull the lever, the odds of your winning are one in four. Practically, this means that you're going to lose 75 per cent of the time, i.e. far more often than the machine pays out. But the payout is random – it's not the case that after every three attempts you will win on the fourth. Instead, it might be the case that your Win/Loss pattern looks something like this:

L W L L L W L L L L L W L W L L

In the above example, after sixteen attempts, you have won four times – on the second, sixth, twelfth and fourteenth rounds – but you have lost twelve times, which averages out to a one in four chance of winning. It might seem like this wouldn't have any reinforcing effect on your behaviour, but two things are against you. The first is that you can never precisely predict *when* you're going to hit the jackpot, which means that you're more likely to carry on playing until you do win. The second is that you win with just enough frequency not to be put off by the number of times you lose. Both of these factors serve to create a situation in which – despite the odds not being in your favour – it's very difficult for you to stop playing. Many freemium games now employ this exact same method. Take a standard 'match-three' game, like *Candy Crush Saga*. On each level, the puzzle board is random – if you play the same level twice, it's likely that you will get a different configuration. That means you cannot devise or memorise a strategy to beat a particular level: whether you win or lose depends on a variable-ratio schedule, because some levels will be easier to beat than others. It might *feel* as though you have some level of control over your chances of success, and can affect the outcome via your skill at the game, but this is largely an illusion, carefully crafted to encourage you to keep playing.

There are other mechanisms that freemium games employ to keep us playing, and some of them are just as counterintuitive. For example, while it might seem that limiting the amount of time you're able to play a game might be a good thing, it can actually increase your desire to play it. Many freemium games frequently use time limits on the number of attempts at a level that you can have – so for example, you might be given five chances, or 'lives', to complete a level, and after the fifth failed attempt you're made to wait for your lives to replenish, which they might do at a rate of, say, one life every half hour. This sort of mechanism provides another opportunity to extract money from players – very often, such games offer you the option to spend a small amount of money in order to unlock your lives immediately. But this sort of gating mechanism has an additional effect – it leaves you wanting more. As games researcher and author Jamie Madigan has written, the effect relates to something known in psychology as 'hedonic adaptation'. This is the idea that over time, if you have unrestricted access to something you really like, the amount of pleasure (the technical term for which is 'hedonia') in it gradually diminishes. Withhold access to that thing though, and the rewarding effect that you get from it stays stable. For example, Madigan has previously highlighted a 2013 study led by Jordi Quoidbach at Harvard University, in which 55 participants were asked to attend two lab sessions spaced one week apart. In both sessions, alongside various questionnaires to fill out, they were given a piece of chocolate: to taste and then rate for enjoyment. Next, sixteen of the participants were told not to eat any chocolate in the intervening week, eighteen were given approximately 900 grams of chocolate to eat over the week, and the remaining 21 weren't given any specific instructions about chocolate eating. When they returned a week later, the participants were again given a piece of chocolate and asked to rate how much they enjoyed it. Quoidbach and his team found that the participants in the 'no chocolate for you' condition reported finding the treat more enjoyable in that second lab session than both the 'eat loads of chocolate' condition and the 'do whatever the hell you want' condition. In other words, restricting access to something rewarding made it more enjoyable later on.

Taking these sorts of psychological exploitations together, my concern is this: that increasingly, games developers are monetising their products by using mechanics that stray worryingly close to the sort used in more traditional forms of gambling. Moreover, developers appear to have become so caught up in the financial prospects of exploiting these systems that very little consideration seems to have been given to the long-term implications of using them, both for the industry, and for the well-being of their player base. This isn't just some esoteric, hypothetical problem, either – it is starting to have clear legal consequences. In the spring of 2018, Belgium's Gaming Commission published the results of an extensive investigation into games that use 'loot box' mechanics (a situation in which players can pay real money to open a virtual box that gives them a random chance of winning new characters, items, or cosmetics to use in-game). Loot box systems are a sort of digital sticker album, like the FIFA World Cup or English Premier League albums that were a school playground fixture when I was younger. Each packet you bought gave you a chance to get new stickers to complete your set, but the distribution of them was never random: some metallic stickers were ultra-rare; other, more basic stickers were so common that you would end up getting hundreds of copies of them. In order to complete your set, you'd either have to trade stickers with other punters or keep buying packets until those elusive rare ones turned up. Loot boxes, and their contents, work in the same way – using the same sorts of variable-ratio schedules that I mentioned earlier to keep you consistently forking over your cash. Every so often during a game, for example after gaining an experience level on a character, you're rewarded with a box full of goodies. Some of the items you receive are common, so there's a good chance you'll get the same thing over and over again. Other items are much rarer: thus much more valuable and desirable. Free boxes are typically earned at a slow rate though, so most games employing a loot box system also allow players the opportunity to buy more boxes for real cash. The outcome of the Gaming Commission report was that the loot box systems in three major games – *Overwatch, FIFA 18* and *Counter-Strike: Global Offensive* were in violation of Belgium's gambling legislation, and are illegal in their execution – because they are games of chance that involve a monetary 'wager'.* Moreover, the scientific research that's starting to be conducted on the effects of loot boxes is showing that there might be good cause for concern. A series of studies by teams led by David Zendle at York St John University in the UK have shown clear links between gambling problems and how people interact with loot box systems. The most recent study involved surveying some 1,200 gamers, and asking them questions about the types of games they play – whether they use loot box systems (both free and paid), or the nature of the loot box systems they use – as well as questions

---

* It's reasonable to ask why these three games were singled out, and not loot boxes more generally. Part of the reason is that there are quite a lot of different ways in which loot box systems can be put into practice. Some games use them, but completely free of charge – you don't ever have to spend money to get more. Some only give you cosmetic items that have no impact on your performance in-game, whereas others contain items that can make it easier for you to win. Some games show you rarer items that you could have won after you've opened a box, whereas others don't. Some games contain loot boxes that provide you with items that have no value outside of the game itself, whereas others contain items that can be bought and traded for real money on external marketplaces. In some cases, such as in *Counter Strike: Global Offensive*, loot box contents have been considered so desirable that they have sold for upwards of $4,000.

about problematic gambling habits. Although the study was pre-registered and the data made openly available, at the time of writing Zendle's work hadn't undergone peer review, so caution is needed before reading deeply into the conclusions. That being said, the study found a correlation between the extent to which players pay for loot boxes and the levels of problematic gambling that they report. About 9 per cent of any symptoms of problematic gambling that players reported could be accounted for by looking at their loot box habits. In the analysis, differences in the way that loot boxes are implemented appeared to make this correlation stronger or weaker, but the overall message was that regardless of how loot box systems were presented in a game, if players are given the option to pay for them, an association with problematic gambling is evident. What these data can't prove is the causal direction of the relationship – it could be that paying for loot boxes causes problematic gambling behaviour, or it could be that people who already have problems with gambling are more drawn to games that have loot box systems in place. Either way, the results suggest that loot boxes are something addiction research should focus on in the near future.

So, should we be worried about video games being addictive? Well: yes and no. Despite the WHO recognising it as one, we don't really have a good handle on what a general 'gaming addiction disorder' might look like yet, which means that it's hard to assess how likely any individual player is to be at risk from it. Our best estimates at the moment though are that the prevalence of such a disorder is low, and so the chances that you would ever come into contact with someone who has a genuine gaming addiction are quite small. And yet, the meteoric rise of freemium-style games and loot boxes presents a very specific concern that video games *could* become unequivocally addictive in the future. Not because of any unique feature of games them-selves, but more because, where developers are willing to accept that they will harm a portion of their player base, they are happy to employ well-established techniques from the gambling indus-try that are very successful at generating money. I think this is an issue that developers have largely ignored in recent years, and to their own detriment. But it's also to the detriment of parents and caregivers who have very real worries about the effects that games can have on children.

Public-facing discussions about this aspect of video gaming largely devolve into hysterical arguments about *all* games basi-cally being like crack for kids. I'm not exaggerating here – in 2016, the British tabloid newspaper the *Sun* ran a story with the headline 'Playing games as addictive as heroin'. This is largely based on a misunderstanding of the underlying neuroscience. You might have heard of a brain chemical called dopamine, which often surfaces in discussions about something being addictive. The story that's put forward is often a simple one: doing something 'pleasurable' (like playing games, or taking a drug) causes an increase in dopamine levels in the brain, and increased dopamine makes us more likely to become addicted to that thing, leading to a vicious cycle. In fact, this is how the *Sun* story interpreted it, even managing to drop in a link to violent video games: 'faster, more violent games are a more intensive experience, so will produce more dopamine', screeched the article.

In reality though, things are much more complicated. Neuroscience has by and large abandoned the idea that dopa-mine is solely responsible for causing the pleasurable feelings that taking drugs entails, and it's not simply the case that an increase in the levels of dopamine in the brain causes a proportional increase in pleasure, or the likelihood of addiction. Regardless, the amount of dopamine that's released by playing video games is nowhere near the levels associated with taking something like cocaine or heroin. But while the conversation is derailed by terrifying stories that liken games to hard drugs, the chances of having a sensible, serious discussion about the way that games are being monetised and marketed, especially to children, is missed. Multiple stakeholders need to be a part of that conversation, and each has their own unique part to play. Scientists who specialise in gaming addiction really need to get their act together – better research needs to be done, research that adheres to scientific best practices like preregistration. Games developers – especially ones that adopt the sorts of frequently-harmful mechanics dealt with in this chapter – need to do a bit of soul-searching and seriously consider the impact that their games will have on the well-being of their player base. If they don't, regulation needs to be put in place to either restrict or curb the use of such mechanics, and restrict who they are marketed towards. But perhaps most of all, each and every one of us who cares about video games, or the effects that they have, has a duty to talk about this in a sensible, level-headed manner. As the Victorian evidentialist philosopher William Kingdon Clifford explained in his 1877 essay *The Ethics of Belief*, as social beings we have a moral responsibility to believe only in things that we have a thorough grounding in, and for which we have sufficient evidence. Tied in with this is a moral responsibility to communicate and discuss those beliefs in a manner that doesn't end up tarnishing our collective knowledge. 'Our words, our phrases, our forms and processes and modes of thought, are common property, fashioned and perfected from age to age ... Into this, for good or ill, is woven every belief of every man who has speech of his fellows,' he explains. 'An awful privilege, and an awful responsibility, that we should help to create the world in which posterity will live.' Nothing is going to change if the kind of discussions that take place on this topic do nothing but devolve into vitriolic ill-informed arguments about how video games turn kids' brains into mush. We can do better than this. We *must* do better than this. And not just in the case of video game addiction.

CHAPTER 9

Screen time

In the summer of 2014, I found myself sitting in the Hard Rock Cafe in Anchorage, Alaska. Anchorage is a beautiful city, nestled perfectly between an unnervingly vast expanse of ocean and unreal-looking mountains. Unfortunately, I wasn't there to escape to the countryside, however tempting a dash to the hills may have been. I was there to attend an epidemiological conference hosted by the University of Alaska. Epidemiology isn't usually my forte, but given that the work I was involved in at the time looking at the potential mental health implications of playing video games, a public health conference seemed like a good fit. An academic conference can be an overwhelming and exhausting experience though, especially if it's in an area of research where you don't know that many people. So, in an effort to make the experience more manageable, I had decamped to a bar to collect my thoughts, and plan out which talks I wanted to listen to over the next few days – partly based on how interesting their titles sounded, but mostly based on how much of a chance I thought I'd have of actually understanding them.

I turned my attention to the music video that was playing on rotation on the bar's screens. It was a song I hadn't heard before, but it was catchy and I liked it. I spied the name of it as it transitioned into the next song – 'The Veldt', by Deadmau5. Something about the name, and the lyrics, felt familiar. After opening up a new browser window and a quick search, the familiarity clicked – the song is based on a short story by one of my favourite science fiction authors, Ray Bradbury. Originally published in September 1950 (under its original title *The World the Children Made*), the story traces the relationship dynamics between two parents, George and Lydia Hadley, their two children, Peter and Wendy, and the fully automated home that they live in. The house does everything for them – down to tying their shoelaces and brushing their teeth – but the focus of the story is the nursery. It's described as something like the holodeck from *Star Trek: The Next Generation* – a vast room in which the walls and ceiling could project any reality you desired. It's the ultimate escapist form of entertainment.

As the tale continues, George and Lydia become concerned with the amount of time their children spend in the nursery, particularly in a recreation of the African veldt. Lions roam constantly, a hot sun beats down from a virtual blue sky, and the parents become increasingly unnerved by familiar-sounding screams emanating from the room. They call on the advice of a friend, a psychologist by the name of David McLean. He rather unhelpfully advises George to dismantle the room and to bring the children to him every day for the next year for treatment.*
After vitriolic arguments with the children, George begins to follow through with his threat of switching off the house. They plead with him to enter the nursery one final time, and he relents (bad idea, George). After being tricked into following Peter and Wendy into the room, the two parents find themselves face to face with a pride of lions, and suddenly realise why those screams sounded so familiar. The story ends with the psychologist returning and asking the kids as to the whereabouts of their

---

* Good one, David. He also precedes this by saying: 'My dear George, a psychologist never saw a fact in his life. He only hears about feelings and vague things,' thus pre-empting the replication crisis by about 60 years.

parents. In the nursery, off in the distance, the lions appear to be feeding, as Wendy flatly asks McLean if he wants a cup of tea.

The story was exceptionally prescient for its time, and I think does a brilliant job of capturing some of the modern-day anxieties about screen-based technologies – worries that extend far beyond video games. Peter and Wendy become obsessed with the virtual reality that the nursery offers them, so much so that they lose interest in everything else. They are painted as lazy, self-centred zombies, only interested in passively absorbing the world around them, rather than taking any active interest in it (at one point, Peter remarks: 'I don't want to do anything but look and listen and smell; what else is there to do?'). Taken at face value, the message of the story seems to be that the consequences of allowing this form of technology into our homes can prove disastrous for the family unit. But the moral runs deeper than that. The story is more about the consequences of using technology as a surrogate caregiver. At the start of the tale, George and Lydia have largely abandoned their children to the substitute 'care' of the house, and so Peter and Wendy are left to their own devices to find and create their own entertainment in the nursery. When the parents realise too late the extent to which this has damaged their relationship with their kids, they go for the nuclear option, rather than attempting to communicate with them about the situation that they have all got themselves into. On top of all of this, the family's breakdown is facilitated by an inept psychologist who doesn't really seem to know what he's talking about.

If all of this sounds familiar, it's because pretty much the same storyline is occurring right now, just on a much larger scale (and with fewer parents being fed to virtual lions by sociopathic children). Over the past decade, as smartphones have enjoyed a surge in popularity, so too has there been an equally explosive rise in the worries that we have about their effects on us. 'Screen time' – the amount of time we spend using smartphones, tablets, laptops, games consoles and computers – has become a catch-all term that encapsulates the fear that society is becoming more regressive, narcissistic, uncaring and unwholesome. We worry about whether video games make us horrible people. We worry that social media isn't actually social at all, and only serves to bring out the darker side of our personalities. We worry that children are becoming glued to their phones, either unwilling or unable to take interest in the real world that exists around them. And we worry that all of this is having a terminal and irreversible effect on our mental health.

Addressing those fears – those very real, and to a certain extent justifiable fears – isn't an easy thing to do. Sure, we can turn to scientific evidence to help us understand what effects screen time is truly having on us, but the story there is a complex one, and objective, dispassionate research often falls flat when it's held up against our personal lived experience. If a scientist comes along and tells us that screens aren't really something to worry about, that's a message that just doesn't fit in with what we see around us – everyone fixated on their phones, unaware of and uninterested in the people around them. These scientists, we can tell ourselves, don't understand the real world of thoughts and feelings and relationships and heartache. Instead, when stories appear in the news where other scientists are sounding the alarm about screens, telling us that social media, games, smartphones and the internet are turning the youth of today into mindless, depressed, narcissistic zombie-like creatures, we listen and take note, because it fits in with our worldview. I'm not here to tell you that your lived experience is wrong. What I will tell you, though, is that the public debate about screen time has become so toxic and vitriolic that it has reached the point where good science – the type of research that can be truly helpful in understanding and managing our worries about screens – has become lost in a sea of misplaced and misdirected scare stories. What I would like you to do, for the next chapter at least, is to park any beliefs you hold about screens – whatever they are – at the door. Yes, I'm going to look at what the current scientific literature is able to say about the effects that screens can have. But science doesn't exist in a vacuum, and as important as it is to understand what the data actually says, it's also necessary to understand why the communication of that science has gone wrong.

In the UK media at least, the charge against screens has been led by the neuroscientist, thriller-writer, and biotech company CEO Baroness Susan Greenfield. Greenfield first crossed my science radar in 2011, after an article hit the national news in which she claimed that video games were causing early-onset dementia in children. She also appeared to make a link between a rise in screen-based technology use and autistic spectrum disorders. Since then, the specific worries she has voiced have changed (for example, in 2017, she claimed smartphones were affecting people's ability to remember things, whereas in 2018, social media was giving children the mentality of a toddler), but her underlying message has stayed the same. Greenfield's prime concern, as outlined in her 2014 book *Mind Change*, is that screen technology can *change our brains*, and that this, broadly, is a bad thing.

Everything that we do changes our brains. My brain is changing as I write these words (whether that's for the better or worse, we'll have to wait and see). Your brain is changing as you read them. To say that our brains are being modified by our environment isn't a particularly interesting or helpful thing to say, because it's that very change that underlies our ability to learn and remember things. To put it simply, if our brains didn't change, we'd be dead. But to make this sort of claim without giving any context or qualification as to *how* it is changing risks unduly scaring anyone who doesn't have a background in neuroscience. To be fair, Greenfield's arguments over the years have been consistent: she claims that yes, this change is a bad thing. Whether this change increases early-onset dementia, depression or anxiety, or causes reductions in attention span or literacy levels, or an inability to communicate, the links she draws have always been negative ones, with only fleeting lip service paid to any potential benefits. Greenfield's are broad-strokes claims. They're not grounded in a thorough read of the scientific research evidence, nor are they particularly useful for science. As I have already detailed, policy and research predicated on a cycle of moral panic tends not to be particularly robust or conclusive.

Over the years, Greenfield's claims have been exposed by a number of science writers and researchers. One of the major criticisms of Greenfield's stance was that if her concerns were serious, then as a research scientist, she is well-placed to lay them out in an academic research paper and to develop a clear set of hypotheses that could be tested by other researchers. She could even do the research herself, and develop the groundwork on which others could build. Unfortunately, she never has – Greenfield has repeatedly rebuffed this suggestion, saying she feels she couldn't do justice to the topic in a single paper. On this final point at least, I agree: no single paper can ever conclusively show the presence or absence of some sort of psychological phenomenon. That's why scientists spend entire careers conducting shedloads of experiments. The rest of her position I've always found mystifying. A scientist, who is clearly passionate about something (which they believe to be having extremely negative effects on society at large), has been seemingly unwilling to do the necessary research to understand what, precisely, those effects are, or how to fix them. As a result, the public has been left with a confusing onslaught of pronouncements from someone who is presented to them as an expert neuroscientist. One who claims screens are bad, and offers little in the way of tangible things that anyone can do to move the debate forward or make things better.

This cycle has repeated itself for many years in the mainstream news – someone (typically Susan Greenfield, but there have been others) makes an unsubstantiated claim about screen technology, which is quickly rebutted by science writers, bloggers and scientists – for example Ben Goldacre or Dorothy Bishop. A few months later, another claim surfaces, and the same would happen again. But then, in around 2017, something changed: there was a more noticeable uptick in public anxieties about the effects that screens can have on us. It was a shift that I think can, at least in part, be traced back to a series of articles written in the popular press by a social psychologist called Jean Twenge. The first and possibly most impactful of these was published in *The Atlantic* under the headline 'Have Smartphones Destroyed a Generation?' in the summer of 2017. In it, Twenge reflects on how a new generation of kids born between 1995 and 2012 – which she colloquially refers to as the 'iGen'* – have

---

* The article was adapted from Twenge's book *iGen*, published the preceding month.

grown up in a world that has never been without the internet, and are seemingly hooked on smartphones and tablets. Both Twenge and Greenfield share broadly similar concerns about the deleterious effects of screens, but where they differ is in the fact that Twenge has actually taken the plunge and conducted her own research into the matter. The picture she paints of the relationship kids have with their screens is bleak. Since the early part of this decade, smartphone ownership has steadily increased. Over the same period, based on questionnaire-based surveys of teenage attitudes and behaviour, happiness has plummeted, as has the amount of time this generation reports that they spend going out with friends, going on dates, and having sex. Loneliness levels have skyrocketed, as have teen depression and suicide rates. In Twenge's view, these are not simply correlations; the blame is placed squarely on the screen.

According to the online content analysis platform Buzzsumo, Twenge's was one of the most widely-shared science and technology opinion articles of 2017, with nearly 700,000 shares on Facebook alone. Since then, there has been a fairly drastic shift in public opinion towards a focus on the negative effects of screen use, with little qualification in terms of any potential benefits. On the advice of Twenge and others, two of Apple's largest investors, Jana Partners and the California State Teachers' Retirement System published an open letter in early 2018 calling for the company to do more to combat the mental and physical effects that smartphone 'addiction' was having on children. In the same year, Apple introduced a 'Screen Time' feature in the newest version of its mobile operating system, iOS 12. The app provides users with data on how and when they use their phone, with the ability to set limits on use. The reasoning behind its introduction was opaque, and it isn't clear that its development was grounded in any decent research evidence – according to *Wired* magazine, rather than consulting with psychologists actually doing work in this area, Apple instead approached advocacy groups such as Common Sense Media, and media figures such as Ariana Huffington, for their advice on the matter. At around the same time, newspaper headlines began to appear about campaigns driven by former Facebook and Google employees to put pressure on their erstwhile employers to combat technology 'addiction'. Meanwhile in the UK, the government's Science and Technology Committee launched an inquiry into the potential impact that screens and social media use are having on children's health and well-being, receiving a huge number of written and oral evidence submissions from scientists, technology companies, parents and schools alike. In a situation that is becoming all too familiar, with so much public anxiety being whipped up about screens, what the scientific research is able to say about what is actually going on was getting lost in the noise. And, echoing everything I've written about video games up until now, the problem is exacerbated by the fact that it can be remarkably difficult to conduct research into screen time that gives clear, meaningful and convincing answers.

'It's a daily struggle, as a psychologist, to try to do good science and use the best methods,' explains Amy Orben, a postgraduate doctoral student at the University of Oxford. 'If you're not careful, you'll get really simple answers and be able to publish them in prestigious journals. But they won't necessarily be the right answers.' Like many people who research the effects of playing video games and using screen technologies, Amy started off on a different route. 'I was studying physics and maths through a natural science degree at Cambridge, but quickly realised I didn't like circuits or planets, or anything to do with things that aren't really living,' she says. 'But I do like the concept of numbers and patterns, things like that.' So she ended up getting interested in psychology instead, which set her on a path to studying the effects that using screens and social media have on us.

Amy's work first came to my attention when she published a blog post in November 2017 which took aim at some claims Jean Twenge had made in a research article, that appeared to provide scientific evidence for the arguments she had outlined in her *Atlantic* piece some months earlier. Twenge's study, published in the journal *Clinical Psychological Science*, used data from over half a million teenagers who responded to two nationally-representative surveys in the United States. The surveys, called Monitoring the Future and the Youth Risk Behavior Surveillance System, have been running since around 1991. Both these surveys use questionnaires to gather a broad range of information from American high school students about their attitudes, values and the health-risk behaviours that they engage in (like whether they use alcohol and drugs or do things that might end up in unintentional injuries or violence). In addition, data about suicide deaths for the age group that corresponded to those who took part in the two surveys were taken from the Centers for Disease Control and Prevention. The aim of the study was to see if there were any correlations between different types of screen-based activities and mental health issues like depression, and what were termed 'suicide-related outcomes,' while accounting for other factors that might have an impact such as socio-economics status, sex or race. 'Suicide-related outcomes' are behaviours that can be linked to suicide in some way, for example thinking about suicide, or planning (or actually attempting) suicide. And, perhaps vindicating Greenfield's views, the data appeared to provide the evidence for the negative link between screens and mental health. According to Twenge's analysis, various measures of teenage depression and suicide-related risk had shown increases between 2010 and 2015. Those teenagers who reported spending more time on social media were more likely to report issues with their mental health. The opposite trend was found for teenagers who reported spending more time on non-screen activities, like going out with friends or engaging in sports and exercise.

The word 'trend' is important here. In these sorts of survey studies, the outcomes that researchers are looking at are largely correlational in nature. What I mean by this is that the researchers are taking a retrospective look at data that have already been collected, and trying to infer potential links between them. It's not possible to account for every potential factor that might have had an impact on that relationship though. Just because both screen use and depression levels go up over the same time period, that doesn't necessarily mean that the former causes the latter. It could be that depression rates were increasing for another reason, and that as a result, feeling more depressed drove teenagers to use their smartphones more. Or it could mean that a third factor – say, austerity – was driving the increases in both. Twenge and her team do point this out in the paper, but confusingly, the language that they use throughout veers towards suggesting that the link between screen use and mental health is more causal than correlational. Disappointingly, this unsubstantiated implication of a causal relationship was elaborated upon further when Twenge wrote popular science articles about the study, that included headlines such as 'With teen mental health deteriorating over five years, there's a likely culprit'.

In her blog post responding to Twenge, Amy's analysis highlighted other issues, though. While the study does show a correlation between depressive symptoms and social media use across all teenagers, this actually seems to be driven by the data reported for female teens. For the male teens in the sample, depressive symptoms actually seemed to have remained stable since 2010, and suicide-related outcomes have decreased. If it's actually the case that the data differ for men and women, then it seems like a real missed opportunity that this was neither highlighted nor explored further in the study. If screens only show clear negative effects for women, then understanding how their technology use differs to that of men could provide a useful target for future research.

Thankfully, the data from the surveys are openly available, which meant that Amy Orben was able to actually reanalyse them for herself. In doing so, she uncovered a deeper problem with Twenge's study. She found that while there was indeed a link between depressive symptoms and social media use, it was vanishingly small. 'I just didn't find any compelling evidence for Twenge's claims,' she explains. In fact, using social media only seemed to explain 0.36 per cent of the variability in the depression scores in the female teenager sample – a point which wasn't reported in the original study. In other words, of any depressive symptoms that the female teens reported, less than 0.5 per cent can be accounted for by figuring out how often they use social media. Well over 99 per cent of those symptoms will be related to other factors that aren't necessarily known about from this research alone.* For the boys in the sample, this social media

---

* This isn't anybody's fault and is simply a hazard of conducting these sorts of analyses. It might be that something that wasn't included in the

use explained even less of the variability in depression – about 0.01 per cent. It's a theme that appears to run throughout the paper: while there are links between using smartphones and various negative mental health outcomes, in general these seem to be quite weak, and it's just as likely that other factors – perhaps difficulties at home, or stress regarding school and work commitments – may have the same or even a much greater effect. To put it another way, as Andy Przybylski said in a 2018 interview with *Wired* magazine about the study: 'I have the data set they used open in front of me, and I submit to you that, based on that same data set, eating potatoes has the exact same negative effect on depression.'

But perhaps there's a simpler explanation for the trends that Twenge found. The way that mental health is discussed in society has certainly changed – in many ways much for the better – in recent years. Although it's unfortunately very difficult to quantify in research, it may well be the case that teenagers nowadays are simply more confident and comfortable when it comes to disclosing information about how they feel. So, while over time it may appear as if depression rates are increasing, there's also a possibility that these numbers simply reflect a societal willingness to be more open and honest about mental health.

At first glance, screen time seems like a simple topic to study scientifically, but there are aspects of screen use that can be remarkably hard to pin down and assess in the lab. 'Screen

---

analysis, or that something that wasn't even captured in the original Monitoring the Future and Youth Risk Behavior surveys is actually the driving force behind depression and suicide risk. What these factors might be is an interesting (and important!) question, and they could be things that aren't easily identifiable by using a questionnaire.

time' itself is a nebulous concept – on the one hand, it can be an appealing one for scientists to use, because it is seemingly easy to get an idea of how many minutes or hours per day an individual might be using a smartphone, tablet or computer. On the other hand, it's a term that's so vague as to be meaningless.

Let me try to explain what I mean with an example. Imagine two individuals who both report using screens for three hours a day. In most research studies, it's likely that both of them would be categorised in the same manner. For example, a research study might classify both of the two individuals as 'medium users', and so not distinguish between them. But how useful is it to just look at the actual amount of time that people use screens? While it gives the researchers an easy number to work with, it misses something crucial about screen technology: that that technology is being used to *do something*. Many scientists have recently started to come to the realisation that it's *what* the screens are being used for, and the context they're being used in, that's important. Here is some more information about the two example participants above. Both are thirteen-year-old girls. One splits those three hours a day into socialising with friends on *Minecraft*, using the internet to do some research for her homework, and watching a Netflix show with her parents. The other spends those three hours on Facebook and Instagram, agonising over her body image, having arguments with friends from school, or trying to find a website that will write her essay that's due tomorrow, but for which she hasn't done any work. All of this is happening without her parents having any aware- ness of what's going on. It's not unreasonable to argue that those three hours of screen time will have very different effects on the two girls, but the chances are that those differences wouldn't be accounted for in any study they took part in; again, they're both classed identically: as 'medium users'. This is just one very obvious problem in screen time research. Why this happens, though, is a sticking point that makes it difficult for research in the area to progress towards more concrete knowledge about any definite screen effects. It might occur because the researchers running the study don't have a clear handle on what screen time actually involves, but for the most part, it happens simply because it's difficult to get any sort of clear and consistent data on contextual factors like the ones in the example above.

That's not to say that good work hasn't been done on screen time. It just tends to get lost in the noise created by some of those bigger and scarier studies. And for any study on the topic, regardless of whether there's a positive or a negative take-home message, it is essential to be mindful of the caveats above: researchers haven't quite yet got a good grip on what it is that they're actually measuring, what it might mean, or how they're measuring it. With all of this in mind, the best currently-available evidence for the effects of screen use on well-being comes from a study conducted by Andy Przybylski and Netta Weinstein, published in the flagship psychology journal *Psychological Science* in 2017. Using the UK government's National Pupil Database as a starting point, the researchers surveyed over 120,000 fifteen year olds, who answered questions on their mental well-being and the types of screen-based activities they took part in in their free time, as well as providing data on various other measures that might have an impact on their mental health (things like ethnicity, gender, and whether they lived in areas of the country that had high levels of unemployment and crime). The study set a gold standard for screen time research. It was preregistered, and all of the data and materials were made freely available for anyone to download and assess themselves.

The researchers set out to test two theories – one pre-existing and one novel – of how screen time affects children. The first theory, and by far the most widely-accepted in both the scientific literature and print media, is known as the 'displacement hypothesis'. First outlined in a paper by the early childhood and literacy education researcher Professor Susan Neuman in 1988, the displacement hypothesis argues that there is a direct and linear relationship between the amount of time a person uses a screen for and the amount of harm that it can cause. More screen time means more negative effects, because using the screens is displacing other (what are assumed to be more wholesome) activities like going out with friends, enjoying nature, or reading books. The second theory is rather felicitously referred to by Przybylski and Weinstein as the 'digital Goldilocks hypothesis'. Rather than arguing for a simple, proportional relationship between screen use and harm, this theory suggests that in today's interconnected world, some levels of screen time are actually beneficial, more so than none at all. It's only at high levels of screen use that other activities start to lose out. In other words, just as with the heat of the porridge in the classic fairy tale, there's an amount of screen time that is 'just right'.

'Screen time' in the general sense is a fairly vague concept for scientists to use, so in Przybylski and Weinstein's study they broke it down into four different types of digital screen activity – watching television and movies, playing video games, using computers (say, to browse the internet or check emails) and using smartphones (say, for using social media or talking to friends). For all four types of screen time, they found evidence in favour of the digital Goldilocks hypothesis, as opposed to the displacement hypothesis.

The paper is important for a number of reasons. First, as I've already mentioned, it set a gold standard for research in this area. Not long after the study came out, I was involved in a fairly divisive interview about it on London-based LBC radio, and one of the questions I was asked was whether the study was biased, because the authors might have received funding from tech companies to pay for it. No such financial conflict of interest existed, but more importantly, because the study was preregistered, and because the data and materials were all made openly available on the internet, any funding source wouldn't have mattered in any case. By registering their intended analysis methods before they collected any data, Przybylski and Weinstein inoculated themselves against any untoward external influence. In other words, an external funder wouldn't have been able to force them to conduct an analysis to give them the 'right' answer, because they were already committed to performing the statistics in a predefined way. In many ways, this is an esoteric point to make, but one that is important for keeping the science in this area (or in any area) honest.

On top of that, the study found that moderate amounts of screen time are better than none at all – and that different types of screen time, at different points during the week, have different effects. For example, the 'extremum' – that is, the amount of time at which well-being scores peak – was about one hour 45 minutes for playing video games on weekdays. On weekends, this number increased to three hours 35 minutes. Similar numbers were found for using smartphones (just under two hours during the week versus just over four hours on the weekend). This increase makes intuitive sense: kids have much less free time on weekday evenings after school than they do during the weekend, so higher levels of screen time will have much less of a negative impact on Saturdays and Sundays, when they have more recreational time. For general computer use, the numbers remained fairly stable: the extrema were four hours seventeen minutes for weekdays, versus four hours 39 minutes for weekends. Similarly for watching television or movies, the extrema were three hours 41 minutes on weekdays and four hours 50 minutes on weekends. Moreover, the drops in well-being that the researchers saw after the extrema had been reached were relatively small, suggesting that even at levels of screen use beyond the times above, levels of wellbeing aren't dropping disastrously – higher levels of screen time accounted for, at most, about 1 per cent of the variability in well-being scores in the sample.

The emerging picture from the research literature, then, is that while screen time does appear to have an impact on things like childhood depression and well-being, these effects are small, and likely not the main driving factors. This is the take-home message from both Twenge's study and the Goldilocks study outlined above, and yet I find it strange that the way such results are presented in the media often takes vastly different routes depending on which expert is chosen to talk about it. Whereas Przybylski and Weinstein's work makes it clear that the effects are small, it's difficult to ascertain why researchers like Twenge instead insist on pointing the finger squarely at screens, when this conclusion is very obviously not borne out by the data. In part, perhaps it's because of the human nature of science. While we (by which I mean researchers) like to think that we look at data in a dispassionate and objective way, it's often very difficult not to allow our own biases to creep into the scientific process. Open science practices help to minimise the effects that such biases can have though – as Amy Orben's reanalysis of Twenge's research attests. 'I think what people have been starting to realise is that you can open up these huge datasets, like the ones we handle, and you can get a lot of high-impact papers from them just by doing some basic correlations,' Amy explains. 'But that doesn't inherently mean that those papers, those analyses are good quality.' In other words, there's a certain level of responsibility attached to analysing large datasets. Often, the best statistical methods to use will end up being quite complex, and the stories that the results tell will be just as difficult to express – it won't necessarily be the case that as screen use goes up or down, something else, like depression, does in the same way. It can be easy, then, for researchers to fall into the trap of running more basic analyses, like the kind that describe more simple correlational relationships. These sorts of analyses don't really tell anyone anything useful though, because they end up simply describing how two factors are associated with each other, rather than providing any insight into whether one factor has a causal effect on the other. But they nevertheless are sometimes published in prestigious journals because of the perceived quality of the large datasets on which they're based. Showing a correlation between screen use and depression in ten people isn't that interesting. Show that same correlation in 10,000 people though, and it seems more like a cause for concern – even if the relationship is so weak as to be almost non-existent. Moreover, if the researcher doesn't have a clear and openly-documented plan for how they're going to go about conducting those correlations, then as I showed in Chapter 5, there is a risk that they end up running analyses over and over again until they get the result that fits with their personal opinions about what the data should be showing them.

The trouble with screen time research isn't just that there isn't enough conclusive evidence on whether screens are good or bad for us. Because screen time is such a complex phenomenon, the problem is also that there are different ways in which we can interpret what the data are telling us. Inevitably then, wherever there is ambiguity in what the science says, we will favour an interpretation that fits in with our own pre-existing beliefs. 'We've got into this situation where people are just always looking for evidence that supports their current view,' explains Amy. 'So if there's a toxic landscape of public discourse around the negative effects of technology, then research that fits in with that view will resonate with us.' By this point in history, we all have lived experience when it comes to screen use, and we've all got stories of situations we've been in where we feel that someone has been using technology in a way we don't agree with – or even where we ourselves have stepped away from the screen thinking, sheepishly, that we've overdone it. People tell me anecdotal stories all the time about how society is crumbling because they were sitting on a Tube train and no one was talking to each other, because they were all staring at their phones. Or that time they went into a coffee shop and saw a mother sitting at a table staring at her phone, while her son was completely detached from his surroundings because he was absorbed in something on his tablet. Or the arguments they have that stem from stopping their teenager playing video games in her room every evening, in a vain attempt to get her to do her homework. Over time, it's completely unsurprising that these sorts of stories coalesce into an opinion that screens probably aren't very good for us.* Then, when we're faced with

---

* Although there are stories that show that screen use is unequivocally bad in some situations. A 2017 paper by economists Mara Faccio and John McConnell examined 12,000 police accident reports in the Tippecanoe

news headlines proclaiming that science shows a link between screen time and mental health issues, we unflinchingly accept it. It's very easy to be critical of something that we disagree with. It is near impossible to even *consider* the possibility of being critical about things that we hold solid beliefs about. But we mustn't confuse anecdotal data with empirical evidence – while opinions based on our informal observations of the world might be an acceptable basis on which we can start to develop testable hypotheses, they can never constitute validating evidence. To assume that they do means we risk missing the reality of situations we are presented with. Perhaps the mother in the coffee shop has a son with autism, and using a tablet is a means to help him communicate with her while filtering out the cacophony of sensory information around them. Perhaps the teenager doesn't want to do her homework because she's having difficulties at school, and it reminds her of what she will have to face in the morning. And let's be honest: no one has ever wanted a stranger talking to them on the Tube – for most of us it's just weird.

Of course, even if it were possible to say that the available research evidence was consistent and unambiguous, we still wouldn't have a particularly detailed understanding about how screens affect us. 'It feels like we're a decade behind,' explains

---

County area of Indiana in the months before and immediately after the launch of *Pokemon GO*. They found a disproportionate increase in the number of crashes near 'pokestops' (in-game locations mapped on to real-world points of interest) in the six months after the game was launched, resulting in an incremental economic and human cost of somewhere between $5 million and $25 million dollars. Their analysis suggested that 31 fewer people would have been injured in that time period, and there would have been two fewer deaths, had drivers not been playing the game. *Don't* use your phone while you're driving.

Amy. 'We're not even in the closing stages of video games research, but people have moved on and now there's something else to worry about. And there will be something else again after that.' Andy Przybylski compares the state of the research field to a bunch of inexperienced kids playing football: we're always running to where the ball is, and not staying in position or strategising about what's going to happen next. That's not to say that things won't improve over the next few years though. As a new generation of tech-savvy young researchers enter the fray, there's currently a lot of talk in academic circles about 'self-replenishing papers'. The idea here is that longitudinal studies could be formulated that get people to use their smartphones and tablets to generate or input data consistently over the course of a few years. As each new wave of information comes through, the paper, located somewhere online, would automatically update itself. The result would be a living record that would allow researchers to document and understand, in real time, how screens are being used, what effects they are having on us, and how both of these things shift and change over the years. For now though, there isn't much good evidence for anyone to be able to say anything about the effects that screens have on us with any certainty.

The frustrating thing is that we are left somewhat empty-handed when it comes to dealing with the very understandable worries that people have about screens. While we're waiting for the evidence to come in though, there are other things we can do to immunise ourselves against the scaremongering effects of online opinion pieces telling us that we should, in fact, be terrified of screen time. The first is to rethink how we critically approach evidence – and this goes beyond discussions about video games and screen technology. One of the most wonderful things about the internet is that it has brought about an era where it's now easier, more than at any other time in history, to easily and quickly access the entire sum of human knowledge. But navigating that information in a meaningful way isn't simple. Search engines help to manage this, of course, but in order to provide us with information that we can understand easily, they necessarily limit, and above all curate, our ability to see the wider picture. What we have to appreciate, then, is that when we search for information about something, the top-ranking hits that the search engine provides aren't necessarily the best evidence. They are also not the complete picture, nor are they devoid of political intent or influence. In other words, search engines don't rank results by quality; but by popularity. 'I'm currently giving a tutorial on aggression, and I provide some information on the "weapons effect",' explains Amy. This effect, briefly, is the idea that the simple presence of a weapon (either an actual physical object, or a picture of one) leads to people feeling or acting more aggressively. 'I remembered that there was some sort of criticism of the effect a while back, so I went onto Google Scholar to check,' she adds. 'But most of the articles that came up were all written by the same author, or were articles edited by that author, and they all confirmed each other.' On the basis of a quick search, it appears as though there is lots of evidence corroborating the idea that the weapons effect exists. However, a deeper, more considered search would reveal the fact that the research literature is actually in much more disagreement about it. It just depends on how you search for information, and what you search for. 'It's hard to get the complete picture,' agrees Amy. None of this is to say that we should be ditching the internet – just that finding good evidence is more than just a quick internet search away.

Identifying good evidence, then, entails taking more time and a more considered approach to gathering information. So the second necessary step is to change the conversation about screen time. Rather than thinking of screens as agents that hold complete control over us, conferring positive benefits (if we're lucky) or negative harms (if we're not), instead we need to remember what they actually are: a tool. And as with any tool, we need to learn how to use them properly in order to get the maximum benefit out of them. For example, despite our worries about it, social media can be a tremendous resource for bringing people together in unexpected and sometimes fortuitous ways. Platforms like Twitter can offer a direct communication link to scientists working at the cutting edge of their fields, who are more often than not more than happy to talk about their work. But with that access comes a level of responsibility to act calmly and appropriately. 'I don't feel like I'm inherently pro-technology – I'm just pro-scientific evidence,' explains Amy. 'In the current media landscape though, that makes us sound like we all love technology, and sometimes people end up thinking or saying we're just shills for Big Tech,' she adds. It isn't a nice thing to have happen, and given the levels of vitriol that can sometimes be spouted online, the risk is that scientists begin to clam up and stop communicating their work because they fear backlash. I've had my fair share of arguments with people on Twitter, and I can tell you, sometimes it really hurts. You start to doubt your own abilities and experience. Sometimes, it makes you wonder whether science communication is actually worth it all. But then again, there are times where the conversations I've had with strangers online have led to opportunities to give talks and presentations about my work to audiences I never even knew existed. Those conversations have resulted in new friendships, new ideas for research, and have even led to some of those ideas coming to fruition. I have, for example, published research papers with co-authors I've never met anywhere other than online. Those opportunities make it worth it, and remind me that nothing is perfect, we always have to find a compromise between the bad and the good.

But it's important to keep the doors to science open for everyone. As much as researchers have a duty to conduct high-quality research, they also have a responsibility to communicate that research – and they must do so in a rational and collected way. At the moment of writing, we don't yet have the full story when it comes to the effects that screens have on us. We will do someday, and when we do I'll orient my position on the basis of the best available evidence. At the moment, that evidence tells us that screen technology is something we shouldn't be worrying about too much. We need to avoid falling into the trap of thinking that banning or limiting screen time will provide an easy fix to the very real and very complex problems associated with rising rates of mental health issues like depression and anxiety. We've yet to uncover the full range of factors driving those rates up, and if we become too fixated on screen time we risk missing out on the positive benefits that things like video games and social media can confer. So in the meantime my friends, stay strong, and don't let the nonsense that you read on and about your smartphone unduly worry you.

CHAPTER 10

Immersion and
virtual reality

Here's another quirk about video games research I haven't yet tackled: no one really has a good idea of how much time people spend playing games. A lot of the studies out there, particularly the longitudinal ones, tend to use what are known as 'self-report measures'. In other words, they ask people directly how much time they think they spend playing games each day or each week. This isn't actually that useful for researchers, because of the very nature of the games that we play.* They are immersive, captivating entities. They are fantasy places that allow you, if you so wish, to escape the confines of the world around you for a little while – or a long while, depending on how deeply you get into them. Getting lost in a good game necessarily means that you're not keeping track of time. Asking people to reflect on their own experiences and put a number on something that is so philosophically opposed to quantification is, therefore, a somewhat fruitless task. I often think of playing video games as a form of time travel. In that bubble, while I'm playing, time stands still. Hours can go by just outside my front door, but for

---

* To reinforce this point, in November 2018 a team of psychologists led by David Ellis at Lancaster University compared a range of smartphone use and addiction scales with actual data about how much time people spent on their phones, measured via Apple's Screen Time app for the iPhone. The correlations were really quite poor, and the research team concluded that existing self-report measures of use aren't actually any good at accurately predicting basic technology use.

me, there's only that single, captivating moment. Simon Parkin, in his excellent book *Death by Video Game*, refers to this idea as 'chronoslip': the idea that games, much like other forms of entertainment, are pastimes in the literal meaning of the word – they cause time to pass. And yet, there's something different, unique about games. Yes, I can lose myself in a movie, or in a book, or in binge-watching *Stranger Things* or *The Good Place* on Netflix. But those experiences never afford the unique experience that a video game can. Video games don't require me to suspend disbelief. Much the opposite – I must become an *active* believer in the world that's presented to me in order to have a fully meaningful experience. That games capture our attention in such a complete way is, understandably, one of the things many people worry about. But that same immersiveness is fundamental to the way games allow us to explore what it means to be human. And, as many scientists are now starting to realise, the virtual realities of video games can offer new ways in which to approach and treat some of humanity's most complex health issues.

It is simultaneously 1989 and 2018, and I am in two places at once. In 2018, I am in a waiting room at a car repair garage, sitting at a round table with my laptop, and a drink that claims to be coffee slowly solidifying in a beige plastic cup next to it. In 1989, I am in a meadow somewhere in Shoshone National Forest, Wyoming. The grass seems dry and bronzed underfoot, and it's quiet here. I can hear the faint burble of a river nearby, and the only indication that this place has ever been touched by other people is the wreck of a snowmobile in a small pond not too far from where I am standing. In 1989 I am 'Henry', a fire lookout* who is trying to solve a mystery in the middle of nowhere, before the burning hell of a wildfire consumes the kindling-dry forest around me. Watching the game unfold on the screen in front of me, I can almost feel the sun beating down on my neck. I try to imagine the smells rising from the grassy carpet of the meadow beneath my feet, but a combination of the aroma from my coffee cup and the slam of the nearby waiting room door snaps me out of my reverie. Because in 2018 I am Pete, and my car is busted. The mechanic looks idly at the laptop, and then informs me that the work won't be done for a few more hours yet. I have no other means of transport, and the garage is so far from home I might as well be in the middle of nowhere. So, after a brief conversation in which I politely pretend to understand what's broken and how it's going to be fixed, he leaves, I put my headphones back on, and return to my game. If I'm going to be lost somewhere, it might as well be in a past version of Wyoming.

Firewatch is one of the most beautiful games I've ever played. It's pretty in an obvious sense – the environment that you're placed in is gorgeous, and serene. But there is a subtler beauty to it that only comes out as the story progresses. As the game begins, you are given a series of text-based choices that allow you to live an accelerated version of the first few years of Henry's adulthood. You start in a bar in Boulder, Colorado, in 1975, where you first meet Julia. You begin dating. Eventually you move in together, and things become more

---

* Someone stationed in a tower in a remote area of wilderness, whose job is to monitor the surrounding area and watch for signs of fires starting. If they spot something, they can radio it in so that fire services can respond before it becomes dangerous.

serious. You get a dog together – either a Beagle or a German Shepherd, depending on your choices. The years go by. One summer evening, in 1979, she asks you about children – it's up to you how to respond. Then the text melts away and you find yourself at the start of a hiking trail. As you begin slowly to head down the path, the text swims into focus again – it is 1980, and you're having arguments with Julia. Things settle down, and you're now back on the hiking trail, hopping over fallen trees as the sun sets over a ridge in the distance. The story returns. Now it is 1982, and you start to notice something subtly wrong with Julia – she seems to lose her words when she gets stressed. Plans for having kids get put on hold when she gets a job halfway across the country, at Yale in Connecticut. The text flashes forward to 1985, and things are getting worse with Julia. She's having memory difficulties at work and gets sent home on leave. After talking to doctors, it seems that she is showing signs of early-onset dementia. The years go by quickly – too quickly. Your dog is getting older, Julia goes back to work, but the dementia starts to get worse and she is sent home on leave in 1987. The text melts away again, and you're back on the trail. As you meander through the forest, you catch sight of a deer on the path ahead of you. It bounds off into the undergrowth as the screen fades and returns to text. Things become more strained with Julia as you try to take care of her, and you start drinking. One evening in 1989 you get pulled over by the police and end up spending the night in jail. Julia's parents, who live in Australia, find out. They fly over and take her back home with them, and you say that you'll visit soon. A few weeks go by, and you see a job advert for a fire lookout in the local newspaper.

You take it, and then the game begins.

The first time I played it, I was crushed by that opening story. It evokes the desperate sense of time passing without you being able to properly take control of it. For a while, things are okay, life is good. Then you start to notice odd little events. They become more frequent, and before you've had a chance to process what's happening, you're dealing with the person you know and love disappearing in front of you, and then its aftermath. I wasn't prepared for it the first time I played – all that I had heard about *Firewatch* was that it was an adventure mystery, played out in the first-person. But that opening text … It immediately brought back memories of my dad, and that sense of prolonged anxiety in the back of my mind, the one that occurs when bad things are happening around you, to you, but there's nothing you can do about them. So it was in the few short years between my dad's diagnosis and his death. It is 1994: life, for the most part, carries on as normal. I go to school, he goes to work. We start to notice subtle things going wrong – he gets out of breath very easily when we play catch in the back garden. Then he starts to get out of breath while walking up flights of stairs. A year passes. I remember the day that he got his first wheelchair. It was meant to be nothing more than an intermittent aid. If he was getting a bit tired, he could sit in the chair instead, and be able to get around. He would still be walking most of the time though. I was twelve, and that's what everyone was telling me was the plan – he would still be walking most of the time. I don't ever remember seeing him walk again after he got that wheelchair.

Another year flashes by, and things are worse. My dad's car – a Vauxhall Cavalier, in British racing green – is still on the drive, but no one has driven it for a while. He's got an electric wheelchair now. It was getting too hard for him to push a manual one around on his own. We have carers who come in to look after him, and my grandparents have moved in with us. Everyone drifts around the house with a sense of quiet sadness. A year or so prior to his diagnosis my parents had gone through a divorce, and one of the more complex negotiations that came out of it resulted in a Byzantine timetable detailing when I would see my mum during the week. An hour after school on Tuesdays and Thursdays, a bit longer on Mondays, Wednesdays and Fridays, unless it was the one weekend in three that I would stay with her, in which case I would be back in time for dinner on Sunday. But as the disease ran its course, I found myself wanting to spend more and more time with my dad. It wasn't something that I consciously realised at the time, just an urge – a frustration when I was late getting home, or in the weeks I knew I was going to be away from him on the weekend. It wasn't my mum's fault; I love her to bits. It's not that I didn't enjoy spending time with her – it's just that I think, deep down, I knew that the remaining time that I had with my dad was limited, and I wanted to squeeze out every last precious drop before he went. Then, quickly – too quickly, it is 1998, and he is gone.

I have played through *Firewatch* many times, and each and every time the opening brings those memories back just as strongly. In a way, I find it a form of catharsis. I'm not saying that I'm a huge fan of persistently dredging up old and very sore memories; obviously, that's not an enjoyable process. But playing the rest of the game allows me to find a certain sense of peace about everything that happened. The world of *Firewatch* is bittersweet and beautiful, and it holds my attention more completely than any other game that I've played. It's somewhere, I think, that my dad would have liked very much. But *Firewatch's* ability to completely capture your attention isn't simply down to its powerful, emotional story. As the games writer Abhishek

Iyer has pointed out, it works extremely hard to place you firmly in Henry's shoes, and to make you forget that you are, in fact, simply playing a video game. All this is achieved with an innovative user interface that provides you with information and options as if you and Henry are one and the same person. It's a great improvement to how players usually navigate around game environments. Invariably, first- and third-person shooter games will provide players with a map they can refer to throughout the course of play. Often, though, checking this can be a jolting experience, because it's clear that the map is only available to you, the human player, and not your in-game character. In *Fortnite* for instance, when a player opts to check the map, it's overlaid on the screen for them. While this is happening, the character doesn't really do anything – they either remain motionless, or carry on running in a straight line. While subtle, this provides an immediate disconnect between the player and the character they're playing. It's the digital equivalent of giving the player a real-world map, but it provides a physical disconnection from the game. Immersion, or that sense of spatial presence within the game, suffers as a result – only slightly, but it suffers nevertheless. *World of Warcraft* uses maps in a similar way, but it makes an attempt to make the disconnect a little less absolute, by having your character pull the map out of their pocket. As the player, you can't really see this happen, but at least it lets other players nearby know what you're doing and why you might have stopped interacting with them.

Firewatch takes something simple like the way a map is presented to a player, and includes it as part of the immersive experience of playing the game. As you walk around the forest, if you want to get your bearings, Henry will pull out a paper map from his pocket, unfold it, and look at it *with* you. When you zoom in to different areas, it's the equivalent of Henry holding the map closer to his face, and more than once I have found myself inching my own head closer to the screen, squinting to take a closer look, as if it were a real thing. As the game progresses, Henry (and by extension, you) annotates the paper with reference points and important information, in much the same way you might scribble on a map if you were actually out hiking in the woods. While it might be a more fiddly way of conveying navigation information to a player, the way that it makes you feel as if you are actually located in the game environment more than makes up for it. If anything, any frustration brought about by using the map brings more realism to the experience – well, at least for me it does. Map-reading and navigation has never been one of my strong points, as I think my wife would agree.* In *Firewatch*, other game mechanics work in the same sort of way. When you stumble upon objects of interest in the forest, rather than you clicking on them to bring up a description of what they are, instead Henry pulls out his radio, and relays a description of them to his colleague, Delilah, who is stationed in another fire-watching tower nearby. Rather than a corner of your screen being filled with a virtual floating compass to help you figure out what direction you're travelling in, Henry has to pull out his actual compass and take a look. For all intents and purposes, you are Henry, and Henry is you.

---

* I have only ever missed one flight in my life: our honeymoon flight, two days after we got married. I missed it because I misread the route to Gatwick Airport, and assumed that I knew a better route than the sat-nav, which was insisting that we would get stuck in major delays if I blindly carried on down the motorway. A three-hour car journey became a six-hour one. I have triple-checked every journey since, on pain of death.

As much as the world of *Firewatch* is about exploring the physical environment of Shoshone National Forest, it's also about exploring the complexities of human emotion. By the time the introductory text hits you with devastating precision as to why Henry has chosen to take a job as a fire lookout, you feel as relieved as he is to be able to pull yourself back together with a solitary ramble through the woods. Throughout the game, not only are you trying to solve the mystery that drives the main story, you're also trying to make sense of the life that you left behind. The dialogue choices you're able to make in your interactions with Delilah allow you to emotionally open up to her, keep your distance, or even at times flirt with her. And while the conversational routes that you decide to take have no major impact on the game itself, oftentimes I have found myself *really caring* about how I let Henry's relationship with Delilah develop. Flirting, game-wise, achieves nothing – you never actually meet Delilah face to face. But the first time I picked that option, I became wracked with guilt. *Henry's still married to Julia*, I thought, *what the hell is he playing at?* I quickly shut down in my later interactions with Delilah, and she quite reasonably became similarly terse. As the game progresses, and their relationship becomes more open and honest, a certain contradiction becomes evident. *Firewatch* is a game where clearly a great deal of time and skill has gone into making your control of Henry feel effortless and enthralling. But at the same time, no matter what you choose to do or say, the ending will always be the same: as the wildfire becomes all-consuming you solve the mystery, Delilah leaves before you get the chance to meet her, and Henry must face his old life and confront his feelings about Julia. The entire game, in a sense, revolves around how you deal with Henry's original decision to run away in the first place. And by placing you in the isolated backcountry of Wyoming, it offers you a safe place to do that, and to interrogate the emotional consequences of your actions. *Firewatch*, in short, allows you to explore what it means to be human, which is what makes it so immersive.

Immersion, then, is about making you feel as closely connected to the game world as possible – even if that sometimes means deliberately breaking the digital fourth wall, that invisible barrier that separates you from the game characters and allows you to observe their trials and tribulations. A memorable game that achieved this in a spectacular way is *Metal Gear Solid*, released for the PlayStation in 1998. *Metal Gear Solid* is a third-person-perspective stealth/action game, following the story of a soldier called Solid Snake as he sneaks around a nuclear weapons facility in order to take down a rogue Special Forces team. One of the boss battles in the game involves a fight with a psychic special-ops mastermind called Psycho Mantis. At the start of the encounter, you find him floating above an office desk deep in the bowels of the military complex wearing a black gas mask and bone-like black armour. Solid Snake doesn't look all that impressed (although he never does), so in order to prove his mental prowess to you, Psycho Mantis reads your mind – or, more precisely, the contents of the memory card inserted into your games console – and rattles off details about the games you've been playing previously. He then instructs you to put your controller down on a flat surface, and, demonstrating his 'telekinetic' powers, moves it around by activating the vibrating rumble motors within. After these shows of bravado, the fight commences. Initially it proves to be nearly impossible, as Psycho Mantis appears able to predict every move you make. The only way to win is to unplug the controller and re-insert it into the second controller slot in the console. When you do, the villain laments that he's suddenly unable to read your mind, and the battle can be won. Whereas in games like *Firewatch* the aim is to keep players immersed by making them feel as though they're in the actual game world, *Metal Gear Solid* achieves a different type of immersive experience by deliberately breaking out of that world. By having characters interact with aspects of the player's environment in the room around them, the room itself becomes part of the game.

Obviously, immersion isn't the sole contributing factor in what makes a good game. As the games scholar Brendan Keogh pointed out in a 2014 paper, mobile games tend to strive for a very different goal to the more traditional console- or computer games in this respect. Whereas one of the aims of the latter is to take you out of the moment and transplant you into a digital fantasy world, the former are instead intended to be subsumed into our daily lives; to fill those idle moments on a train, or when we're waiting for a friend to join us. But for me, immersion is important. The best games that I've ever played – and you may disagree with me on this – are the ones, like *Firewatch*, that are able to completely transport you to another life and another world.

From a psychological point of view, conducting research on immersion, and understanding how it is achieved in games, is fraught with difficulty. It doesn't help that terms like 'immersion' and 'presence' are used somewhat interchangeably. Some scholars have argued that immersion is best thought of as a form of spatial presence; a sense of feeling physically located within the game. This is different to, for example, social presence (the extent to which you interact with other players or characters within a game as if they are real) or self-presence (the extent to which you merge your actual self with your digital avatar). How do you measure something so seemingly evanescent? Sure, there are questionnaire scales out there, but as with many psychological phenomena, asking people to rate themselves on something that by its very nature is nebulous and transient feels a little pointless. Are there any other ways, though? Can it be assessed experimentally, for instance? This is a question I have grappled with for a number of years now, with little success. Perhaps the closest to a satisfactory experiment on immersion that I have seen had nothing to do with video games, but with movies.

In my postdoctoral years, I worked in a motion capture lab at the University of Bristol. My departmental PhD examiner, Professor Tom Troscianko, along with his doctoral student Stephen Hinde, were conducting a couple of pilot experiments to try to develop more real-time measures of immersion, which could be used to assess different factors that might affect our experience of watching a television screen. As I've already mentioned, using questionnaire-based methods for assessing something like 'presence' – that feeling of actually being *in* the game – has its limits. If nothing else, the questionnaires tend to be administered *after* the immersive activity has finished, which makes them susceptible to all sorts of confounding problems. As scientists with research expertise in understanding how the human vision system works, Troscianko and Hinde were instead interested in whether there was a way to measure immersion more directly – and specifically, while the activity is being undertaken. The two experiments they conducted looked at the effects of a fairly simple factor: given that television screens have increased in size over the years, does size actually matter? Are bigger screens better? Participants were seated in a darkened lecture theatre, and asked to watch the first 45 minutes of *The Good, The Bad and The Ugly*. The first experiment was, in essence, a feasibility check to determine whether screen size actually did have any effect on immersion, using a self-rated measure of 'presence' similar to questionnaire studies. At sixteen separate points throughout the movie, a bright red light would appear above the screen for a second. When participants saw the light, they had to place a mark on a straight line in front of them to indicate how 'present' they felt in the movie as the light came on. It was a simple experiment, and with it came a simple finding: participants rated themselves as feeling more immersed in the movie when they viewed it on a bigger screen. Doubling the size of the screen resulted in an increase of between around 43 per cent and 63 per cent in those subjective ratings.

Having established that the basic principle behind the study worked, the second experiment then introduced two novel real-time measures of immersion. This time around, the setup was similar, but instead of a red light appearing above the screen, a loud beep was played at the same sixteen points throughout the movie. As soon as the participants heard the beep, they had to press a button – the idea being that if they were more immersed in the story, it would take them longer to snap themselves out of it, register the beep and thus react to it. About two seconds before the beep sounded, the experimenters also took a more surreptitious measure: an infrared camera recorded a brief video of the participants' eyes, and the diameter of their pupils was measured after the experiment had finished. Psychologists have known since the 1960s not only that our pupils dilate when we're thinking hard about something, but also that there is a link between the amount of dilation and the relative amount of brain processing that's happening on a moment-by-moment basis. Part of this, at least, seems to be due to the involvement of memory processes; for example, the Nobel prize-winner Daniel Kahneman (he of *Thinking, Fast and Slow* fame) showed in work early in his career that pupil size seems to be especially responsive to tasks that involve our short-term memory. It stands to reason, then, that if we become particularly involved in the storyline of a movie we are watching, our immersion in it might be reflected in our eyes.

Troscianko's study found precisely that. Just as in the first experiment, these two more objective measures of immersion showed that there were differences depending on the size of the screen used. In other words, participants showed both increased reaction times (they were slower to respond to the beep) and more dilated pupils when watching the 'big' screen as opposed to when they watched the 'small' screen. Although it was only a pilot study (only 30–40 participants took part in each experiment), it nevertheless provided a promising addition to research looking at how we might best assess something as ephemeral as immersion in a more objective way. Unfortunately, Tom Troscianko's work in the area was to go no further than this. In November 2011, while the study was still undergoing the review process at the journal they had submitted it to, Tom had a heart attack and died in his sleep at the age of 58. It was sudden and very much unexpected, and for many of us at Bristol and beyond, it left a huge hole in our lives. At the time, my office was just a couple of doors down from Tom's, and I acutely remember the days and weeks after we had found out that he had gone. Usually, his door would be open, and he was always more than happy to welcome visitors for a chat. In the weeks following his death, most days I would walk past his door, expecting to see his big beaming smile. But the door was closed, and the corridor was a little quieter. Occasionally, serving as a jolting reminder of our loss, his office phone would ring for a while, and then cut out. It would take a while before we were actually able to get someone into his office to disconnect it.

To the best of my knowledge, no one has taken the study design that Tom and his team developed and adapted it to try to understand video game immersion. That's not to say that other work hasn't been done in the area, and obviously I'm glossing over a broad section of studies that have similarly tried to measure presence and immersion in other media. Certainly, there have been some attempts to objectively quantify immersion in video games, and they, too, use principles from vision research. For example, a 2008 study by a team led by Charlene Jennett at UCL used eye-tracking methods to look at whether immersion could be measured in a more objective fashion, by studying the pattern of people's eye fixations while they were playing a computer game. As our attention becomes more focussed on a task, we tend to make fewer eye movements, and instead fixate on objects of interest for longer. The hypothesis in Jennett's study was that people who engaged in an immersive task (in this case, playing the game *Half-Life*) would show a fewer number of fixations on the screen, compared to those engaged in a non-immersive task (clicking a square that would appear randomly on-screen). The results bore that out. Again, it wasn't a perfect study (the researchers only tested 40 participants, and there are outstanding questions about whether their two study conditions differed in ways other than one being immersive and the other not), but it did show that there might be properly objective methods of testing immersion, more so at least than the standard self-report questionnaires. Nevertheless, understanding how video games generate immersive experiences remains an elusive goal for researchers.

At this point, it's reasonable to ask why anyone should even care about all of this fluff. Games are games, right? Who cares how, whether or why they're immersive? Well, if we care whether games might be addictive, or whether violent games might harm us or change our behaviour, then understanding how they capture our attention is an important part of that puzzle. It will become even more important as the technology that drives video games evolves and improves, and this will be of particular interest given the revival of virtual reality as a viable technology platform in recent years. To date, relatively little work has been done in this area though, and the majority of what has been done has, again, been devoted to violence and aggression. Yet again, the results have been too mixed for any clear conclusions to be drawn. For example, a 2004 study by Ron Tamborini at Michigan State University asked participants to play the first-person shooter *Duke Nukem 3D*, either in virtual reality or using a more traditional gaming platform. The study then looked at the effects on self-reported measures of presence, hostile thoughts and aggressive behaviour. The results of Tamborini's study suggested that playing a game in virtual reality didn't have much of an effect on any of these outcome measures. By contrast though, work conducted a few years later by Susan Persky at the National Human Genome Research Institute and Jim Blascovich at the University of California, found precisely the opposite. In their study, participants who played a custom-made game using a virtual reality system reported higher levels of both presence and aggressive feelings than those who played the same game on a desktop computer (i.e. not in VR). So while there might be good reason to think that more immersive video games might have a more substantial effect on our behaviour, this idea isn't supported by the available research base. The science needs to come to a conclusion one way or the other though, because the ways in which we interact with games are changing at a rapid pace, and they don't show any signs of slowing down.

'Have you seen *Westworld*?'

I'm talking to Bill Roper again. Bill, if you recall, is Chief Creative Officer at Improbable Games, who specialise in creating new computational platforms on which more complex gaming experiences can be built.

'It's the horrifying example of what can go wrong,' he explains. 'But when I was at Disney, you can bet that every Imagineer was watching that series and thinking "that's what we all wanna make".' He isn't talking about creating an army of robots that suddenly become sentient and start murdering lucky visitors in the Magic Kingdom.* He's talking about the dream of every games developer: the ultimate goal of making an immersive experience so real, that for the time you're in it, you feel like you're really there, and that you are a different version of you. Bill refers to this as the idea of a 'multiversal self' – that as virtual reality becomes richer and more powerful, it will augment human experience, becoming every bit as real and as meaningful as our offline lives. It's a concept that has permeated science fiction for decades. Ernie Cline's *Ready Player One*, for example, tells the story of a not-too-distant future in which humanity, faced with a world on the brink of environmental collapse, escapes into a worldwide virtual reality simulator called the OASIS that offers players the ability to become whatever

---

* At least, I hope he isn't.

and whomever they wish. As far as Bill is concerned, when it comes to the technological side of *Ready Player One*, we aren't that far away.

'Some of the technologies that are essential to building elaborate virtual worlds are the kinds of things that we're working on right now – or at least, the backbones of those technologies,' he explains. 'Like, how do you get not just hundreds, but millions of players into a single virtual world, and have everything work smoothly?' Bill's work at Improbable focusses on just that: how to solve some of the big issues in distributed computing in order to run mind-bogglingly huge shared virtual environments, complete with non-player characters who have artificial intelligences so advanced that you can interact with them as if they were real people. But there are responsibility issues that need to be worked out as virtual reality becomes a viable technology. 'One of the easiest things for VR developers to do is to find ways to scare players, for example,' Bill points out. As far as emotions go, fear is one of the easiest to elicit in virtual reality games. Whereas in horror movies it's easy to detach yourself from the scary stuff that's happening on-screen, in virtual reality the aim is for you to be living that moment. 'But if that's all that VR ever focussed on, then wow! What a horrifying thing that would be. Like: I really wanna be inside this mind-altering immersive place, but oh my God, every time I am, I just come out of it a jangle of nerves.' He goes on to explain that there have already been a lot of discussions inside the industry about the responsibilities that VR developers have: to ensure that they're doing more than just cynically tapping into primal emotions in order to make their games interesting. At the 2016 Game Developers Conference in San Francisco, for example, a panel of industry experts pointed out that while drawing out a visceral reaction might be something that people enjoy when it happens in a movie or a more traditional video game, it can actually become a hugely uncomfortable experience in virtual reality. Two years earlier, at a similar panel at the same conference, Denny Unger, the creative director of Cloudhead Games, claimed that virtual reality games peddling in jump-scares could very easily lead to someone with a heart condition being literally scared to death. Developers, he argued, shouldn't underestimate the immersive power of the medium, which necessarily requires a greater consideration for the people who use it. 'It's the same as in any game development,' Bill adds. 'How do you keep it engaging and fun, but still be very aware of the fact that people actually have lives?'

Not that the discussion about immersion and the future of virtual reality is completely negative. In many ways, a thoughtfully-realised multiplayer virtual reality game – something on the truly worldwide scale of *Ready Player One*'s OASIS – could provide a whole new way of thinking about how we live our lives in the future. As virtual worlds become more immersive, it stands to reason that people will spend longer and longer in them. At face value, this seems like a bad thing, right? The whole idea that people might become disconnected from reality feels extremely uncomfortable, especially if it's predicated on systems (like those that came up when I looked at addiction) that exploit people in ways that aren't in their best interests. But the creation of a virtual environment built on positive principles (that is, centred on the experience of the player themselves), and which embraces the fact that they want to stay in that environment for as long as possible, could offer a very different way of looking at things.

For developers like Bill Roper, building more immersive virtual worlds isn't about escapism. Instead, it's about thinking of new ways to create opportunities and experiences for people. We are already in a situation where many basic or unskilled tasks and jobs are being replaced by automation or artificial intelligence. And the discussions have already started about what this means for the workforce of the future – will there be enough jobs for everyone? If not, how will we pass our time? What does this mean for the economy? Arguably, one solution to this is for people to find a new form of work in the virtual environment. If there are fewer jobs in the offline world as a result of AI automation, and people have more time to spend doing other activities, as Bill suggests, 'there's an opportunity out there for some extremely clever developer to figure out: "how do I give people real jobs in my MMO?"' Say you have someone who, in a virtual reality game of the future, plays a bartender. And they are great at it. They make weird and wacky space drinks, they're lots of fun to be around, and everyone loves chatting to them. So they get tipped for their time – not just in an arbitrary game currency, but in actual, real-world money. As a result, the amount of time that they spend in the game has a tangible value to it, over and above the inherent entertainment value. It becomes a source of income, and one that anyone with an interesting idea can tap into. Moreover, where people may be unable to generate income in the offline world due to a lack of jobs, they can make up for this in the online world, thus maintaining the economy. Bill provides another example: 'Say you had an economy or game mechanic where characters actually had to eat. If you were an excellent [virtual] hunter or farmer who could provide food supplies, there would be a real exchange rate for that. Whether that's in real-world dollars or in cryptocurrency, those are the things that the future starts sorting out.'

I appreciate that this may seem like an overly naïve idea in some ways, and I'm not blind to the issues that such a future could bring with it. The dystopian undertone to *Ready Player One* is that a world that we have ravaged is being ignored and left to rot while we fritter away our time in a virtual world. Clearly, we have responsibilities as custodians of an environment that future generations will be born into. But my point is this: I think it's inevitable that a completely immersive, hyper-realistic virtual world will be created sooner than we anticipate, and it will be one that many people will want to get lost in. The conversations that we need to have now are about how we achieve that in a socially and environmentally responsible way. Will we end up with a society split into players and non-players, and how will we reconcile those two existences? How do we make true virtual reality a positive and healthy experience? I don't have answers to these questions yet, but what I can tell you is that there are already examples of virtual reality being used as a force for good out there, and perhaps we can start the conversation by taking a lead from them.

I stare out of the windows of the sixth floor of the Wellcome Trust's headquarters. The biomedical research charity, founded by an endowment from pharmaceutical giant Sir Henry Wellcome in 1936, is situated on Euston Road, one of the main transport arteries through the heart of London. The large open-plan room I'm in is relaxed, with people quietly milling about and conversing with each other in hushed tones. On any other day, you might reasonably expect academics to gather here, engaging in discussions about their latest research, or making the case for why their project is most deserving of funding from the charity. This isn't that far off the mark, but as I look over to one corner and see a particularly unfortunate individual face-plant the floor in a VR headset, I'm reminded that this is a fairly unique event.

The Developing Beyond competition is the product of a unique collaboration between the Wellcome Trust, one of the world's largest research funders, and Epic Games, the development company responsible for games such as *Fortnite, Unreal Tournament*, and the *Gears of War* series. The aim of the competition is to bring games developers, scientists and scholars together, in order to develop new video games that take inspiration from real-world scientific research and ideas. The winners get to take home a prize pool of $150,000, along with help to fully develop their game idea into a commercially viable product. Today's event is a showcase of the three semi-finalists, and one in particular catches my eye: a VR game called *Seed*. Developed by the independent games house All Seeing Eye, *Seed* takes its inspiration from the do-it-yourself movement of biotechnology 'hackers' spawned in the last century – people would grow and tinker with plants in their garden sheds, engaging in an amateur hobby in much the same way as others would create model trains or rockets. *Seed* acknowledges that history by placing you in the humble surroundings of a simple garage, allowing you to grow and generate new types of plants – often in unexpected ways.

'There's a drawer that has radioactive clocks in it,' explains Ollie Kay, associate creative director of All Seeing Eye. 'You can hold a seed over that, and it will change the properties of it. The idea was taken from a crazy story about a guy in the late 50s who was scraping radium off watch faces, and using that to make his rose buds mutate.' It was through their collaboration with

Cambridge researcher Dr Helen Anne Curry that All Seeing Eye were able to add quirky little elements like this* that pay homage to the history of bio-hacking. Helen's research is in the history of plant breeding, and more broadly, the history of science. 'The setting, the whole concept of what the game is – that just comes straight from her ideas of garage biotech,' explains Ollie. 'The game, fundamentally, is the science of how plant breeding works.'

The ill-fated player I saw earlier is still lying in a crumpled heap on the floor. A couple of onlookers help her, and she takes the headset off. Apparently, she was trying to lean over the workbench and grab something on a shelf a bit further away. She was so involved in the game, she leaned all the way forward, using her hand to balance on a table that didn't actually exist. Virtual reality offers up a fascinating new way to tell stories and foster an interest in science, but clearly there are some hazards.

Later in the day, I get the chance to sit down with the European Territory Manager for Epic, Professor Mike Gamble. 'Actually, this is our third competition with Wellcome,' he explains. The previous event, held in 2015, was the Big Data VR Challenge. That competition tasked developers with finding new ways to allow people to manipulate, navigate and ultimately make better sense of extremely large datasets in real time. The winners, LumaPie, created a way to visualise and interrogate a

---

* Although in a paper outlining the history of the garage biotech movement published in 2014, she points out that in reality, using watch radium to mutate flowers wasn't the most successful of endeavours – she quotes amateur plant breeder John James, who after trying out the procedure, noted 'it was the most deformed, black spot-susceptible rose I have ever known'.

vast treasure trove of data from the longitudinal study I mentioned earlier – the Children of the 90s dataset.

The Big Data VR Challenge showcased how development concepts from the world of video games could be used to inspire new ways of managing and analysing scientific data and research. But the aim of the Developing Beyond competition at the Wellcome was something different. 'It is actually just a game competition,' explains Mike. 'We wanted the science to be seamlessly integrated, but first and foremost, the entries should be games – fun, entertaining, and potentially sellers in the market'. To my mind, this was an interesting shift in thinking. Far too often, the way scientific research has tried to interact with games development has been by co-opting basic design concepts in gaming – things like introducing a scoring system, competing against other players – in order to generate experiments that are more 'fun' for people to take part in. And more often than not, this type of 'gamification' produces rather sad-looking products that no reputable game player would ever want to play. 'That's where Wellcome *get* it,' agrees Mike. 'They get that good science in entertainment doesn't have to mean it's an educational product. It just reflects the correct use of science.'

Ultimately, the aim of Developing Beyond is to allow this sort of thing to happen more naturally. The competition at the Wellcome Trust was very much a deliberately engineered situation. Developers were specifically paired with scientists in a way that would maximise the chances of a successful game being created. But there's no reason that games developers can't contact people in the scientific community and do this on their own. 'Hopefully games developers will start thinking about this,' Mike adds. 'If they're going to use science, or if there's any sort of scientific background in their games, hopefully they'll just automatically decide, "Let's talk to some scientists."'

It isn't just biomedical charities who are showing an interest in how we can best use games and virtual reality to help science. Scientists themselves are using the technology, and adapting it to help those in need. Two of the most interesting examples of this in recent years have used the very essence of virtual reality – that it is a completely immersive experience – to tackle complex problems connected to mental and physical health. In 2008, a team lead by Hunter Hoffman at the Human Interface Technology Laboratory at the University of Washington published research that looked at whether virtual reality games could be used as a treatment for pain in burns patients. One of the many awful things about burns injuries is that the process of treating wounds and refreshing bandages itself can be an excruciatingly painful experience. Dressings are applied to the damaged area, but as the wound heals, new skin becomes attached to them. When the patient goes in to have those bandages replaced, as they are removed, so too is the new skin, along with any infected material underneath. Apart from the purely physical factors, a range of research studies have shown that psychological factors can have an impact on our subjective experience of pain. Put simply: if we focus our attention on a wound or injury, we also focus on the pain that it is causing. However, if we are able to distract ourselves, our subjective feelings about how painful the injury is subside. Hoffman's team took this concept and developed a virtual reality game called *SnowWorld* in order to see whether they could reduce the pain that burns victims experience in a non-pharmacological way. The game involves players moving around a winter wonderland environment full of penguins, woolly mammoths and snowmen.

The object is simple; as they move along a fixed path, players use the VR headset to look around the environment, and a joystick to shoot snowballs at the various objects of interest they see. So much is going on around the patient that they simply don't have enough attention left over to think about anything else – and, critically, they can't watch the process of the wound redressing happening. In Hoffman's study, patients were asked to provide subjective ratings about how much pain they were experiencing, and did so during two brief pauses in the wound redressing process. The results showed that patients reported feeling less pain after being immersed in *SnowWorld*.

Elsewhere on the west coast of the United States, other researchers have been developing virtual reality tools in order to help alleviate other types of pain caused by mental health trauma. Over the past decade and a half, work led by Albert 'Skip' Rizzo at the University of Southern California has led to the development of a clinical tool called *Bravemind*. At its core, *Bravemind* is a form of exposure therapy, operating in virtual reality, with the aim of treating cases of post-traumatic stress disorder (PTSD) in war veterans. Exposure therapy is a treatment method that is used to help patients confront things they fear. The basic idea is that if someone continually avoids that thing (be it an object, person or situation), then over time their fear of it becomes increasingly worse. In extreme cases this can lead to situations in which the object of fear causes panic attacks, anxiety, nightmares, flashbacks and other psychological issues that can become completely debilitating. Exposure therapy creates a situation in which the patient gradually comes into closer contact with the object of their fear in a safe environment, with the aim of breaking the pattern of avoidance and, ultimately, the fear itself. Traditionally, this might have been achieved by placing the physical object in the room with the patient. If someone is afraid of snakes, the first step might be to sit them in a room and talk about snakes for a bit. After a few sessions, the next step might be to look at cartoons of snakes. Then real pictures. Then sessions might involve bringing a toy snake into the room. The process can be paced in different ways, but the idea is that sooner or later, the patient is asked to be in a room with a real snake, and that the therapy will have helped them to overcome their fear of it.

Useful for something tangible like a snake, or a spider. But combat-related PTSD is a little harder to overcome in the same way. This is where *Bravemind* comes in. Combining the principles of exposure therapy with video game design, *Bravemind* is a completely immersive environment that uses sights, smells, sounds and vibrations in order to gradually re-introduce war veterans into the situations that may initially have caused their PTSD to develop. Because it occurs in a fully-controllable virtual environment, the rate at which patients are exposed to the trauma-inducing situation can be as gradual as required. The process might start with a relatively benign scenario – for example, driving down an empty street. Over repeated sessions, more and more elements can be added to the situation: buildings, then perhaps children running down the street, people shouting, maybe the sound of a gun firing in the distance. Each element is only added providing that the patient has successfully adjusted to previous, simpler elements. Eventually, the idea is for the scenario to culminate with the trauma-inducing event: for example a roadside bomb attack, represented in 3D space, with all of the accompanying sights and sounds, the smell of burning rubber, and so on. All of this can be controlled by a clinician, in a completely safe environment for the patient. Rizzo's studies have shown that there is a huge amount of promise in this approach; in a clinical trial of an early iteration of *Bravemind* for example, sixteen out of twenty PTSD patients no longer met the diagnostic criteria for the disorder at the end of the treatment. Other studies have shown similar rates of recovery, and a randomised controlled trial testing the newest version of *Bravemind* is currently underway. The emerging picture is one that suggests that VR offers a safe and effective way of delivering exposure therapy for cases of PTSD.

I don't think that it is naïve to suggest that the future of virtual reality is exciting and promising. Yes, there are difficult conversations that will need to be had in the next few years, centring specifically on how virtual worlds are created such that they don't exploit individuals – especially vulnerable individuals. I agree with people like Bill Roper, that VR worlds can potentially offer us new ways to earn a living and to foster new and meaningful relationships with other people. At the same time, though, I worry that, because gambling mechanisms that exploit human weaknesses and fuel unhealthy obsessions are so easy to employ in games, they will not only be the first thing to appear in VR worlds, but also constitute a major focus for the shaping of those worlds. This, I fear, would only serve to hinder what could otherwise be a huge boon for humanity. We're still right at the beginning of virtual reality, and developers have a collective responsibility to work out, right now, what the rules are, and what constitutes good practice. Perhaps scientists can provide the right sort of moral compass to help inform those rules. As researchers, we are bound by ethics rules to do no harm to our participants – their welfare must always take precedence over the scientific knowledge that we seek. In the same way, in the runaway excitement to produce the ultimate immersive virtual reality, the welfare of those that will use it must be held up as the most important consideration of all. How we would bring this idea into effect isn't a trivial question. It would require an immense amount of collaboration, not just between games and VR developers, but also with psychologists, behavioural scientists, clinicians and policy-makers. The seeds of such partnerships are already there, in some ways – initiatives such as the Fair Play Alliance show that developers are capable of crossing corporate boundaries in order to come together for a common good. It also clearly brings into focus that need to draw the public conversations about games and technology back into a sensible, reasonable arena, lest we remain stuck in the hamster wheel of 'violent video game' hyperbole for years to come. If we can do all of that, and get it right, then the future of virtual reality – the scientific and medical benefits that it could afford us, as well as the opportunities for unleashing our creativity in unimaginable new ways – will be a truly exciting thing to behold.

CHAPTER 11

Wayfaring and wayfinding

I grew up in the North of England: in a quiet old mill town called Glossop, snuggled up against the desolate expanses of the Dark Peak and Kinder Scout, about a half-hour trip from Manchester. For a time, in some misguided attempt to entice hapless tourists to its perpetually damp and grey streets, Glossop billed itself as the 'gateway' (presumably one of many) to the Peak District national park. It was a PR strategy that always gave me pause for thought – the sort that made me think that they should've just gone the full distance and branded the town as the 'Gateway to Literally Anywhere Else'. The peaks were a vast, untouched wilderness, ripe for exploration. *That's* the place you wanted to go. Glossop was just something quaint to look at as you sped through on your way.

Given the complete lack of anything interesting to do in the town, I spent those formative years doing what any teenager would: finely tuning a persona that matched the weather – bleak, grey, and occasionally windy. I went to school in a town just over an hour away, far enough to be inconvenient for seeing friends on a social basis. The few friends I did have nearby were transient, moving in and out of the town as parental marriages disintegrated or jobs changed. So for a few short years in my mid-teens, I was stuck there; feeling too old and socially awkward to start a new community hobby, too young to be able to abandon myself to a night out in Manchester. Losing my dad affected me in ways that I didn't understand or even have any awareness of at the time. But the effects were there.

I retreated, becoming engrossed in sci-fi and fantasy stories. Books like Terry Pratchett's *Discworld* series became a place to run away to, where even things like death didn't seem all that bad. I would latch onto any television show that allowed me the possibility to imagine what it was like to have an actual father-like role model in my life, for all the faults that such a pursuit entails. Everything from *Due South* (the greatest comedic police procedural ever created, with a lead character who was the embodiment of a moral compass) to *The New Yankee Workshop* (a woodworking show where host Norm Abrams seemed to be on a mission to systematically build an entire town's worth of furniture using every piece of wood in New England), became essential watching.

Games didn't offer the same opportunity to find someone worth looking up to, but they did provide something else: a way to escape the confines of my hometown for a while and become a virtual tourist. That video games can present us with landscapes and vistas that have no limits other than our own imaginations is well known: a piratical adventure on the high seas, perhaps, or an alien war in a far-flung region of the galaxy. In video games, we get to satisfy one of the deepest of human urges – to explore and discover things about the world around us, and perhaps about ourselves. For me, the digital vista that best encapsulated this idea didn't involve the magnificence of an otherworldly cityscape, or the ultimate grandiosity of outer space. It was a view of a simple field.

The Legend of Zelda: Ocarina of Time was the first video game to give me the sense that I was free to explore other worlds – and that not only was this not a scary thing for me to do, I was actively encouraged to do it. Where years earlier I had felt almost trapped by some games – locked into the linear corridors of *Blake Stone*, scared of facing the next monster in the next room, for example – *Ocarina of Time* instead took me by the hand and eagerly showed me what it was like to be a digital sightseer. It conveyed to me, for the first time, that sometimes it's okay just to get lost in another world for a while. Set in a fantasy land called Hyrule, *Ocarina of Time* follows the adventures of the silent protagonist, Link, as he tries to save the world from the malevolent King of Thieves, Ganondorf. In the early stages, you play as a young Link, trying to collect a set of three spiritual stones that will allow you to enter the Sacred Realm and retrieve a holy relic known as the Triforce and a weapon of great power called the Master Sword. However, as Link retrieves the mythical sword, he is placed in stasis, too young to fully wield its power. At the same time, Ganondorf enters the Sacred Realm and steals the Triforce for his own gain. After seven years, Link is finally reawakened to a Hyrule ravaged by monsters and ruled with an iron fist by the evil King of Thieves. In order to save the world, the older Link must awaken five sages, save a sixth, Princess Zelda, and ultimately confront Ganondorf atop Hyrule Castle, who in the final battle uses the Triforce's power to become a demonic embodiment of evil known simply as Ganon. After he has succeeded in the task, the sages banish Ganon to another realm, and Zelda transports Link back to his childhood, forcing him to actually suffer through puberty this time around, just as anyone else would.

The opening levels of *Ocarina of Time* are fairly linear in nature – after being gently guided through the control system to acquire a sword and shield, you're tasked with cleansing the Great Deku Tree of a curse residing within. It's at this point that you get to explore the wider world, through the central hub of the game that is Hyrule field. The first time you see it, it is a true wonder to behold. The grass rolls out before you with what feels like almost endless possibility. In the distance, you can see what appears to be a volcano stirring to the east. To the northwest, but some jog away, you can spy a drawbridge inviting you in to the relative safety of Hyrule Castle. Time flows freely here – wait long enough, and the sun will set, the drawbridge will close, the gorgeous music will fade into silence, and undead monsters will start to rise from the ground and attack you. This isn't just a gimmick. It matters what time it is, because some parts of the game are only accessible at certain points during the day or night. That first time I got to experience the field though, to explore in any direction I wanted – it felt like I was a part of a huge, living, breathing world, as fragile as it was awe-inspiring. I had never really experienced anything like it. It was beautiful. My own little virtual world that I could cruise around to my heart's content, without having to be driven anywhere by my mum. I would spend hours there – sometimes playing the game, but sometimes just meandering around the field and its surroundings, taking in the sights and sounds of this fantastical other place. For teenaged me, in a naïve and sheltered sense, it felt like the start of real, adult-like freedom – or at least provided a hint of some of the good bits.

Ocarina of Time was considered by many to be the pinnacle of a series of video games that come together under the broad title of *The Legend of Zelda* and stretch back to 1986. That first eponymously-titled game was, in many ways, revolutionary. It was the first game that allowed players to save their progress at any point, and not have to start each session afresh every time the console was fired up. This new freedom was straightforwardly achieved by the addition to the game cartridge of an internal battery pack. It changed the nature of how console games could be played. Before that point, many games were limited to short or repetitive levels, all of which could be completed relatively quickly – providing you were skilled enough, of course. With the new 'save' ability though, *The Legend of Zelda* could afford an experience that was more complex, less frantic, and ultimately more exploratory. In that sense, it was the one of the first games that offered players a nonlinear experience. You could choose when and where you wished to go and in what order to complete dungeons, as opposed to being restricted to a fixed path. It was a game that combined this sense of exploration with puzzles, a rudimentary levelling-style system, and fighting, and although these elements could already be found in other games of the time, none brought them together in the unique way that *The Legend of Zelda* did. It was a formula that would prove successful for the next 30 years, with *Ocarina of Time* being a particularly noteworthy addition to the series – this was the first three-dimensional *Zelda* game, and it introduced many features that would become industry-standard. But as much as I love *Ocarina of Time*, as much as I have a nostalgic soft spot for it, it isn't the greatest game in the *Zelda* series. That accolade goes to the most recent instalment: *Breath of the Wild*.

Released in 2017, *Breath of the Wild* follows the same loose storyline, but it took everything that was good with *Ocarina of Time*, and amplified it. In a way, that feeling of complete freedom that had bubbled up the first moment I stepped onto Hyrule field in my younger days had been something of an illusion. Yes, you could travel anywhere you wanted to – *on the field*. Beyond the grassy confines of that central hub though, *Ocarina of Time* gently nudged you to complete certain dungeons, at least in the first half, in a specific order. But with *Breath of the Wild*, the world truly is yours to do with as you wish. Hyrule field is now so vast that it takes over 100 hours of play to fully complete the game. Barring the initial hour or two it takes to get to grips with the control system, there are no restrictions on where you can go. Quests can be completed in any order you wish, and there are numerous side quests and goals to keep you occupied in the meantime. The Hyrule of *Breath of the Wild* is a world that demands your attention – you can, if you wish, forge a direct path to and between each of the major dungeons, but to do so is to miss the most important part of the game. The value of *Breath of the Wild* isn't in its completion; it's in the journey itself. Hundreds of mini-puzzles crop up around the world as you wander, but you have to be actively exploring, *really looking* at the environment in order to spot them. It's almost as if the puzzles aren't there for the sake of being puzzles; they are there to trick you into getting lost in the beauty of the world you're immersed in. And it truly is a breathtakingly beautiful world, both in sight and sound.

Coming to it nearly twenty years after playing *Ocarina of Time* though, I experienced a tinge of sadness as well as that sense of exploration. Throughout the game there are distant echoes of that past adventure. For example, if you capture and ride a horse around, a simple piano ditty starts to play. It's rudimentary enough at first, but if you ride long enough it gives way to a haunting string rendition of the original *Zelda* theme tune. It's a fleeting moment, very easy to miss, but one that gives you pause to think about where in time this particular version of Hyrule sits within the pantheon of *Zelda* games.*

* The chronology of instalments in *The Legend of Zelda* series is somewhat convoluted, involving alternative timelines and multiple revisions over the years. In 2011, Nintendo published an official history of the games,

Further clues can be found in the derelict remains of civilisation that pepper the landscape. In the area in which the game starts, you come across the ruins of the Temple of Time, an abandoned collection of collapsing walls and broken windows, all slowly being reclaimed by moss and ivy. In *Ocarina of Time* however, the temple was alive; a grandiose and pristine building that marked the entrance to the Sacred Realm. Another such area, labelled somewhat simply and innocuously as 'ranch ruins', bears a striking resemblance to Lon Lon Ranch, a cheerful little set of stables and barns in *Ocarina of Time*, where, in that game, you can find the iconic horse Epona. The ranch ruins of *Breath of the Wild* are clearly the burned-out remains of somewhere that had seen happier times. The crumbling corner of a stone house greets you as you enter the area, the last remnant of a once-thriving farmhouse. A few dusty pots litter the pathway to your right. Broken pieces of wooden structures provide a skeletal outline of a stable and paddock. While Nintendo have never officially confirmed that the ruins are indeed those of Lon Lon Ranch,* for me the resemblance was enough to make me stop and reminisce

---

Hyrule Historia, complete with a comprehensive timeline of where each sits with respect to each other. However, even this has been met with contradictory statements by the games' developers at times, and there is much disagreement and debate among fans.

* Nintendo have even gone so far as to state that they will never say where *Breath of the Wild* exactly sits in the *Zelda* chronology. In a hardcover art book, *The Legend of Zelda: Breath of the Wild – Creating a Champion* published in late 2018, the series producer Eiji Aonuma argued that formally including the game in a 'restricted' (as he put it) timeline would stifle players' imaginations. The development team, he said, were sympathetic to the fact that players were enjoying the process of piecing together their own interpretation of the story, through the 'fragmental imagery' that was provided to them.

about that more innocent time I had spent playing *Ocarina of Time* when I was younger, and wonder how things might have gone so wrong in Hyrule in the interim. In a sense, both the temple and ranch ruins were a nod to the very real passing of time in the offline world, a poignant counterpoint to the idea that games are eternal entities in which time has no meaning.

I am wary of returning to the games of my childhood; the rose-tinted lens through which we view them as adults so often gets shattered by the realities of archaic technology, cumbersome games controllers, and modern-day expectations of high-definition visual experiences. *Breath of the Wild*, whether intentionally or not, offers a way to experience at least one of those childhood wonders in a more fitting way. It affords the possibility of re-visiting that feeling of freedom that *Ocarina of Time* once presented us with, while reminding us that we cannot stop the onslaught of the seasons, that all good things must inevitably come to an end. And for me at least, it preserves the experience of *Ocarina of Time* for what it was – a game from a formative moment in my past that cannot be experienced in the same way ever again.

In a way then, *Breath of the Wild* offers a paradox, at least in the context of how we view time. On the one hand it's an archetypal immersive experience, allowing us to spend hours – days even – getting lost in our virtual travels. Time loses a certain sense of importance when an entire evening, spent scouring a fantasy world that exists on a small screen before us, can seemingly flash by in an instant. On the other, acknowledging and appreciating the time that we have is at the core of what makes *Breath of the Wild* a captivating experience. For players of a certain age, who came to the game at a certain point in their lives, the melancholic nature of a Hyrule that is slowly returning to nature reminds us that time is a fleeting, precious thing that should never be taken for granted.

Certainly, when it comes to science, one of the most valuable things that you can give a researcher is time. Time to develop ideas for experiments, time to write research funding applications in order to get money to do those experiments. Time to actually run the damn things. Perhaps more important than all of these things, the time that research participants willingly relinquish to you in order to take part in your studies, helping you to paint an incremental layer onto the edifice of human knowledge. Time is a precious commodity, but one that we also often take for granted, especially when we're young. As with anything of this nature, it's easy to forget how important it is until it's gone, and perhaps nowhere is this idea more salient than in the case of Alzheimer's.

For something so prevalent and well known, we still know frustratingly little about what causes this disease, and it can be difficult to make a completely definitive diagnosis. Early symptoms – sufferers misplacing objects, having trouble trying to find the right words, finding it difficult to make decisions, or forgetting having had conversations with people – can simply be put down to stress. When we're under large amounts of pressure, we all suffer from these things from time to time. They're also hallmarks of other disorders, like depression, or even nutritional deficiencies. It can take many months, and many appointments, in order to get a complete diagnosis. When that does happen though, when a definitive diagnosis is actually made, the average life expectancy for someone with the disease is around six years. It's very much a disease that robs people of their identity: as it progresses, people with the condition can become confused, disorientated, forget the names of loved ones, and to the outside observer it can feel that the person we knew is disappearing. But more than that, Alzheimer's disease robs people of their past. Short-term memory loss – getting confused and misremembering things that are happening to us in the here and now – can be a common indicator, but as the condition progresses, it eats into long-term memories from earlier in our lives.

As Alzheimer's progresses, it isn't just time that becomes an issue, space can be a problem too – specifically, spatial navigation. The ability to successfully move around our environment is an easily overlooked, but incredibly important skill to have. For the most part, we don't appreciate how amazing we are at doing it. From the simple task of finding your way around your home, avoiding bumping into tables or chairs, right up to figuring out how to get to work or where to walk with the dog, effortless spatial navigation is integral to normal everyday life. For the most part, there are two frames of reference that we use to achieve this. The first is known as an 'egocentric' frame of reference, and involves remembering the locations of objects in relation to our own bodies. Let's say you walk to work every day by a fixed route. After doing this repeatedly over a few days, you start to learn to navigate your route via important landmarks – you turn left at the end of the road, past a post box, and then later on you turn right when you reach a petrol station. You perceived everything in reference to where *you* are located – so on your way home, everything is perceived in reverse: left at the petrol station, right at the post box. The second frame of reference is called 'allocentric' navigation. This method relies on creating a mental map of your surrounding environment, so instead of objects being represented in relation to your own body, they're represented in relation to other objects in the world around you. In the example above, you might construct a mental map of your route to work wherein the post box is north of your house, the petrol station is west of the post box, and work is north of the petrol station. Different people use a combination of these navigational strategies in different ways, but when it comes to Alzheimer's, problems begin to arise in the way that patients use both strategies as the disease progresses. The trouble is, researchers don't (yet) completely understand the precise way in which these problems begin to manifest. There are good reasons for this lack of understanding. First, we don't really have a good grasp even of how *healthy* individuals use these systems. And while a great deal of research has been devoted to trying to understand deficits in spatial navigation caused by Alzheimer's, because of the difficulties inherent in diagnosing the disease when it's at an early stage, we also don't have a clear idea of precisely how this ability might decline as the condition progresses.

The reason I'm talking about all of this is that over the past few years, video games have started to play a role in our understanding of Alzheimer's disease, as well as featuring in discussions about how they affect our ability to navigate our environment. These discussions haven't always been positive: for example in 2015, the UK news media got whipped up into a frenzy after a research study suggested that playing games like *Call of Duty* could actually increase the risk of developing Alzheimer's. It was an extraordinary and quite terrifying claim to make, not least because a couple of years earlier, Activision (the publishers of the *Call of Duty* series) had boasted that since 2007, some 100 million people had played the game series. If there was even the merest suggestion that it could cause serious long-term issues with the brain, then an enormous number of people would be at risk. As is so often the case when video-game-related research is covered in the media though, the reality of the situation was much more complex, and not nearly as worrisome. The study in question, led by Gregory West, an associate professor at the University of Montreal, had partici-pants searching for objects in a virtual reality maze, and simply showed that people who played action video games for more than six hours per week were more likely to use an egocentric navigational strategy, whereas non-players were slightly more likely to use an allocentric strategy. Although they claimed in the study and subsequent press release that using egocentric strategies was associated with an increased risk of Alzheimer's, this wasn't what West's study was actually about. Neither did the study test anything specific about *Call of Duty* – that link arose out of over-exuberant journalists looking for a sensationalist hook they could use to make the study sound more interesting.

In other instances though, there has been a much more positive story to tell about research relevant to the role that video games can play in our understanding of conditions like Alzheimer's disease. This isn't research that looks at the effects that playing games can have on us, though – it takes a more novel approach. It uses a fascinating and unique video game as a virtual laboratory – one that has the potential to provide us with those insights into spatial navigation that have so far remained elusive for scientists.

In late spring 2016, to great fanfare, a team led by Professor Michael Hornberger at the University of East Anglia and Professor Hugo Spiers at UCL launched a new mobile game called *Sea Hero Quest*, available as a free download for both iOS and Android-based phones. A visually beautiful game to play, its narrative is heartbreakingly familiar to many; the story puts you in the shoes of an unnamed sailor whose father, a fantastical seafaring explorer, is slowly losing the memories of his former life. For players, the aim of the game is to travel around cartoonish waterways in search of fragments of his old journal, to try to help him keep hold of the memories of his past. Each level takes the form of a little maze through which you need to navigate your boat. At the start of some levels, you're given a top-down map of the watercourses in the area, pinpointing a number of buoy markers that you will later need to navigate through. After a few moments, once you've had time to memorise the map, you're transported to the boat and your task is to travel around the 3D world and visit each buoy in a specific order. In other levels, the task instead is to navigate to a single buoy, reorientate your boat to face the direction in which you think the start point was located, and fire a flare. A simple game, but one that generates a rich amount of data. Everything you do – the information about the route you take, and what course of action you decide on if you end up getting lost – is saved and transmitted to the research team for further analysis. While the game can't be used as a way to diagnose dementia, the plan is for it to be used to create a benchmark for navigation behaviour in a vast number of healthy people all across the world. The aim of the research underpinning the game is to understand what 'normal' navigation abilities look like, so that scientists can figure out what is going wrong in people with Alzheimer's. By understanding how healthy people find (and lose) their way around novel environments, and by figuring out whether there are any systematic patterns in the way that spatial navigation ability deteriorates over time, in the future it might be possible to better adapt the environments that people with Alzheimer's disease live in – from care homes to entire towns.

As with any sort of study that attempts to do something groundbreaking on a grand scale, *Sea Hero Quest* was serendipitous in its conception. 'I got a phone call one day from Michael [Hornberger], who's an old friend,' explains Spiers, who is the co-lead researcher on the project. Hornberger, he tells me, had been approached by the advertising giant Saatchi & Saatchi, to see if he was interested in working with one of their clients to develop a new type of citizen science project. The client, Deutsche Telekom (a telecommunications company that owns brands such as cellular network operator T-Mobile), wanted to do something positive, and they'd identified that maybe dementia would be a good area to focus on. The problem was, they didn't really know what any potential project would actually look like. Saatchi & Saatchi were project-managing the whole process.

Prior to contacting Hornberger, the advertisers were trying to figure out if they could do something useful based on more traditional citizen science projects, wherein willing participants are used more as sophisticated computers, rather than as active data-generators. An example of that model was a mobile game called *Reverse the Odds* commissioned by the British TV broadcaster Channel 4 in 2014, as part of their annual fundraising event Stand Up To Cancer. The game itself was fairly simple, and involved getting people to play a series of *Othello*-type puzzle games in order to help a species of cute cartoonish bugs improve and upgrade the little world they live in. However, before they could start each successive level, players would first have to do a little bit of scientific sleuthing. They would be shown a series of images that contained a combination of blue- and orange-coloured cells, and after a brief tutorial, would be asked to identify some key features in those pictures – for example how many blue-coloured cells there were, how strong the colour was, and whether they could spot any unevenly-shaped cells. The images were based on samples from hundreds of bladder cancer patients who were being tested and treated by various research teams at Oxford University. Each sample came from a bladder tumour, which was first set in wax, and then cut into a series of extremely fine slices. A special dye was applied to each slice, which in the image was represented by the cells being coloured blue or orange, depending on whether a specific protein was present. That protein, the researchers believe, could be an important marker that could help to figure out whether a patient will respond better to bladder-removal surgery, or whether they would be better off opting for radiotherapy. Crucially, the samples were taken from patients who subsequently received one of those treatments, so researchers were able to compare the levels of that protein in each patient alongside how successfully those patients responded to their treatment. By getting a better understanding of this relationship, the hope is that the protein marker could be used for future cancer patients – to help make the process of coming to a treatment decision a little easier.

The actual task of detecting and matching particular patterns within an image is surprisingly difficult to automate on a computer, and there are entire areas of research in computer science devoted to it. It's definitely possible for a computer to do, but for complex images such as the protein markers, the process is time-consuming and expensive, and it's difficult to figure out what the computer algorithm might be getting wrong along the way. Even the most powerful, artificial intelligence-based pattern-matching algorithms that exist pale in comparison to the ability that humans have in doing this sort of task. By recruiting thousands of people then, it's possible to quickly and accurately categorise a huge number of images. Admittedly, staring at a bunch of blobs on a screen is a fairly tedious thing to do, but *Reverse the Odds* incentivised the process by mixing in the pattern-matching task with a fun and engaging game. Over the course of two years, the game's players classified around 4.75 million images, contributing a total of 20,000 hours to cancer research in the process. And research based on the game that was published in the *British Journal of Cancer* in 2018 showed that *Reverse the Odds* players were able to successfully identify not one, but two markers that could be used to predict bladder cancer survival.

Sea Hero Quest is different though. Instead of getting players to act as sophisticated computer processors to sift through data that has already been collected, Hornberger's idea was to make the players themselves the source of that data. 'As I understood it, Saatchi & Saatchi had contacted a number of different academics around the UK to try and find somebody who might work with them,' explains Spiers. 'Michael's suggestion was to potentially develop a diagnostic tool for Alzheimer's that was placed inside a video game. They really loved the idea.' After a games developer – a small independent London-based company called Glitchers – was brought on board to actually create the game, the project evolved. From thinking about the game as a method of diagnosing Alzheimer's, it became more about understanding how some of those specific spatial navigation strategies we use every day might start to go wrong as the disease develops. Importantly, the game isn't a mask or diversion. It's not just something to keep you engaged while periodically performing a more menial but scientifically relevant task. Launched to much fanfare in spring 2016 (and helped in part by advertising and PR from Deutsche Telekom), *Sea Hero Quest* is a living, breathing, virtual lab, where the game itself is the experiment. At the end of each play session, anonymised data about a player's moment-to-moment coordinates and orientation on the map (what they were actually doing while they were playing the game) are sent to a state-of-the-art secure server in Germany. If they so wish, players can provide additional data in the form of information about their age, sex and geographical location. All of this is collected and collated by the research team for further analysis. So far, they've only scratched the surface of what this treasure trove of information can tell them. 'When we started out, we talked to people who had done big citizen science projects in the past – the ones who had promoted it with TV spots, advertising in the media, all the usual things. They got about 20,000 participants,' explains Hugo Spiers. 'We figured, "Well we've got a lot more backing behind us, *Sea Hero Quest* is going to go global. Hopefully we get 100,000 participants after six months or so."' The developers, Glitchers, managed to hit that target just two days after the game was launched. 'We were just blown away by the response,' says Spiers. By the summer of 2018, over 3.7 million people had downloaded the game, from every single country in the world.

Within six months of launch, *Sea Hero Quest* was generating preliminary findings that, among other things, suggested that in fact our spatial navigation abilities begin to deteriorate from our early twenties onwards – previously, scientists had thought that this decline set in at a much later age. More recently, the research team has published work that has started to look at whether differences in wayfinding abilities might depend on where we live in the world. This is where the game really comes into its own; most clinic-based cognitive tests that are used to assess dementia are language-based, which often means that it can be difficult to compare data from different countries. *Sea Hero Quest*, however, transcends linguistic boundaries. In a landmark study published in the journal *Current Biology* in August 2018, Hornberger and Spiers's team used data from just over 550,000 *Sea Hero Quest* players, spread across 57 countries, to develop a general measure of performance that captured various aspects of spatial navigation ability, while correcting for any prior video gaming experience players may have had.

The team found clear and striking differences in performance based on geographical location – players from Finland, Denmark, New Zealand, Canada and Norway generally performed best, while players from Egypt, India, Macedonia, Iraq and Romania generally performed worse. Dividing the world into five clusters based on game performance, the study showed that there was a positive correlation between navigation abilities and a country's GDP (although this wasn't the only influencing factor). Across all nations, the study again found a general decline in navigation ability from nineteen years old to 60 years old. But more than this, and rather strangely, there seemed to be an advantage based on sex – although men and women showed the same linear pattern of decline, women generally showed worse performance at all ages. Looking at data on a country-by-country basis, Hornberger and Spiers's team found that there was a positive correlation between the size of the difference between performance in men and women, and the level of gender inequality, which they assessed by looking at the World Economic Forum's Gender Gap Index.* In other words,

---

* The GGI is a benchmark assessment which looks at a country's progress in terms of gender equality in four areas: educational attainment, political empowerment, health and well-being, and economic opportunities.

in countries where there is a high degree of equality between men and women, there was generally only a small sex difference in navigation ability. In countries where there were high levels of inequality, the difference was much greater. *Sea Hero Quest*, then, had found evidence that sex-based differences in some cognitive abilities, far from being innate, were instead due to the culture that people are living in.

'This is the most interesting thing from the paper, in my mind. We were able to take a cognitive skill like spatial navigation and look at how our ability in that is distributed worldwide,' says Spiers. With these findings as a foundation, Spiers's team hopes that in the future, data from *Sea Hero Quest* can be used to develop new diagnostic and treatment tools in patient populations.

Aside from the results themselves though, one of the most important things to come out of this first study is that the only way for huge, worldwide projects like this to be viable is if they are open and collaborative. 'The one thing that's really, really struck me about this project is the amount of data we're sitting on,' Spiers explains. 'There's no way we'll get through it all, even in the next ten years. The whole idea of open science? This couldn't be a better example.' Perhaps more than anything, *Sea Hero Quest* shows that video games really can help scientists to gain a richer and vastly more complex understanding of human psychology than ever before. For Professor Spiers, it's certainly got him thinking about how games can be used to ask the big scientific questions of the future. 'I'd love to work with a large-scale games company to do some mass online experiments – say on the PlayStation,' he explains. 'With *Sea Hero Quest* for example, there isn't any interaction between people. I would really love to look at something like that.' But for the moment, he is just happy with the runaway success of the game. 'My goodness, 3.7 million people,' he says excitedly. 'There are so many possibilities. We can start to really pin down human experience in some quite remarkable ways.'

For all of their faults then, for all of the worries about them, video games offer opportunities to do some amazing things. They tap into that deeply-seated human desire to travel, seek out new experiences and absorb new knowledge about the world – and about ourselves. They provide a safe place where we can relax as digital tourists within the comfort of our own home, visiting places that might only otherwise be accessible in the wildest reaches of our imagination. And where video games found their origins in the scientific frontiers of the middle of the last century, now they are returning the favour: by offering scientists, for the first time, a way to explore and understand what it means to be human on a planet-wide scale.

CHAPTER 12

Digital spectator sports

If you've ever wondered if there's anything more acutely bor-ing than watching paint dry, grass grow, or God forbid, trying to sit all the way through *Prometheus*,* go to a casino and see how long you can last watching a poker tournament. Nothing happens. A bunch of people who insist on wearing sunglasses despite being inside a room that has no windows or natural light, sit around a table in grim silence. The only sound is the incessant click-clack of chips as the players, awaiting the next deal of the cards, fiddle with their gains to pass the time. Some perform elaborate stacking and flicking tricks. Others simply riffle through their chip piles, neatly arranging them into tee-tering columns ready to be wagered. Cards are dealt around to everyone, but you, as an observer, can't see what's on them. Nobody says anything, nobody moves. Occasionally someone will quietly leave the table, their hoard of chips having been reduced to nothing by more adept players. Barely anyone smiles,

---

* I've tried understanding it, I really have. But Ridley Scott's 2012 prequel to the excellent *Alien* just doesn't make sense to me. It dragged on for ages, was full of plot holes, and the science was all wrong – even from the very beginning. As geneticist and broadcaster Adam Rutherford pointed out in *Aliens: Science Asks: Is There Anyone Out There?*, the opening sequence shows DNA from an otherworldly progenitor swirling into the primordial soups that begat life on Earth. Except that the DNA helix twisted to the left. All life on Earth has DNA that twists to the right. It was, he said, 'a fact that betrays its singular origin and the shared ancestry of all life on this planet.'

or looks as if they're having a good time. Watching poker in a casino is really, really boring.

I'm actually a huge fan of *playing* poker. In many ways, it's the quintessential game: easy to pick up, difficult to master, scalable to any number of players, with a nice balance of skill- and luck-based elements. It can also be exceptionally entertaining to watch, provided that it's watched through the right medium: screens trump real life when it comes to card games. At the turn of the millennium, televised poker experienced a dramatic rise, going from relative obscurity to being one of the most popular spectator sports on the planet. I'm convinced that were at least two reasons for this: one obvious, the other not so much.

Before around 1999, watching poker on television was just as dull as watching it in person, but then *Late Night Poker*, a quirky little show from the UK broadcaster Channel 4, revolutionised the way people could engage with the game. The producers placed tiny cameras under the table, and suddenly a new world of data was opened to us. Whereas before, viewers had been limited to guessing what cards a player *might* have, what strategy they *might* be using, now we were privy to that information in real time. All of a sudden, a closed spectacle unfurled into a drama – the viewer, like an omniscient but impotent god, had all of the knowledge, but was unable do anything with it. The thrill of watching in agony as players walked into carefully-constructed traps, or of smirking triumphantly at a well-placed bluff, refashioned poker-watching from a seemingly seedy vice into a legitimate form of sports entertainment. By bringing the human element to the fore, televised poker transformed the game into something that everyone, no matter their skill, could relate to and enjoy. It became an improvised drama, where the stories and the people were more important than the game itself.

Nowhere was this more evident than in 2003, when a previously unknown amateur player with a brilliantly apt name – Chris Moneymaker – took home the grand prize of $2.5 million in the World Series of Poker's main event. Moneymaker's story was captivating. An accountant by trade, his road to fortune had started relatively innocuously, with him winning a qualifying event in an online poker room that he had paid just $39 to take part in. Going on to win a series of qualifying tournaments thereafter, Moneymaker would end up in a fairytale situation in the finals, eventually squaring off in a head-to-head situation with the professional poker player Sammy Farha. It was the classic underdog tale, but in real life and for a life-changing sum of money. You didn't need to be an elite athlete to play poker, nor did you necessarily need to devote your entire life to it in order to become an expert. The possibility of being at the main event – as Moneymaker showed – could happen to anybody.

Poker suddenly had the potential to draw people in, but it needed something else: exposure. So here's the second reason I think poker exploded in popularity: ice hockey. Well, actually, a lack of ice hockey. In 2004, North America's National Hockey League (NHL) got caught up in a major dispute over pay. The resulting ten-month strike meant that a staggering 1,230 games weren't played during that missing season (NHL teams play a gruelling schedule of fixtures: in the previous season, 30 teams played 82 games each over the course of seven months). This posed a problem for sports television networks: if 1,230 games weren't being played, 1,230 games couldn't be televised, and so something else was needed to plug the gap. As it turned out though, ESPN had secured the long-term broadcast rights to the World Series of Poker (the game's equivalent of a World Cup) the previous year; and so it was a relatively simple solution to expand their coverage in the strike year. Coupled with the development of new ventures such as the World Poker Tour, and the so-called 'Moneymaker Effect', the golden years of televised poker began.*

Obviously, a societal shift in preferences for one pastime over another will never come down to a simple or limited number of factors, and there will be all sorts of other reasons that poker started to become a more mainstream pursuit at that time. But the crux is this: we like stories we can relate to, and we appreciate watching people do the things that we like, especially when they can do them at an extraordinary level. This applies to anything: poker, football, ice hockey and, obviously, video games. Or perhaps not so obviously – I often have conversations with friends and family who find it difficult even to grasp the idea that watching people playing video games can be fun or meaningful. I don't think this is a generational issue, more that it's an experiential one. It's true that video games are still relatively new, and they are evolving relatively quickly. Despite their now being such a mainstream form of entertainment, though, there's still an element of counter-culture to them. It still seems weird to many people that anyone would want to spend their time playing video games at all. To take that a step further, though, and explain to them that many people just enjoy watching others play? It's entirely understandable how that can come across as an alien concept. But from their very inception, video games were designed to be multi-person, social, shared

---

* Of course, it wasn't just poker that benefited from the NHL lockout. By many accounts, Major League Soccer started to become profitable in 2004, with many commentators directly attributing this to sports fans needing something else to occupy their time.

experiences. The idea of games as a digital spectator sport is baked into their very existence.

The history of competitive gaming – or e-sports, as it has now become known – can arguably find its roots in the early history of video games themselves. In 1972, for example, the 'intergalactic spacewar olympics' were held by students at Stanford University. A couple of dozen competitors huddled around a console in a dimly lit, broom-cupboard-like room adjacent to the university's PDP-10 computer. Two events were held: a five-person free-for-all and a team competition, with the winners taking home a year's subscription to *Rolling Stone* magazine (the co-organiser, Stewart Brand,* was then a writer at the outlet). It was a humble affair, but one that gained a certain amount of public awareness due to Brand's coverage of it in a subsequent article for *Rolling Stone*, and provides an early demonstration that video games had the potential to be as enthralling as any other competitive sport. E-sports would find a mainstream audience a few years later in 1980, when Atari hosted the inaugural *Space Invaders* Championships in the United States, where more than 10,000 competitors at regional events across the country vied for the title of World Champion. The championships would eventually be won by seventeen-year-old Bill Heineman, who would go on to spend a long career in video game programming and development (creating games such as the 1986 cult classic *Tass Times in Tonetown* and 1989's *Dragon Wars*).

---

* Brand would later go on to have a successful career as a writer (most notably of the *Whole Earth Catalog*, considered to be a major influence on the formation of the internet), and is a co-chair of The Long Now Foundation.

Throughout the 1980s and 1990s, as games consoles became more commonplace in the home, rudimentary e-sports events would be held as part of magazine-style television shows that had a focus on video games. Shows such as the UK's iconic *GamesMaster*, which ran from 1992 to 1998, would pit players against a series of challenges – a one-on-one match in *Street Fighter 2*, for example, or having to speed through the fourth level of *Chuck Rock* before a timer ran out – with the aim of winning a coveted Golden Joystick trophy. As desirable as it was to actually be a competitor on the show, the draw of video games as a spectator sport was evident in the crowds of kids in the studio who were there to cheer contestants on and share in their experience. In that sense, shows such as *GamesMaster* highlighted the fact that video games were like any other sort of competitive sport. As much as people enjoy playing them, they enjoy watching, especially when other people can play them at a more elite level. Although *GamesMaster* enjoyed considerable success, after it was cancelled competitive games broadcasting, at least in the UK, fizzled out. According to *GamesMaster*'s creator Jane Hewland, the decision to shut down the show was mutual between the commissioning editors, producers and presenters. 'You get to a point with any television show,' she said 'where it's getting derivative and you can't think of anything else to do.'

In the same year that *GamesMaster* was cancelled in the UK, Blizzard released *StarCraft* to worldwide acclaim. A multiplayer online space-based strategy game that plays out in real time, *StarCraft* found particular success in South Korea – partly due to the rapid investment in (and growth of) the broadband internet infrastructure in that country in the mid-1990s. The popularity of the game (and others) among young Koreans drove the creation of dedicated local digital television stations, which placed a focus on broadcasting and commentating on gaming events. In combination, these factors fostered the start of a gaming culture in South Korea that produced players with cult-like followings, much like the fanbases of professional players in more traditional sports in the West. As a result of this explosion in the popularity* of competitive gaming, the Ministry of Culture, Sport and Tourism founded the Korea e-Sports Association in 2000, a body that both promotes and regulates e-sports tournaments in the country.

However, despite its success in the east, televised coverage of games still seemed to sputter elsewhere in the world. The reasons for this aren't entirely clear. The growth in popularity of online gaming in South Korea can partly be explained through the combination of the 1997 Asian financial crisis (a huge surge in redundancies and lay-offs pushed people into both opening, and spending their time in, new and lucrative internet cafes) with the hypersocial nature of Korean culture, so perhaps it was simply the absence of these sorts of factors which meant that televised gaming didn't take hold elsewhere. Or it may be the case that there was a creative spark missing from the way that video games were presented on television in the West. Where Korean gaming shows had extremely high production values with enthusiastic, over-the-top presenters, shows in the West, like *GamesMaster*, tended to focus on the

---

* By 2002, around 5 million Koreans (just over 10 per cent of the population) were playing *StarCraft*. According to reports in *Wired* magazine, by that point around 26,000 online gaming cafes, or 'PC baangs' as they are known locally, had popped up around the country (up from a mere 100 just five years earlier).

actual gameplay itself. Being a passive observer while someone sits at a computer screen isn't particularly fun – it's like watching a live game of poker. For e-sports to become a truly global phenomenon, it needed the thing that televised poker had found: a way to bring the human element of video games to the fore.

This was eventually achieved, partly thanks to the development of online streaming platforms (such as Twitch), which meant that e-sports tournaments didn't need to organise expensive, time-limited and unwieldy contracts in order to be televised. Instead, it became relatively easy to broadcast events to potentially huge audiences over the internet.* Twitch, if you've never used it before, is a website and mobile- or console-based application that allows you to broadcast live videos about anything you want: chat shows, real-time painting, programming advice, cooking, eating, crafting, whatever you like. The vast majority of streams are gaming-related, though – channels are organised by game title, and the videos themselves usually involve real-time output of the game screen as the player sees it, with the player providing additional commentary about what's going on. Each stream is accompanied by its own text chat window, so that viewers can talk to each other (and, critically, the player) about the game, the performance, life, whatever they wish. It's this element that has helped to bring a more human aspect to e-sports: by allowing spectators to interact with each other, an instant community is created based around a shared common interest. No longer is it the case that watching

---

* The arrival of Twitch did something else, echoing the Moneymaker Effect: any player, no matter their level of expertise, could broadcast their gaming sessions to a potentially limitless audience.

someone play a game is a passive process; instead, spectators get to feel as though they are part of the experience.

So far so good, but a flexible streaming service and giving viewers the ability to chat to their favourite gamers is only part of the reason that e-sports began to garner a wider audience. Another important factor was the fact that the creators of the games had come to the realisation that people wanted to watch games being played, and they began to facilitate this by incorporating new spectator-orientated mechanics into the games themselves. These started off as simple concepts, like allowing players who had been killed during the course of a match to view the rest of the game through the lens of a teammate or competitor. But over time, spectator modes became more complex: some games now provide options for the spectators to include commentary over the course of play, or to give you full control over an in-game camera that allows you to wander around and view the action from whichever angle you wish. This ability stems from games as far back as 1993's *Doom*, in which players could record 'demo files' – a data file which tracked every single keyboard click or mouse movement – which could then be given to other players (say, on a floppy disk) to play back on their own computer. These were used either to guide them through walkthroughs of difficult levels, or simply to boast through demonstrations of in-game prowess.* Games like 2007's *Halo 3* popularised the concept, taking it much further with the introduction of a 'theater mode': after a player had completed a

---

* Although demo files would give the appearance of a video recording, in reality the player would start a new 'live game', and the keystroke data from the demo file would be used to control the in-game character, as opposed to the player themselves providing the input.

multiplayer game (or single-player level), they could use a virtual theatre to completely replay the entire session. 'Theater mode' gave players the option to view the action from the perspective of any other player in that particular game, or to take a free-roaming camera around the level to find a good vantage point to fast forward or rewind the best moments at will. Other games, like Blizzard's *Overwatch*, provide 'play of the game' highlight reels at the end of each match to showcase some of the best moments. And as spectatorship started to become more engrained in the very fabric of the video game experience, the popularity of e-sports began to skyrocket.

In 2018, analytics firms estimated the global e-sports market to have a value of over $900 million, with a worldwide audience of 380 million viewers, of whom over 200 million were classed as occasional viewers. Alongside the financial benefits, e-sports seems to offer other positives. Over the past year, the British E-sports Association (a not-for-profit national body promoting e-sports in the UK) has been piloting a national tournament in schools across the country (similar work is also currently underway in the US, with researchers at UC Irvine evaluating the impact of the North America Scholastic E-sports Federation). The preliminary evaluations to come out of the UK pilot have suggested that getting kids involved in these sorts of competitions can help in all sorts of positive ways: from building confidence to developing teamwork and communication skills, and in some cases, even improving attendance at school. E-sports, it would seem, are here to stay.

I'm waiting in what feels like a forgotten break room area somewhere deep in the bowels of Blizzard HQ. Three long, high benches with teetering stools punctuate the middle of the space, and off to one side are a couple of beanbags placed neatly in front of a PlayStation 4 and a huge projector screen. The introduction screen to *Overwatch* is looping silently, and a small part of me wonders whether I have time to play a quick game to calm my nerves. I'm here to talk to Jeff Kaplan, *Overwatch*'s lead designer. Jeff's route into games development was an unusual one. After attaining two degrees in creative writing from the University of Southern California and New York University, he spent a good proportion of his early adulthood trying to break into writing. It wasn't a particularly successful time – speaking to *Rolling Stone* magazine in 2016, he admitted that in one year alone, he had 172 rejections from different magazines that he was trying to get short stories published in. Understandably, in his mid-twenties he decided to take a break from it all for a while. Having been an avid gamer for most of his life, and abruptly finding himself with a lot of free time on his hands, Jeff started playing *EverQuest*, a fantasy-based MMO. It was there, through sheer coincidence, that he would join a group of players who happened to include Rob Pardo, who was working for Blizzard at the time, as lead designer on *Warcraft III*. After they had got to know each other through the game, Pardo suggested that Kaplan apply for a newly-posted job at the games developer – quest designer for the company's then recently-announced MMO, *World of Warcraft*. 'Quest design' involves developing an idea for a mission for players to embark on, which usually ends up in some sort of reward (a new weapon, a piece of armour, or other in-game item of value). A good quest is one that has an interesting backstory to it, and feels fun and engaging to complete. For Kaplan then, it seemed like the perfect job: one that effortlessly amalgamated his love of games with his background in creative writing. In 2009, he was assigned to other projects, which would eventually result in the development of *Overwatch*, released in 2016 to great fanfare. It's a fast and furious game, and one that has been built from the ground up with professional e-sports in mind: *Overwatch* has been designed to be played in front of crowds, both online and in person.

Having played *World of Warcraft* for close to ten years, I'll admit that I was a little nervous in the run-up to this meeting. Partly because I'm an anxious person, and I get nervous whenever I interview someone, but also because I've always been wary of the idea of meeting people who have been involved in creating the things that you love – if the encounter doesn't go to plan, it can end up blighting the memories of something you once cherished, or dulling the enjoyment you might get out of it in the future. Jeff wanders into the room through a door I hadn't spotted, and catches me by surprise as I stand there in anxiety-tinged reverie. He greets me with a warm smile and a hello, exuding a relaxed Southern California attitude that puts me immediately at ease. As we head over to a meeting room, we drop into a conversation about ice hockey. Jeff is a huge fan of the local NHL team, the LA Kings, while I've been following the Anaheim Ducks from afar for the past decade. The night before, I got the chance to see them live for the first time in my life. 'It's a feedback loop, right? Part of what elevates my love for playing hockey is watching it, and part of what elevates my love of watching hockey is playing it,' he explains. 'It's the same with video games – there are a lot of elements that draw people into playing them, but one aspect is challenge and mastery.' The idea that there's a pinnacle that you haven't personally reached, but that you can watch others attain, reflects that idea of mastery. It can be a hugely exhilarating feeling, and one that in Jeff's eyes is no different for e-sports than it is for ice hockey or any other sport.

'Watching e-sports has become this social thing, where everyone can talk to each other in a chat channel, and I think that's really important. Watching sports should be a social experience,' he points out. He gives me the example of his love for the LA Kings. Growing up in LA, both he and his brother had been fans of the team all their lives. The Kings, though ... let's just say that they had a bad run for a time. 'They were *terrible*. For most of my adolescent and adult life, they were terrible,' he laments. Their fortunes changed in 2012. Despite a stumble of a start to the season, that year they would go on to win the Western Conference (one of two subdivisions used to split up teams within the NHL) and make it through to the Stanley Cup finals, played at the Staples Center in downtown LA. 'My brother and I went to that game. We barely got in, we had the worst seats, but we were there,' recalls Jeff. The Kings would win the game 6–1, and lift the trophy for the first time in the club's 45-year history. 'It was one of the most emotional experiences of my life,' says Jeff. 'It wasn't just about the Kings winning the Stanley Cup – that was the centre of it, sure – but it was about sharing that with my brother.' They had been following the team together their whole lives, and now they got to share that unique, overwhelming moment with each other. 'My point is, those moments can happen in e-sports too,' he explains. 'I've never personally had the same feeling that I had in 2012 in the Staples Center, but something close happened at Blizzcon last year when South Korea played the USA.'

Blizzcon is Blizzard's annual gaming convention, held every November in Anaheim, just up the road from their headquarters. The company uses it as a vehicle to promote entirely new games, or new releases in their major franchises such as *StarCraft*, *Hearthstone*, *Heroes of the Storm*, *Diablo*, *Warcraft* and *Overwatch*. In 2017, it was also host to the second *Overwatch* World Cup. Thirty-two countries participated in qualification stages held around the world, with the final sixteen progressing to the main tournament in Anaheim. South Korea had dominated the inaugural tournament the previous year, and faced off against the USA in a quarter-finals matchup. The US team took the first round, and for a fleeting moment it looked as if they might pull a spectacular upset, but two losses in a row for the US team would eventually give the win to the Koreans. The scoreline didn't matter though. 'It was this breakthrough match, super close and really exciting,' explains Jeff. 'I think it was a moment where a lot of people went "Wow, e-sports can be amazing. *Overwatch* can work as a league." It was a really emotional experience.'

In many ways, Blizzard considered the *Overwatch* World Cup as a prototype for something bigger that they'd had in mind since the game's inception: a fully-developed league, structured and monetised in a similar way to traditional sports. Part of this vision included the company's own 450-spectator capacity e-sports stadium in Burbank, California, which they opened in October 2017, about a month before the World Cup was staged. As a permanent base, the Blizzard Arena ensured that the games developer had a guaranteed home for any and every live e-sports event they wished to run. The arena would also play host to the inaugural *Overwatch* League (OWL) season, which launched in early 2018 with twelve teams and a $3.5 million prize pool. It certainly isn't the first time a game has tried to break out into what feels like more traditional competitive sports. Nor, necessarily, was the stadium's capacity overly ambitious. In 2013, the world finals of the real-time strategy game *League of Legends* had been hosted at the Staples Center in LA with a crowd of 12,000 in attendance. Two years later, the same finals were held in Seoul's Sangam stadium, this time with 45,000 people watching in person, and a further 27 million watching online. But what seems to set the OWL apart is Blizzard's deliberate intention to model it on other, more traditional North American sports leagues. Adopting less of a tournament structure and more of a season structure* than previous gaming leagues, the OWL ran from January to June, with teams placed in two divisions, playing a total of 40 games each. Borrowing heavily from concepts in other sports, each team has a 'home' town (although in reality, all of the teams are based in LA).** Every team also has their own dedicated branding, logos and livery – London Spitfire playing, for example, in turquoise, orange and black, with a Supermarine Spitfire motif emblazoned on their chests. *Overwatch* itself was modified to accommodate this, such that not only do the team's players wear branded uniforms, so too do in-game characters, making it much easier to figure out which

---

* In this sense, tournaments can best be thought of as standalone, short-term events that usually involve some sort of elimination mechanism; losing teams are knocked out such that the pool of teams gradually gets smaller, until a winner is declared. A season structure, on the other hand, involves teams playing a fixed number of games against each other over a much longer period of time, with the results being accumulated over all the games that take place. The teams with the most points will then usually progress to an end-of-season knockout stage to declare a winner.

** For convenience and control, more than anything. Having the teams all based in the same city means that they can play every game at the Blizzard Arena, which in turn means that Blizzard has full control over the production and broadcast of the season. It also cuts down on the hefty costs that would be involved in transporting teams around the world.

characters belong to which team during the course of play. In addition, an AI-operated in-game camera was developed that could be strategically positioned to offer spectators the best view of the action (for example, rather than providing a first-person view from a particular character, the camera could instead pan out to offer a third-person, birds-eye view of a section of the map where multiple players are fighting), as well as providing instant replays of key events in otherwise frenetic matchups.

If this seemed like an outrageously ambitious project that might never get off the ground, behind the scenes there was old knowledge and expertise coming into play. One of the co-owners of the Boston Uprising team is Robert Kraft, who has owned the NFL's New England Patriots since 1994. Philadelphia Fusion are owned by the sports company Comcast Spectacor, who are former owners of the 76ers basketball team and current owners of the NHL's Philadelphia Flyers. There are similar ownership overlaps between *Overwatch*'s New York Excelsior and the National Basketball Association's New York Mets. Given the managerial experience and business acumen that such investors command, as well as the knowledge of what a successful sports league model actually looks like, it's perhaps unsurprising that the OWL enjoyed a largely successful inaugural season. The first night of live broadcasts was watched by just under half a million people, and the viewing figures never dropped below 285,000 for the rest of the season. By comparison, in 2017 the US broadcaster NBC reported an average of 417,000 viewers per game (both TV and streaming) for its NHL coverage. And popularity aside, by most accounts the first iteration of the e-sports league was a lucrative one – for Blizzard, sponsors and players alike. No official figures have been released, but some sources have reported that the games developer charged franchisers around $20 million per team, and that the broadcast deal between Blizzard and Twitch was worth somewhere in the region of $90 million. League players are currently earning a minimum salary of $50,000 per year, with their teams also providing them with housing, health insurance and other benefits. For the eventual winners of the first season, the London Spitfire, players would earn an average bonus of around $83,000 each. Not bad for playing a video game.

Nevertheless, it feels like there's something missing from the league. Perhaps it's just time. The NHL has been around since 1917. The UK's football Premier League started much more recently, in 1992, but it wasn't a new concept – professional football in England had been organised into divisions, televised and marketed, for years beforehand. The *Overwatch* League certainly builds on a rich history of e-sports and competitive gaming, but it doesn't feel as though this has evolved as gradually or as naturally as in other sports. It feels jarring, for instance, that the London Spitfire aren't actually based in London. Or perhaps there's a deeper issue. Look at a sport like football, and it's easy to see that the aspirational value of it doesn't just involve the game or the teams. The players are at the heart of it. We cheer them on, we boo them when they do things we don't like, we watch them grow as athletes. They are the heroes and the villains of the story – Messi, Pelé, Beckham, Zidane, Cruyff are all household names for those who love the game. But with e-sports, it often feels as though it's the game itself that's the 'personality'. Or, as videogames journalist Dave Thier has argued, the *Overwatch* League needs to somehow get past the fact that it's all about *Overwatch*.

Let me try to explain with an example that elaborates on Thier's argument. In the summer of 2018, English football fans were treated to a spectacle that they hadn't seen in 28 years: the national team made it to the semi-finals of the FIFA World Cup. As the years since England's 1966 win have dragged on, the expectations of the nation have become an increasingly crushing pressure on the team. Alongside a seemingly chronic problem in discovering and developing exceptional players, on the world stage, the team has consistently found itself dismissed relatively early. This World Cup seemed different though – England was a young, hungry team that actually seemed to be playing for the pure joy of the game. In an early fixture against Colombia for example, there were times when the goalkeeper, Jordan Pickford, seemingly morphed into a cat as he stretched lazily across the goal to bat away incoming shots. Harry Kane, the captain, who seemed older and wiser than his 25 years, was stalwart in the face of a villainous opposition that was all too intent to start a scrap. The narrative that came out of the tournament wasn't simply about the scoreline. It was about the real people who made up the team: their personalities, histories, foibles and strengths.

In contrast, one of the biggest pieces of news about *Overwatch* in the same summer was the introduction of a new and rather controversial character, 'Wrecking Ball': a hamster with a genius-level intellect who rolls around in a giant metal ball of death. Elsewhere, tweaks were made to existing characters to make them more playable and balanced. This was in the wake of an earlier controversy that year, when Mercy, a healer-type character, was drastically reworked. Professional and amateur players alike were divided in their opinions about all of these changes. Would the tweaks to Mercy change the way the game is played? Was she the best healer to pick, or was it better go with another character? Was Wrecking Ball too ridiculous a character, and did it make the game look too childish? These are the kinds of debates that ran through the gaming community. And while these are stimulating, and often passionately argued topics for people who have a deep love of the game, nevertheless there is a certain human element missing.

Competitive video games aren't static entities – they constantly shift and evolve as players find ways to push at the rules in order to gain as much of an edge as possible. The competitive gaming community often talks about something called 'the meta', which is an emergent form of gameplay that considers general strategies about how best to use certain characters in certain situations. The 'meta' is something that never stays still; as new characters or maps are added to a game to keep it fresh, players often find ways to use already-existing character abilities in new and potentially unintended ways. As a result, developers are often engaged in a sort of digital arms race, releasing updates and tweaks in order to maintain a balanced gaming environment. Let's say a new character is introduced to *Overwatch* who has ridiculously overpowered abilities. Everyone would end up playing that character, and the game would become something that it shouldn't be – it's no longer about creating a well-balanced team, but instead about which player can use that character to the best of their ability. 'Games designers often talk about protecting players from themselves', explains Jeff. 'Sometimes this is in reference to things like addiction or compulsive behaviours, but more often than not it's just in reference to the fact that players will do really terrible, boring things if they're given the chance.' He gives an example from *World of Warcraft* to highlight the point. The way that the game is intended to be played is for players to move their character through a series of storylines that take them to a diverse array of lands and adventures. 'But if it was possible to get your character from level 1 to 110 just by killing a single wolf over and over again, they would do it,' he explains. Thus, the experience changes, becoming something not in the intended spirit of the game, and, arguably, grindingly dull. An inevitable side effect of all of this is that the game itself becomes the focal point of community discussions, with players (and by extension that much-needed human element) becoming secondary actors.

That's not to say that e-sports athletes don't enjoy a certain degree of celebrity. It's just that this is largely self-generated, through avenues like personal Twitch streams and social media branding. However the somewhat informal nature of this process, the breakdown of that line between private and professional life, can sometimes put players in the spotlight for all of the wrong reasons. Just two weeks after the OWL launched in January 2018, the Dallas Fuel team member Félix Lengyel was suspended after launching a homophobic attack on another player, Austin Wilmot, who is openly gay. The tirade happened on Lengyel's personal Twitch stream, apparently in response to Fuel's loss against Wilmot's team, the Houston Outlaws. The OWL took a zero-tolerance approach to the situation, fining Lengyel $2,000 and suspending him for four games (with Dallas Fuel later extending that suspension). Almost immediately on his return, however, he was fined and suspended again, this time for racially disparaging, and generally derogatory, language. At about the same time, two other OWL players were fined for using homophobic and xenophobic memes – again, all on personal Twitch streams or other personal social media accounts. Other sorts of player-centred controversies plagued the league even before play started. In November 2017, the manager of San Francisco Shock, Max Bateman, was fired after allegations of sexual misconduct surfaced. Then, in March 2018, Boston Uprising's Jonathan Sanchez was fired after damning allegations involving sexual misconduct with underage girls came to light. While the OWL rightly took hard-line action in all of these situations, it nevertheless cast a long shadow over the long-term aim of the league becoming something that appeals to a broad audience.

It also didn't help matters that of the 100-plus number of players who started the season, none were women. This wasn't down to a banal question about ability; one of the all-time best *Overwatch* players is the nineteen-year-old South Korean Kim 'Geguri' Se-yeon, a player so adept at the game that she ended up being inundated with accusations of cheating – and, outrageously, death threats. To silence her critics, in 2016 she hosted a livestream that simultaneously showed in-game footage and the movements her hands were making on the keyboard to prove that there was no cheating involved. She is simply an excellent player. During a media day shortly before the start of the inaugural OWL season, a number of teams were asked why they hadn't signed her up. Excuses ranged from there being too much of a language barrier (which was strange considering both New York Excelsior and London Spitfire boasted all-Korean teams), to there being concerns over teammates of opposite sexes sharing accommodation together (by no means an insurmountable problem, but one that in some ways seems a little creepy to highlight). As the games journalist Nathan Grayson noted at the time, the general narrative coming from the team camps appeared to be that the OWL would definitely be open to women players one day. Just not right now, and not without women putting in more work than everyone else. It was a lazy attitude that trickled out in various comments from that media day. For example, one manager shifted the focus to the media, pointing out that if a team were to sign a female player, the press might question whether it was just a PR stunt. Echoing that sentiment, Houston Outlaws player Jacob Lyon vaguely suggested that it would have to be the right person being picked at the right time, so that people wouldn't 'doubt the intent' – whatever that means. Geguri would eventually enter the league later in the season, signing to the Shanghai Dragons in mid-February, but the kinds of excuses given for why women were not involved earlier are pathetic. Video games ought to be a great leveller. They are not just physical shows of strength – they involve feats of mental agility, rapid reflexes and excellent communication and coordination skills with teammates. None of these things are the exclusive domain of men. The misogyny on display throughout the first season of the *Overwatch* League was infuriating to observe for many reasons, not least because from its very inception *Overwatch* has had a secondary goal of being an inclusive game.

'It's something we don't like to overly focus on, but we try to represent people of the nations of the world, and people of different orientations,' explains Jeff Kaplan. 'Because our game is a big part of popular culture, I feel like we have a responsibility to show normal things as normal.' Fundamentally, inclusivity and open-mindedness have always been at the core of *Overwatch*. Characters from all walks of life are very deliberately included, but the developers are keen to never make a big deal about these aspects. For example, the support character Symmetra – an Indian architect who uses a photon projector to create sentry turrets, teleportation devices and shields for teammates – was gradually revealed to have autism through a series of comic strips that provided a richer background into each of the major characters in the game. This fact wasn't paraded about; it was simply dropped in as one facet of a complex and fascinating individual. 'We've had so many people identify with her as a character and *Overwatch* as a game, because it's important to show that somebody with autism could be heroic,' Jeff points out. 'There are all these awesome heroes. They also happen to have these things about them. That's not the point of them, but they're awesome. Can we all just continue?' The impression that I got from talking to him is that the *Overwatch* developers are hugely sensitive to the nature of their fanbase. It isn't a game that tries to be overtly political, nor is it one that tries to make impactful societal statements. Nevertheless, there is an appreciation that because it's a game that enjoys mainstream popularity, it will inevitably attract some impressionable young players. Some of them will be full of self-doubt about their identity. Maybe some are bullied or criticised for how they look, who they're into, or what they're into. In its own way then, *Overwatch* – the game – is trying to simply normalise the different ways that people *are*, through its storytelling and through their character choices, and cater to these audiences.

Overwatch (the league) therefore, has all of the right ingredients for something truly unique in e-sports: a game that can be played by anyone, and because of the nature of its in-game characters, one that can appeal to anyone. In the drive to generate a sustainable sports entertainment venture though, perhaps the league has lost the developers' original ethos along the way. Problems with the behaviour of some of the game's real-life characters have cast a glaring spotlight on the misogyny that has plagued gaming for far too long, and shown that unless pre-emptive systems are put in place from the start, no game or competition is immune. These problems aren't insurmountable, and perhaps sunlight really is the best disinfectant here. I firmly believe that the *Overwatch* League has the potential to become a much-needed paragon of effortless diversity in competitive gaming. To do so, it needs to not only acknowledge the wrongs that have happened so far, but to actively rectify them. It needs to seek out players from a diverse range of backgrounds, who both passively and actively contribute to creating a more inclusive atmosphere around the competition, normalising the fact that anyone and everyone can enjoy the entertainment. In other words, the league needs to embody the principles of the very game that sits at its core.

CHAPTER 13

Loss

B lythe House feels more like a high security bank vault than a museum collections store. Located in a leafy corner of West Kensington in London, the impression that the imposing, red-brick behemoth of a building gives isn't accidental. There's an industrial beauty to it though; as well as a certain sense of familiarity to the muted white stone archways that comprise the main entrance. Among other movies, Blythe House was a location featured in the 2013 Marvel action movie *Thor: The Dark World.** Originally built at the turn of the last century, it was the headquarters of the Post Office Savings Bank for nearly 75 years. Nowadays, it acts as a store for three of London's most important institutions: the Victoria and Albert Museum, the British Museum and the Science Museum. I'm here to view some of the archived collections of the latter, but I get stuck trying to negotiate my way past an unimpressed security guard at the entrance to the first. He gives me a pitying look as I wave a scrappy piece of paper with some directions scribbled on them in front of his face, and points me down the road, to another entrance around the corner of the block.

After a brief yet anxious wait in the (correct) security office, my guide for the day arrives. Abbie MacKinnon is the Science Museum's Assistant Curator for Technologies and Engineering. As she leads me through a labyrinthine trail of fusty corridors,

---

* Definitely not the best Marvel movie (that would be *Captain America: Civil War*), nor even the best Thor movie (that would be *Ragnarok*).

she explains to me that the Science Museum is in the midst of relocating their entire collection to a state-of-the-art new facility in Wiltshire. As beautiful and as iconic as Blythe House is, it wasn't built for preserving the 320,000 scientific curios that currently reside there. As a result, the museum's curators are now undergoing the painstaking process of cataloguing and relocating some of the world's most important scientific arte-facts. Part of that process involves creating digital records for every object, with the aim of producing one of the world's most extensive and universally-accessible online scientific archives. I feel a little sheepish taking up Abbie's valuable time in light of the move, but she's a very gracious host: as eager and excited to sift through the Nintendo archive as I am.

The holding area that we arrive in is a long, dark corridor filled with shelving units stretching from floor to ceiling. *This* is what I always thought a museum archive would look like. Typewriters and music players, radios and television monitors adorn the racks, silently awaiting categorisation and a move to their final resting home. In one section I spy a herd of obso-lete mobile phones – everything from the chunky black plastic blocks that were the early 90s carphones, up to the iconic Nokia 3310. And on a trolley, near the caged door to the area, sits the equipment I'm after: an assortment of Nintendo memo-rabilia, anonymously donated to the museum in dribs and drabs over the past few years. My initial assumption was that an insti-tution as large and as important as the Science Museum would already have a fairly extensive collection of video games mater-ial – but the way in which it acquires objects for the archive isn't always a straightforward process. The museum can sometimes go out on specific drives to acquire items through auctions, especially for older or more historically important artefacts, but much of the time it's also hostage to the whims and caprices of fortune: reliant on generous yet unpredictable donations from unknown benefactors. While the assortment in front of me doesn't represent the total sum of the Science Museum's video game collection, it is nevertheless a testament to that process.

The trolley holds a seemingly random array of ancient toys from Nintendo's previous life as both a toy and board game manufacturer, along with three or four copies of the company's first foray into the video game industry – the 'Colour TV-Game 6 console', launched in 1977. Everything is fragile here. Abbie lets me open up a box containing the 'Ultra machine', a Nintendo-branded plastic baseball bat and ball launcher. We carefully extract all of the pieces from the decaying cardboard, and piece the launcher contraption together. We exchange a brief, conspiratorial glance as I hold the bat up. I think to myself: *We could totally start playing this!* Then I re-evaluate the look on Abbie's face which appears to be saying: *Oh God, I hope he doesn't start playing with this!* I tentatively return the bat to the trolley – something was missing from the launcher anyway, and we couldn't get it to work. I turn my attention instead to the fleet of games consoles. Some of the controller leads are frayed, and the consoles themselves show the grazes and smudges of a life spent sitting precariously in front of a television as a beloved family plaything. These were evidently not collector's items, consigned to a life of pristine but solitary confinement, away from the grubby hands of the young. These are things that were actually played with: they were enjoyed, as they were meant to be. 'We don't really know much about this particular donor,' Abbie tells me. 'It's a shame.' She tells me that the Science Museum used to be a lot more about showing *how* things work, so would, for example, have exhibits teaching people what a computer does. But it's hard to make that sort of exhibit sustainably interesting. 'It's a niche group of people that is interested in that sort of thing,' she explains. 'When actually, what people want to hear is stories about other people. People who are like them, people who are different from them. That's what's interesting. More and more we're trying to tell that kind of story.' Wearing gloves, I handle the consoles gently, looking at them in an engrossed silence. I think to myself that, just one last time, it would be nice to give them a chance to be played, before they are meticulously filed away, never to be used again.

As I place the console back on the trolley, I think about what it means to preserve video games for future generations. At first glance, it might seem like a completely trivial thing – all we need to do is to source consoles, games cartridges and disks, controllers and other peripheral devices, and carefully store them for other people to take a look at in the future. But the patchy collection on display in front of me shows that preservation is a much more difficult process than that: because video games are dying. Not dying *off*, of course – the video games industry is stronger now than ever, with gamers spending a reported $138 billion in 2018. But on an individual level, each console or controller or cartridge or disk starts dying right from the moment they're made. Think about that console that you had when you were a child – where is it now? Parts get broken, cables go missing. The battery packs inside games cartridges – that save our progress – run down. The very plastic that they are made from goes yellow, becomes brittle, and eventually starts to crack. Nothing lasts forever. The fugacious nature of video games presents a quandary for preservation specialists like Abbie MacKinnon. On the one hand games, by their very nature, are to be played. In that sense, it seems an abomination to lock consoles up behind Perspex and glass, only to be viewed and never to be touched. On the other hand, as each successive generation of games consoles falls out of production, what's left is a finite and dwindling resource, along with the problem of how to maintain them for an indefinite amount of time.

I talk to Abbie about this, mentioning that I find it heartbreaking that the consoles we're looking at will never be played again. 'You could really say that about anything that we've got here though,' she points out. 'Our radios don't play music any more. We have some of the first computers here. They don't work any more.' Inadvertently, I pull a distraught face and she laughs at me. 'Yeah! It is kinda sad, isn't it? ... But ask anyone who works in a museum, and they'll tell you that there's always merit in preserving things like this – even if it means their original purpose is no longer served.' Abbie's view is that preserving these objects and cataloguing how we used them in their own times and context will provide future generations with stories about what they meant to us. She points to the Color TV-Game 6. 'Preservation isn't just saying, for example, that this is Nintendo's first games console. It's [also] about the story of where that console has been, how it ended up here, and who had possession of it along the way,' she explains. 'It's not just about the physical object. It's about the story of that object.' For this collection though, the story is a patchy one. Without much in the way of details about who donated the Nintendo memorabilia, piecing together how, where and when they were used is an impossible task. I find it lamentable in a way. On reflection, that seems like an odd thing to feel. These are only pieces of inanimate plastic, after all. But as I thank Abbie for her time and leave the museum, I reconsider: as with anything that we feel a personal connection to, it's only natural to mourn the passing of something that brought us great joy. There's no doubt that games preservation is an important thing, in much the same way that art conservation is worthwhile, or protecting sites of historical importance is essential. Whether you play them or not, video games are an integral part of our culture, and cataloguing stories not just about how people played them, but the attitudes and beliefs that were held about them, is an indispensable part of chronicling the late 20th and early 21st century for future generations. The tricky part, it would seem, lies in exactly how to preserve those stories. Thinking about the lost story of the Science Museum's Color TV-Game 6 collection on the train home, I find some comfort in the idea that although they will never be played again, eventually they may become part of a larger story that's told about Nintendo's early video game history. As long as the memories of these things can be preserved in the right way, then it's okay to let go of the physical objects of our past. Or, to put it another way, and as the noted video games scholar Professor James Newman has put it: if video games are dying, perhaps we should just let them die.

Professor Newman is a man who talks quickly, softly and passionately about video games. A few days after my adventure at Blythe House, I meet up with him while taking a walk through the university campus (I'm fortunate enough to work in the same institution as he does). It's a cool, breezy spring day in May, a contradictory time at university. As the season surrounds us with new life after a particularly cold and dreary winter, gaggles of final year students walk past us, faced with the existential crisis that is brought to their own lives by the end of their studies, looming in just a few weeks' time. I invite him into the relative calm of my office so that we can tease apart the idea of why letting video games 'die' might be a good thing.

'There's a set of conditions that a game needs [in order] to work,' James explains to me. 'Some of them are technical: there's a console or a PC with a graphics card and operating system. There's a TV or a CRT monitor. But there's a finite period where that stuff exists in the world.' Perhaps, then, the thing to do with video games is to accept that they are going to disappear at some point. Rather than trying to get them to last forever, James explains, the better thing to do is to document them as much as possible, in as many ways as possible, while we still have them. 'It's analogous to something I saw in a documentary about manatees,' he adds. 'There would be a point in our lifetime where they weren't around any more, so we needed to find out all of the information that we could about them before it was too late.' Thankfully, manatees aren't endangered any more, but the principle is a solid one, and echoes what Abbie MacKinnon explained to me at the Science Museum: our accumulated knowledge and lived experience needs to be catalogued, and *that* information needs to be preserved for future generations. With games, not only would the game itself be safeguarded, but the context of the period it was placed in would also be retained. The preservation process becomes not just about what it is (or was) like to play the game, but also about the surrounding culture that was in place when the game was designed and published, and about the communities of fans that built up around it. In other words, as James argues, rather than thinking in terms of *game* preservation, it would be better to think about *gameplay* preservation.

While this may seem like an eminently sensible – and obvious – approach to take, in many ways it's a process that can be hampered by the very industry that gameplay preservation seeks to help. As James notes in his 2012 book *Best Before*, the video game industry engages in a sort of 'planned obsolescence'. Because it involves a rapid cycle of development, production and innovation, the industry is necessarily reliant on current technologies becoming redundant in order to make way for newer, better ones. As a result, the idea of games rapidly becoming out-dated is almost baked into their very existence, and along with it, an implicit attitude that preservation isn't something worth spending much time thinking about. And yet, somewhat paradoxically, the industry has experienced a boom in recent years precisely thanks to those old, obsolete technologies. For example, you can now buy a mini Super Nintendo console, packed with around twenty of the best games of the early 1990s, and without the added hassle of trying to find an outmoded television to get it to work on. Games are emulated – reproduced and tweaked so that they can be played on modern computers, allowing the mega hits of the past, like *Star Fox*, or *Donkey Kong Country*, to be played anew. But, perhaps counter-intuitively, the revival of retro video games isn't necessarily all that helpful to gameplay preservation either.

'It sort of denies the possibility of thinking about how the games changed,' James points out. He uses the example of *Pac-Man* to explain his point. Although the basic game design didn't itself alter much in the years after its release, the way in which people approached playing it did. 'In the early 1980s, you would get these pulpy books coming out, just full of patterns that you could take through the maze. You'd have to rote-learn it,' he explains. Guides such as Penguin's 1982 *How*

To Win At Pac-Man would be full of complex-looking maze patterns, tips and tricks, that players would need to memorise and then practice, repeatedly, in order to perfect. A year earlier, one of the more substantial books in this genre – *Mastering Pac-Man* – was published by Signet, featuring some 120 different predetermined routes through *Pac-Man*'s mazes. *Mastering Pac-Man* was written by a man called Ken Uston, a well-known and notorious blackjack player, banned from numerous casinos in the 1970s for perfecting extremely effective team-based card-counting techniques. Learning these patterns was effectively a brute-force method of trying to beat the game – like memorising thousands of potential chessboard configurations. In other words, at this point in *Pac-Man*'s life, playing the game was entirely about the maze. But over time, James tells me, players – and games scholars – moved their focus away from the maze, and onto the four computer-controlled ghosts that haunt *Pac-Man* as he navigates the game environment. 'The algorithms that governed their movement were utterly deterministic, and once people started to really look at how the ghosts behaved, you could then start to play against them,' James explains. Once those routines were learned, there was a shift in the way that people approached gameplay, which would eventually lead to the first 'perfect' *Pac-Man* games being played in the later part of the 1990s. 'Because of the way it was programmed, the game breaks at level 256,' James adds. 'Nobody knew that when it first came out. Everyone thought the levels went on forever.'

In *Pac-Man*, each level consists of a maze full of dots, all of which the titular character needs to devour to get to the next stage. So as long as a player had at least one life remaining, the thinking was that new levels could be generated indefinitely.

However, due to a bug in *Pac-Man*'s code,* when a player completes level 255 the game crashes. A 'perfect' game, then, is one in which a player scores the maximum possible number of points (3,333,360, to be precise) after 255 levels. So although *Pac-Man* never changed, the way players approached it did. Where in the early 1980s it was seen as a game with seemingly no end, in which players concentrated on memorising complex patterns of pathways through the mazes, in the late 1990s it became a game with a 'win condition', with top-level players focussing on how quickly they could reach that perfect score.

The problem with the emulation currently going on in the world of games is that all of this rich history and contextual background is lost in favour of a quick fix of nostalgia. It allows us to play the games we knew and loved when we were younger – but they're not quite the same. There are free versions of *Pac-Man* you can play online now: emulations of the original for your smartphone, but when you're playing something that uses different code (and perhaps that fixes the level 256 bug), as well as different controllers and different hardware to the original, are you really playing the same game? Emulations of *Pac-Man* are more about providing people with a brief opportunity to reminisce about playing a couple of levels of the game

---

* The bug is technically known as an 'integer overflow' error. An internal level counter in the game is stored as a single byte, which in computing terms, means that it can only hold 256 numbers (from 0 to 255). Other calculations in the game (such as figuring out how many fruit to display at the bottom of the screen) are based on this counter, and go haywire when trying to increment certain numbers above 255. Practically, this means that when a player progresses to level 256, the game screen becomes corrupted, with the entire right half of the maze filled with jumbled symbols, letters and numbers – any further progression is impossible.

they experienced when they were younger, rather than the story and cultural impact of the game itself. In other words, while it may seem that emulations are about rekindling happy memories of youth, they are really more preoccupied with the object – the game itself. In the drive to force games to live forever, there is a risk that they inadvertently become locked in a kind of stasis, existing only as they did at a very specific point in their past.

In saying that video games should be allowed to 'die', James Newman isn't suggesting that they should be forgotten or disregarded. Instead, he believes that preservation should focus on the context of the game. Documenting the evolution of gameplay (for example, showing how players figured out the programming design of particular games, and how the communities that built up around those games shared information about how to play them in new ways) results in a much richer historical account of something that should be seen as an important cultural and social phenomenon, rather than a passing fad or waste of time.

Clearly, a more nuanced approach to games preservation like this makes the entire enterprise a vastly harder and more time-consuming task. Acknowledging not just the game itself but the experiences people have had with it opens up countless avenues for investigation and categorisation. It isn't only that the way we play a given game generally changes over time. The way each of us approaches games individually also differs, and what a particular game will mean to us at different moments in our own private play – or lives – can go through seismic shifts: for example, as we get better at it, or as the circumstances in which we play it change. I've spoken at length in previous chapters about what games like *Firewatch, World of Warcraft*, and *Ocarina of Time* have meant to me. Those will be very different experiences to the kind that you might have had if you have played those same games. *Minecraft* is another good example. By and large, I've only ever played it in quiet moments on my own, in single-player mode, largely isolating myself from anyone else. My enjoyment from *Minecraft* comes from the simple escapism that the game offers, the ability to be somewhere else for a little while, to build something inconsequential, and perhaps, in the process of creating that little log cabin in the middle of a snowy ravine, take a bit of time to think about my dad. For others, it's a vastly different experience – for the students who used the game to develop MolCraft, it was a chemistry learning tool, a medium through which science communication could be explored. And for many kids, it's essentially a glorified social network: a virtual playground where they can hang out and mess around with their friends. By documenting the many ways in which the game could be played, future generations would be able to see *Minecraft* for what it really was – not just a mindless or antisocial waste of time, but a novel way for people to connect with each other.

How museum curators and game preservation specialists would go about documenting this is no easy task though, and would likely require bespoke sets of resources to accomplish. As an example, James tells me about a new type of interactive exhibit that he helped to develop at the National Videogame Arcade. 'Game Inspectors', as they're termed, look a little bit like a games console – visitors are presented with a screen and a controller box with a joystick and numerous colourful buttons. The controls allow people to explore numerous aspects of a video game – things like how levels were designed and where enemies and items were placed, as well as how players figured out how to navigate and complete levels in different ways – without actually having to play the game themselves. Games are hard, after all, and especially so for newcomers. By coupling interactive videos of experts playing the game with background information about how those same players could exploit the way it was designed (in order to, for example, complete levels at diz-zyingly fast speeds), the Game Inspector achieves two things. It allows visitors to experience video games as they were originally realised, while at the same time providing them with the more human stories of how, and why, gameplay changed over time.

For the most part though, video game exhibits tend to be a combination of static displays explaining the history of video games, and exhibitions that offer people the chance to play on the consoles of years gone by. 'It's expensive to put on these sorts of displays,' explains James. 'And it usually ends up being a carefully-curated set of games that either happen to be the best-known ones, or the ones it was easiest to source.' In a sense, these are the same sorts of difficulties that any museum cura-tor will encounter. I think back to my time at the Power Up exhibit at the Science Museum, and my curiosity as to why the Binatone TV Master was positioned at the start of the timeline of consoles. Perhaps it was just a simple matter of resources – there was no Magnavox Odyssey there because it's difficult to source one that works and can be reasonably maintained. 'Yeah, you're always going to find a Spectrum in those sorts of collec-tions, but you probably won't see a Dragon 32 or an Oric-1,' he laments. 'And there's a whole bunch of other stuff that just slips through the cracks.' If you never actually encountered any of these consoles in your youth, maybe this isn't so much of a prob-lem. But curators need to be careful that they don't inadvertently rewrite the story of video games – that it doesn't become solely about, for example, the Sinclair ZX Spectrum, just because the Spectrum succeeded where other consoles of the time didn't.

Without that context, without that accompanying background history of who played these games consoles, and how and why they played them, it ends up being difficult – understandably so – for visitors to these sorts of exhibits to encounter them as anything other than niche retro curiosities.

As much as I'm loath to say it then (for I so very much love going to exhibitions like Power Up), perhaps it's best to let old games and old consoles die in dignity. By trying to keep them alive as long as possible, something intangible but important about them is lost. They have experiential value, right here in this moment. They offer us ways to escape, to travel to far-off places rich in adventure and wonder. They provide us with a medium through which we can find kindred spirits, forge new friendships and maintain old ones. They offer us a way to find ourselves, and sometimes they offer us a way to lose ourselves. These things aren't without risk, but when is *anything* that's worth doing in life? In being all of these things and more, in time games can become those very aspects of life that they reflect – treasured memories that we can look back on through the soft glow of nostalgia. They are a part of us, and when we play, we are a part of them. And as with anything fleeting and cherished in life, sometimes, in order to keep the memory strong, we just have to let go of them.

It's inevitable that something as powerful as the notion of loss could form the narrative of a video game itself, and there are numerous examples of games that attempt this. Some do it intentionally and directly – games such as the beautiful *Last Day of June*, released in 2017. This tells the tragic story of a couple: Carl and June, who live in an idyllic, watercolour-like village with four other people. After a blissful evening spent together by a dock not far from home, the two end up in a car crash on the drive back, which is fatal for June. The game is played primarily through the eyes of Carl, now wheelchair-bound, as he travels back in time to relive memories of that day through the actions of the other village folk, desperately trying to force them down different paths to avoid the crash and save his wife – all to no avail. In the early parts of the game, for example, the accident is caused by a child playing with a ball which ends up bouncing out onto the road, with Carl swerving to avoid hitting him. As Carl nudges the child instead to play with a kite earlier in the day, the crash instead happens when his best friend, moving out of the village, skids on the road and causes boxes to fly into their oncoming path. As difficult and as dark as this may seem, *Last Day of June* is a touching and powerful meditation on loss, and treats the subject with the sensitivity and gravity it deserves. It taps into that deep-seated belief that we hold when we lose someone close to us, that whispering voice that asks what might have happened if things were different. However, as the game progresses, it becomes increasingly apparent that we cannot change the things that have happened in the past. Instead, the underlying message is that it's more important to hold on to the memories of what we had. It's a masterpiece of storytelling, told through the actions and interactions that characters have with each other and their surroundings. No words are spoken in *Last Day of June* – at least, none that are intelligible. Instead, you become drawn into the narrative through the gentle movements of the characters and their stop-motion animation-like world. There are very few games that have made me cry out loud. This is one of them.

Other games can come to represent loss completely unin-tentionally, rather than via an explicit storyline that guides your actions through grief. Instead, some games offer the freedom to impose your own narrative on the virtual worlds that they allow access to. For me, the game that best offers this freedom isn't a sandbox game like *Minecraft*, or an open world like *World of Warcraft*. It is instead a much less obvious choice, and so requires some explanation.

Just over ten years ago, I had the very good fortune to meet an experimental psychologist called Dr Robbie Cooper. I was a postgraduate student at the time, an awkward proto-scientist on the verge of embarking upon a PhD for reasons that weren't quite clear to me, save for a desire to stay within an academic system that, up to that point, had been a pretty fun ride. I studied at the University of Bristol, an exciting place to work, full of interesting people doing fascinating things. One of my fondest memories of that institution was the close-knit community of staff and students within the psychology department. It was to prove to be a crucial part of getting through my degree, too – if I can offer would-be doctoral students one piece of advice, it's this: if you want to do a PhD, for the love of God find a strong motivation. Do it for the love of the science. Don't do it if all you really want is to be called doctor. PhD programmes are intellectually and emotionally brutal, and you need to have a clear goal to get you through the difficult times. On top of that it turns out that in the real world no one actually cares whether you're a doctor or not.

Having a strong and caring community around you is essential to getting through the low moments: when an experiment just isn't working, or when you feel so hopelessly lost in a sea of scientific jargon and computer code that you feel like there's no possibility of seeing the end. For me, Robbie was the backbone of that support. A giant of a man with a gentle Scottish accent, he was often a calming presence in the departmental coffee room; someone who could be counted on to offer brotherly advice or much-needed comic relief. Aside from anything else, Robbie was *cool*. He played basketball. He was a brilliant drummer, playing most notably for the rock band Laeto in the early 2000s, and later on as one half of the excellent drum/guitar duo Iron Crease. He was a creative researcher, too. One of the wackiest experiments that I ever had the opportunity to take part in was about how we perceive human facial expressions. Most of the research that has been carried out in this area involves getting participants to sit in a dark room, in front of a computer, while various experimental tasks get them to respond to pictures of faces that pop up on the screen. Robbie's problem with this methodology, though, was that this isn't how we interact with actual faces in the real world – at the very least, faces are three-dimensional things. So to see whether this was an important factor or not, he and a colleague devised an experiment, titled 'FaceReality', in which participants would have their eye movements tracked while they looked at an actual face. To be specific, Robbie's face. Peering out at you from the darkness of the laboratory, pulling smiles, frowns and everything in between. It was a wholly disconcerting experience, and I couldn't help but burst out laughing the first time the lights went up to reveal his goofy face.

While Robbie was many things to many people, he was also a gamer, and it was in this role that I got to know him best. After his postdoctoral position ended in 2009, he moved back to Scotland to take up a lectureship at Edinburgh Napier University. We still kept in touch, through the medium of *Halo 3*, and its later successor, *Halo: Reach*. We would spend hours online, chatting to each other about everything and nothing. Playing *Halo* alone, I would often get sucked into a state of really caring about unimportant aspects of the matches I was playing – trivial things like how many games I'd won, or how many kills I'd scored took precedence over the sheer fun of just being entertained. I played it differently when I played it with Robbie though. Who scored what, how many games we won, those things didn't matter. Sometimes we would barely even play the game – instead we'd just get our characters to jump into an armoured car, and drive around a multiplayer map for a bit while we spoke, occasionally firing off a rocket-propelled grenade vaguely in the other team's direction to show willing. They were some of the happiest times that I can recall playing a video game, and that was solely down to the person that I was playing with.

Robbie died in 2014 at the age of 36, from a particularly rare and aggressive form of cancer called anal adenocarcinoma. Nothing about it was fair, but then nothing about cancer ever is. It was too fast, and Robbie was too young. For everyone who knew him, it was an immeasurable loss, and I still think about him often, in the quiet hours of the evening, when there's nothing else to think about apart from the ghosts of our past. I don't play *Halo 3* any more, not after Robbie logged off. At least, I don't play it like we used to play it. Sometimes though, I might load up one of my old, favourite multiplayer maps that we used to frequent. The appropriately-named Valhalla is a gorgeous level, set in a ravine with two monolithic bases at opposing ends, both towering into a cobalt sky. A shallow river splits the valley floor in two, and a small cave system tracks through the cliffs to one side, before spilling out onto the crash site of a downed transport ship, a silent monument to a war that, at least for today, isn't affecting this place. On the other side of the ravine, a huge dam-like wall plunges down, deep into the ground. At the far end of the map, behind one of the bases, lush grass gives way to a rocky beach, and a caldera-like lake spreads out before you. There's a gentle breeze here, constant yet comforting. Across the water, mountains drift off into the distance, and just before the haze casts the landscape into oblivion, you can make out the gentle rise of a huge arc of land that traces up into space, looping around at an impossible rate to, eventually, meet you from behind. A reminder that you're not on Earth – you're not even on a planet. You're on an alien installation, a 'Halo' structure, for which the game is named. Sometimes, I like to wander through that empty landscape, crouch down by the waterside, listen to the wind, and think about Robbie. It isn't the same since he died, but then, I'm not there to try to recapture something that I lost years ago. Just for a moment, in those timeless surroundings, I imagine what it was like to see his name popping up on my screen as he logs on, and I think back to the times when we wouldn't even think of that occurrence as something precious – just a prelude to us both jumping into a tank and going for a pyrotechnic jaunt over to the other team's base. And so for me, Valhalla stays quiet, a virtual memorial to an amazing person who touched my life for the briefest of times.

We play video games for all sorts of different reasons. We play them to connect with people; we play them for the joy of discovery. We play them because we like the sense of achievement they give us when we win. We play them to find ourselves, and sometimes we play them to lose ourselves. When we lose someone close to us, sometimes we can't play them at all. And when we can finally pick up the controller again, sometimes we play to remember. In a way, video games are a lens through which we can make sense of the world around us. Over the course of this book, I hope that I have communicated a sense of how they are able to achieve that. Some games have the power to remind us to take stock of the memories and people that we hold so dear, and they can often do so in unexpected or unintended ways. Others can challenge us to become better versions of ourselves, and can offer us a quiet shelter in times of need. They can fix us, and yes, they can also break us, and because of their immersive nature they can perhaps do this more strongly than any other form of media. However, we aren't yet at a point where we possess a completely satisfactory way of talking about video games. Likewise, we're not yet at a point where they have gained true cultural acceptance. We see this manifest itself most directly in the countless news articles claiming that video games are the driving factors for all of the negative things in society. And for the most part, I think it's safe to ignore these sorts of stories. But that isn't to say I think that it's a good idea to simply ignore any and all concerns that people might have about their effects on us, and as I write, the UK government's Digital, Culture, Media and Sport Committee have announced that they will hold an inquiry into the potential future impact of immersive technologies like virtual and augmented reality, as well as the potentially addictive nature of video games. Clearly, there are important societal questions that still need to be answered: for example about whether there are certain types of exploitative mechanisms that should be barred from use in games, or whether the industry should be more stringently regulated. But, given that the scientific research still seems to be stuck on that age-old question of whether violent video games make us more aggressive, there's still a long way to go before it can provide clear and conclusive answers to any of these sorts of queries.

Are games good or bad for us? The honest answer is that we don't convincingly know either way, and it's probably a bit of both. As much as they're a form of entertainment, they're also a tool: one that must be treated with respect and responsibility, in the full knowledge that if used improperly or without due care and attention, they may cause as much damage as good. But it's worth remembering that, as with any such device, they are not the sum total of our being, however strongly we might identify with them. Nor are they intended to be. Not every story of what it means to be human can be told through our experiences with video games, which are after all but one small aspect of our complex, rich, and multifaceted lives. Whatever our views on games are, we need to remember that the conversations we have about why we play them and what they can do for us are still in their infancy: needing all of the care, compassion and guidance that such a young entity requires.

I never did manage to find the Time-Lost Proto Drake, you know. Sometimes, in the hushed moments before I drift off to sleep, I think about rousing myself just enough to log into *Warcraft* and search for it once more. Those thoughts, more often than not, lead me back to thinking about why I was searching for the Drake in the first place. In many ways, writing this book has forced me to re-evaluate the relationship that I have with video games. For better or worse, over my life I've tended to use them as a coping mechanism; a way of dealing with unexpected and at times catastrophic loss. You could argue that this isn't necessarily a good thing – that using games as a distraction isn't a particularly good way of dealing with death. And while I would agree that getting truly, deeply lost in a game is an unhelpful form of escapism, I also believe that playing the right game, at the right time, can act as the perfect outlet through which to explore and understand grief. It's worked for me so far, at least. And if you ever find yourself in a similar position,

I truly hope that you find something that works for you too. But the real value in video games, as I have come to realise, is not in their power to distract or captivate us. The real value is in their ability to connect us; to provide us with a way to foster new friendships and maintain old ones, to allow us to tell stories about interesting and amazing people, and to help us remember those we hold closest to our hearts.

Acknowledgements

A few years ago, I found myself in a pub in London, not far from the Royal Institution, with Alok Jha and Ed Yong, who are two of the best science writers it is my pleasure and privilege to know. I was wittering on about possibly, maybe, finally getting around to finishing a pitch about a book on video games, and they gave me a much-needed kick up the arse to actually get on with it. I am very thankful that they did.

Through the process of writing this, numerous other people have been amazing sources of support, information, guidance and wisdom. In no particular order, my thanks go to: Graham Russell, Hayley and Chris Ware, Alex and Debbie Chong, Adam Smith, Lauren D'Rozario, Dean Burnett, Adam Rutherford, Kevin Fong, Sarah-Jayne Blakemore, Roger Highfield, Tilly Blyth, Joe Walsh, Jermaine Ravalier, Aileen Fraser, David Schofield, Dean Burnett, Megan Evans, Stu Evans, Kerry Harben-Evans, Tony and Christine Evans, Maggie and Keith Halliday. Special thanks also go to Martin Evans, Scott Jones, Suzi Gage and Chris Chambers for providing comments and feedback on earlier drafts of the manuscript. Thank you to Sam Bandah, Steven Khoo and Vanessa Vanasin at Blizzard for orchestrating some key interviews, and to everyone featured in these pages for taking the time out of their busy days to talk to me.

As I have been writing this book, my friend Tom Chivers has also found himself in a similar situation, grappling with a fascinating book about artificial intelligence. Despite our messages to each other mainly comprising panic-induced sentiments like 'oh God I can't do this' and 'what the hell were we thinking', his companionship and encouragement has been a source of great comfort, and I am thankful that we got to walk part of this road together. His book, *The AI Does Not Hate You*, is brilliant and you should read it.

In 2012, I won an online science communication competition called I'm a Scientist: Get Me Out of Here. The prize was a small grant, which I ultimately used to purchase some much-needed recording equipment, and without which many of the interviews for this book would have been much harder and stressful to deal with. It is, hands down, one of the best public engagement activities that I've ever had the opportunity to be a part of, and I am indebted to Shane McCracken and the team at Gallomanor for all of their guidance over the years.

To James Randerson, Tash Reith-Banks, Alok Jha, James Kingsland and Ian Sample, thank you for giving me the opportunity to cut my writing teeth at the *Guardian* – the science blog network experiment may have finished, but I think we did a good job of it.

My heartfelt thanks also go to all of the brilliant people at my publisher, Icon, who have been so enthusiastic and encouraging about the manuscript, and in particular to my editor Tom Webber. I am a better writer as a result of his skill, experience, and steady guiding hand.

When I first decided that I wanted to write a book, the one consistent thing that people kept telling me was that I would need an excellent literary agent on my side. To that end, I am tremendously lucky that Will Francis at Janklow & Nesbit took me on board. Will has been integral in shaping the ideas and the stories I've written about, and he has been a constant and unwavering source of support and sage advice since the very beginning. And on top of everything else, he's an excellent *Mario Kart* player. This book is richer from his influence.

To my Mum, thank you for being there for me over the years, and for our recent conversations about my Dad, remembering all of the silly things that he got up to. Most of all, thank you to my wife, Frances. Writing this has been one of the hardest things I've ever done, and I genuinely believe it wouldn't have come to fruition without your enduring support and love. In many ways, this book is about my past, but you are everything that I'm looking forward to about the future.

Bibliography

Aarseth, E., Bean, A.M., Boonen, H., Colder Carras, M., Coulson, M., Das, D., Deleuze, J., Dunkels, E., Edman, J., Ferguson, C.J. & Haagsma, M.C. (2017). Scholars' open debate paper on the World Health Organization ICD-11 Gaming Disorder proposal. *Journal of Behavioral Addictions*, 6, 267–270

Adachi, P.J. & Willoughby, T. (2011a). The effect of video game competition and violence on aggressive behavior: Which characteristic has the greatest influence? *Psychology of Violence*, 1, 259–274

Adachi, P.J. & Willoughby, T. (2011b). The effect of violent video games on aggression: Is it more than just the violence? *Aggression and Violent Behavior*, 16, 55–62

Adachi, P.J. & Willoughby, T. (2013). Demolishing the competition: The longitudinal link between competitive video games, competitive gambling, and aggression. *Journal of Youth and Adolescence*, 42, 1090–1104

Adorno, T.W. (1954). How to look at television. *The Quarterly of Film, Radio, and Television*, 8, 213–235

Alderman, N. (2013). The Existential Me. BBC Radio 3. https://www.bbc.co.uk/sounds/play/b03h3p4q

Alexander, J. (2016). Blizzard clears high-ranking teenage Overwatch player in cheating scandal. *Polygon*. https://www.polygon.com/2016/6/21/11996752/blizzard-overwatch-zarya-cheating

Alexander, J. (2018). Overwatch League player fired after sexual misconduct allegations. *Polygon*. https://www.polygon.com/2018/4/8/17213638/overwatch-league-suspends-player-jonathan-dreamkazper-sanchez

Anderson, C.A., Sakamoto, A., Gentile, D.A., Ihori, N., Shibuya, A., Yukawa, S., Naito, M. & Kobayashi, K. (2008). Longitudinal effects of violent video games on aggression in Japan and the United States. *Pediatrics*, 122, e1067–e1072

Baer, R.H. (2005). *Videogames: In the Beginning*. Rolenta Press

Baker, C. (2016). Stewart Brand recalls first 'Spacewar' video game tournament. *Rolling Stone.* https://www.rollingstone.com/culture/culture-news/stewart-brand-recalls-first-spacewar-video-game-tournament-187669/

Bartle, R. (1990). Early MUD History, https://mud.co.uk/richard/mudhist.htm

Bartle, R. (1996). Hearts, clubs, diamonds, spades: Players who suit MUDs. http://mud.co.uk/richard/hcds.htm

Bartle, R.A. (2004). *Designing Virtual Worlds.* New Riders

Bartle, R.A. (2010). From MUDs to MMORPGs: The history of virtual worlds. In: *International Handbook of Internet Research*, J. Hunsinger, L. Klastrup, M.M. Allen eds. Springer, pp. 23–39

BBC. (2017). Teen's death at Chinese internet addiction camp sparks anger. BBC News. https://www.bbc.co.uk/news/world-asia-china-40920488

Beatty, J. (1982). Task-evoked pupillary responses, processing load, and the structure of processing resources. *Psychological Bulletin*, 91, 276–292

Beck, K. (2018). *Overwatch* League is already disciplining players for hateful behaviour. *Mashable.* https://mashable.com/2018/01/22/overwatch-league-homophobic-suspension/

Bell, V., Bishop, D.V.M. & Przybylski, A.K. (2015). The debate over digital technology and young people. *BMJ*, 351, h30964

Bem, D.J. (2011). Feeling the future: experimental evidence for anomalous retroactive influences on cognition and affect. *Journal of Personality and Social Psychology*, 100, 407–425

Billieux, J., Van Rooij, A.J., Heeren, A., Schimmenti, A., Maurage, P., Edman, J., Blaszczynski, A., Khazaal, Y. & Kardefelt-Winther, D. (2017). Behavioural Addiction Open Definition 2.0 – using the Open Science Framework for collaborative and transparent theoretical development. *Addiction*, 112, 1723–1724

Bishop, D. (2011). An open letter to Baroness Susan Greenfield. http://deevybee.blogspot.com/2011/08/open-letter-to-baroness-susan.html

Bishop, D. (2014). Why most scientists don't take Susan Greenfield seriously. http://deevybee.blogspot.com/2014/09/why-most-scientists-dont-take-susan.html

Boyd, A., Golding, J., Macleod, J., Lawlor, D.A., Fraser, A., Henderson, J., Molloy, L., Ness, A., Ring, S. & Davey Smith, G. (2013). Cohort profile: the 'children of the 90s' – the index offspring of the Avon Longitudinal Study of Parents and Children. *International Journal of Epidemiology*, 42, 111–127

Bradbury, R. (1950). The Veldt. *Saturday Evening Post*

Brand, S. (1972). Spacewar: Fanatic life and symbolic death among the computer bums. *Rolling Stone*

Bräutigam, T. (2018). *Overwatch* League exceeds revenue expectations, gets bigger and more expensive. *Esports Observer*. https://esportsobserver.com/overwatch-league-gets-bigger-more-expensive/

Bushman, B.J., Gollwitzer, M. & Cruz, C. (2015). There is broad consensus: Media researchers agree that violent media increase aggression in children, and pediatricians and parents concur. *Psychology of Popular Media Culture*, 4, 200–214

Carpenter, N. (2018). Dallas Fuel player xQc suspended again from the *Overwatch* League, others fined. *Dot Esports*. https://dotesports.com/overwatch/news/overwatch-league-players-banned-fined-21753

Carras, M.C. & Kardefelt-Winther, D. (2018). When addiction symptoms and life problems diverge: A latent class analysis of problematic gaming in a representative multinational sample of European adolescents. *European Child & Adolescent Psychiatry*, 27, 513–525

Cavanagh, S.R. (2017). No, smartphones are not destroying a generation. *Psychology Today*. https://www.psychologytoday.com/gb/blog/once-more-feeling/201708/no-smartphones-are-not-destroying-generation

Chambers, C. (2017). *The Seven Deadly Sins of Psychology: A Manifesto for Reforming the Culture of Scientific Practice*. Princeton University Press

Chambers, C.D. (2013). Registered reports: a new publishing initiative at Cortex. *Cortex*, 49, 609–610

Chambers, C.D., Feredoes, E., Muthukumaraswamy, S.D. & Etchells, P. (2014). Instead of 'playing the game' it is time to change the rules: Registered Reports at AIMS Neuroscience and beyond. *AIMS Neuroscience*, 1, 4–17

Chan, E., Baumann, O., Bellgrove, M.A. & Mattingley, J.B. (2013). Reference frames in allocentric representations are invariant across static and active encoding. *Frontiers in Psychology*, 4, 565

Charlton, J. & Danforth, I. (2007). Distinguishing addiction and high engagement in the context of online game playing. *Computers in Human Behaviour*, 23, 1531–1548

Chiodini, J. (2015). Introducing Low Batteries, a series about mental health and gaming. *Eurogamer*. https://www.eurogamer.net/articles/2015-08-26-video-introducing-low-batteries-a-series-about-mental-health-and-gaming

Chuang, T. (2007). Blizzard makes WoW wish virtual reality. Orange County Register. https://www.ocregister.com/2007/05/22/blizzard-makes-wow-wish-virtual-reality/

Clifford, W.K. (1877). The Ethics of Belief. *Contemporary Review*, 29, 289–309

Cline, E. (2011). *Ready Player One*. Random House

Condon, E.U., Tawney, G.L. & Derr, W.A., Westinghouse Electric Co LLC. (1940). *Machine to play game of nim*. U.S. Patent 2,215,544

Consumer Guide. (1982). *How to Win at* Pac-Man. Penguin.

Cooper, R.M. (2012). Banal cancer. https://robbiemcooper.wordpress.com/2012/10/20/banal-cancer/

Coutrot, A., Silva, R., Manley, E., de Cothi, W., Sami, S., Bohbot, V.D., Wiener, J.M., Hölscher, C., Dalton, R.C., Hornberger, M. & Spiers, H.J. (2018). Global determinants of navigation ability. *Current Biology*, 28, 2861–2866

Cover, R. (2006). Gaming (ad)diction: Discourse, identity, time and play in the production of the gamer addiction myth. *The International Journal of Computer Game Research*, 6, 1–14

Curry, H.A. (2014). From garden biotech to garage biotech: amateur experimental biology in historical perspective. *The British Journal for the History of Science*, 47, 539–565

Dear, W. (1984). *The Dungeon Master: The Disappearance of James Dallas Egbert III*. Houghton Mifflin Harcourt

Deci, E.L. & Ryan, R.M. (1985). *Intrinsic Motivation and Self-determination in Human Behavior*. Plenum

Dixon, D. (2011). Player types and gamification. In: *Proceedings of the CHI 2011 Workshop on Gamification*

Doll, B.B., Hutchison, K.E. & Frank, M.J. (2011). Dopaminergic genes predict individual differences in susceptibility to confirmation bias. *Journal of Neuroscience*, 31, 6188–6198

Ellis, D.A., Davidson, B.I., Shaw, H. & Geyer, K. (2018). Do smartphone usage scales predict behaviour? *PsyArXiv*. doi: 10.31234/osf.io/6fjr7

Elson, M., & Ferguson, C.J. (2014). Twenty-five years of research on violence in digital games and aggression. *European Psychologist*, 19, 33–46

Elson, M., Mohseni, M.R., Breuer, J., Scharkow, M. & Quandt, T. (2014). Press CRTT to measure aggressive behavior: The unstandardized use of the competitive reaction time task in aggression research. *Psychological Assessment*, 26, 419–432

Enhancing exposure therapy for post traumatic stress disorder (PTSD): Virtual reality and imaginal exposure with a cognitive enhancer. (2011). Retrieved from https://clinicaltrials.gov/ct2 (Identification No. NCT01352637)

Epstein, R.A., Patai, E.Z., Julian, J.B. & Spiers, H.J. (2017). The cognitive map in humans: spatial navigation and beyond. *Nature Neuroscience*, 20, 1504–1513

Etchells, P. (2013a). The Next Level. *Story Collider*. https://www .storycollider.org/stories/2016/1/4/pete-etchells-the-next-level

Etchells, P. (2013b). What is the link between violent video games and aggression? *Guardian*. https://www.theguardian.com/science/ head-quarters/2013/sep/19/neuroscience-psychology

Etchells, P. (2015). 'Needs less shock and more substance': Susan Greenfield's tech claims criticised. *Guardian*. https://www .theguardian.com/science/head-quarters/2015/aug/13/susan -greenfield-bmj-editorial-digital-technology-video-games-need -less-shock-and-more-substance

Etchells, P. (2016). Sea Hero Quest: how a new mobile game can help us understand dementia. *Guardian*. https://www.theguardian .com/science/head-quarters/2016/may/19/sea-hero-quest-mobile -game-dementia-alzheimers-disease-spatial-navigation

Etchells, P. & Chambers, C. (2014a). Is there any evidence of a link between violent video games and murder? *Guardian*. https://www.theguardian.com/science/head-quarters/2014/ may/06/violent-video-games-murder-aggression-ann-maguire

Etchells, P. & Chambers, C. (2014b). Susan Greenfield: Why is she reluctant to engage with 'mind change' critics? *Guardian*. https://www.theguardian.com/science/head-quarters/2014/oct/03/susan-greenfield-mind-change-technology-evidence

Etchells, P. & Chambers, C. (2014). Violent video games research: consensus or confusion? *Guardian*. https://www.theguardian.com/science/head-quarters/2014/oct/10/violent-video-games-research-consensus-or-confusion

Etchells, P. & Chambers, C. (2015). No, there is no evidence for a link between video games and Alzheimer's disease. *Guardian*. https://www.theguardian.com/science/head-quarters/2015/may/20/no-there-is-no-evidence-for-a-link-between-video-games-and-alzheimers-disease

Etchells, P.J., Gage, S.H., Rutherford, A.D. & Munafò, M.R. (2016). Prospective investigation of video game use in children and subsequent conduct disorder and depression using data from the Avon longitudinal study of parents and children. *PLOS ONE*, 11, e0147732

Faccio, M. & McConnell, J.J. (2018). *Death by Pokémon GO: The Economic and Human Cost of Using Apps While Driving* (No. w24308). National Bureau of Economic Research

Fanelli, D. (2010). 'Positive' results increase down the hierarchy of the sciences. *PLOS ONE*, 5, e10068

Ferguson, C.J. (2015). Do angry birds make for angry children? A meta-analysis of video game influences on children's and adolescents' aggression, mental health, prosocial behavior, and academic performance. *Perspectives on Psychological Science*, 10, 646–666

Ferguson, C.J. (2018). Children should not be protected from using interactive screens. In: *Video game influences on aggression, cognition and attention*, C.J. Ferguson ed. Springer, pp. 83–91

Ferguson C.J. & Colwell, J. (2017). Understanding why scholars hold different views on the influences of video games on public health. *Journal of Communication*, 67, 305–327

Ferguson, C.J., Coulson, M. & Barnett, J. (2011). A meta-analysis of pathological gaming prevalence and comorbidity with mental health, academic and social problems. *Journal of Psychiatric Research*, 45, 1573–1578

Ferguson, C.J., San Miguel, C., Garza, A. & Jerabeck, J.M. (2012). A longitudinal test of video game violence influences on dating and aggression: A 3-year longitudinal study of adolescents. *Journal of Psychiatric Research*, 46, 141–146

Ferranti. (1951). *Faster Than Thought: The Ferranti Nimrod Digital Computer.* Ferranti Ltd

Fox, J. A. & DeLateur, M. J. (2013). Mass shootings in America. *Homicide Studies*, 18, 125–145

Friedman, R. & James, J.W. (2008). The myth of the stages of dying, death and grief. *Skeptic*, 14: 37–42

Gebremariam, M.K., Bergh, I.H., Andersen, L.F., Ommundsen, Y., Totland, T.H., Bjelland, M., Grydeland, M. & Lien, N. (2013). Are screen-based sedentary behaviors longitudinally associated with dietary behaviors and leisure-time physical activity in the transition into adolescence? *International Journal of Behavioral Nutrition and Physical Activity*, 10, 9

George, M.J. & Odgers, C.L. (2015). Seven fears and the science of how mobile technologies may be influencing adolescents in the digital age. *Perspectives on Psychological Science*, 10, 832–851

Gibson, E. (2013). GamesMaster: The inside story. *Eurogamer.* https://www.eurogamer.net/articles/2013-06-04-gamesmaster -the-inside-story

Goldacre, B. (2011a). Serious claims belong in a serious scientific paper. *Guardian.* https://www.theguardian.com/ commentisfree/2011/oct/21/bad-science-publishing-claims

Goldacre, B. (2011b). Why won't Professor Susan Greenfield publish this theory in a scientific journal? *Guardian.* https://www .badscience.net/2011/11/why-wont-professor-greenfield-publish -this-theory-in-a-scientific-journal/

Goldsmith, T.T. & Mann, E.R., Du Mont Allen B Lab Inc. (1948). *Cathode-ray tube amusement device.* U.S. Patent 2,455,992

Gonzalez, R. (2018a). It's time for a serious talk about the science of tech addiction. *Wired.* https://www.wired.com/story/its -time-for-a-serious-talk-about-the-science-of-tech-addiction/

Gonzalez, R. (2018b). Why Apple can't tackle digital wellness in a vacuum. *Wired*. https://www.wired.com/story/apple-screen-time/

Good, O. (2013). Sandy Hook killer's video gaming obsession: Not what you'd expect. *Kotaku*. https://kotaku.com/sandy-hook-killers-video-gaming-obsession-not-what-yo-1471421158

Goode, E. & Ben-Yehuda, N. (1994). *Moral Panics: The Social Construction of Deviance*. Wiley-Blackwell

Goodeve, P. (Undated). The NIMROD machine – some facts and figures. https://www.goodeveca.net/nimrod/facts.html

Granic, I., Lobel, A. & Engels, R. (2014). The benefits of playing video games. *American Psychologist*, 69, 66–78

Grayson, N. (2018). No *Overwatch* League team signed the game's most notable female pro to their roster. *Kotaku*. https://compete.kotaku.com/no-overwatch-league-team-signed-the-games-most-notable-1821968992

Green, H. (2018). No girls allowed: Dissecting the gender divide in *Overwatch* League. *Paste*. https://www.pastemagazine.com/articles/2018/01/no-girls-allowed-dissecting-the-gender-imbalance-i.html

Greenfield, S. (2014). *Mind Change*. Random House

Griffiths, M. (1997). Video games and clinical practice: issues, uses and treatments. *British Journal of Clinical Psychology*, 36, 639–641

Griffiths, M.D., Van Rooij, A.J., Kardefelt-Winther, D., Starcevic, V., Király, O., Pallesen, S., Müller, K., Dreier, M., Carras, M., Prause, N. & King, D.L. (2016). Working towards an international consensus on criteria for assessing internet gaming disorder: a critical commentary on Petry et al. (2014). *Addiction*, 111, 167–175

Hall, R.C., Day, T. & Hall, R.C. (2011). A plea for caution: Violent video games, the Supreme Court, and the role of science. *Mayo Clinic Proceedings*, 86, No. 4, 315–321

Hamari, J. & Sjöblom, M. (2017). What is Esports and why do people watch it? *Internet research*, 27, 211–232

Hamari, J. & Tuunanen, J. (2014). Player types: A meta-synthesis. *Transactions of the Digital Games Research Association*, 1, 3

Handrahan, M. (2016). VR devs call for restraint on horror games and jump scares. *Gamesindustry.biz*. https://www.gamesindustry.biz/

articles/2016-03-14-vr-developers-advise-caution-on-horror
-games-and-jump-scares

Harris, S. (2017). How phones make us dim: Brain scientist says
excessive use of high-tech appliances stops us remembering
details. *Daily Mail*. https://www.dailymail.co.uk/sciencetech/
article-4867190/Smart-phones-making-dim-say-scientists.html

Herz, J.C. (2002). The bandwidth capital of the world. *Wired*.
https://www.wired.com/2002/08/korea/

Hess, E.H. & Polt, J.M. (1963). Pupil size in relation to mental activity
during simple problem solving. *Science*, 140, 1190–1192

Hoffman, H.G., Patterson, D.R., Seibel, E., Soltani, M., Jewett-Leahy,
L. & Sharar, S.R. (2008). Virtual reality pain control during burn
wound debridement in the hydrotank. *The Clinical Journal of
Pain*, 24, 299–304

Horkheimer, M., Adorno, T.W. & Cumming, J. (1944). *Dialectic of
Enlightenment*. Continuum

Hulatt, O. (2018). Against popular culture. *Aeon*. https://aeon.co/essays/
against-guilty-pleasures-adorno-on-the-crimes-of-pop-culture

International Software Federation of Europe (2017). GameTrack
Digest: Quarter 3. https://www.isfe.eu/sites/isfe.eu/files/
gametrack_european_summary_data_2017_q3.pdf

Ives, M. (2017). Electroshock therapy for internet addicts? China vows
to end it. *New York Times*. https://www.nytimes.com/
2017/01/13/world/asia/china-internet-addiction-electroshock
-therapy.html

Ivory, J.D. (2015). A brief history of video games. In: *The Video Game
Debate*, R. Kowert, T. Quandt eds. Routledge, pp. 1–21

Ivory, J.D., Markey, P.M., Elson, M., Colwell, J., Ferguson, C.J.,
Griffiths, M.D., Savage, J. & Williams, K.D. (2015). Manufacturing
consensus in a diverse field of scholarly opinions: A comment
on Bushman, Gollwitzer, and Cruz (2015). *Psychology of Popular
Media Culture*, 4, 222–229

Iyer, A. (2017). How Firewatch's UI enhances immersion. *Medium*.
https://medium.com/the-cube/how-firewatchs-ui-enhances
-immersion-18feddbc7857

Jenkins, H. (2012). *Textual Poachers: Television Fans and Participatory
Culture*. Routledge

Jennett, C., Cox, A.L., Cairns, P., Dhoparee, S., Epps, A., Tijs, T. & Walton, A. (2008). Measuring and defining the experience of immersion in games. *International Journal of Human-Computer Studies*, 66, 641–661

John, L.K., Loewenstein, G. & Prelec, D. (2012). Measuring the prevalence of questionable research practices with incentives for truth telling. *Psychological Science*, 23, 524–532

Jozuka, E. (2015). This *Minecraft* world teaches kids the basics of biochemistry. *Motherboard*. https://motherboard.vice.com/en_us/article/d7ygwz/this-minecraft-world-teaches-kids-the-basics-of-biochemistry

Kahneman, D. (1973). *Attention and Effort*. Prentice-Hall

Kaplan, J. (2017). Developer update – play nice, play fair. https://youtu.be/rnfzzz8pIBE

Kardefelt-Winther, D. (2017). How does the time children spend using digital technology impact their mental well-being, social relationships and physical activity? (Vol. Innocenti Discussion Paper 2017-02). Florence: UNICEF Office of Research

Keogh, B. (2014). Across worlds and bodies: Criticism in the age of video games. *Journal of Games Criticism*, 1, 1–26

Kim, W.K., Liu, X., Sandner, J., Pasmantier, M., Andrews, J., Rowland, L.P. & Mitsumoto, H. (2009). Study of 962 patients indicates progressive muscular atrophy is a form of ALS. *Neurology*, 73, 1686–1692

Kleinman, Z. (2013). Screen use is bad for brain development, scientist claims. BBC News. https://www.bbc.co.uk/news/technology-22283452

Kneer, J., Elson, M. & Knapp, F. (2016). Fight fire with rainbows: The effects of displayed violence, difficulty, and performance in digital games on affect, aggression, and physiological arousal. *Computers in Human Behavior*, 54, 142–148

Kowert, R. (2016). *A Parent's Guide to Video Games: The Essential Guide to Understanding How Video Games Impact Your Child's Physical, Social, and Psychological Well-being*. CreateSpace

Kübler-Ross, E. (1969). *On Death and Dying*. Routledge

Kuss, D.J., Griffiths, M.D. & Pontes, H.M. (2017). Chaos and confusion in *DSM-5* diagnosis of internet gaming disorder: Issues, concerns, and recommendations for clarity in the field. *Journal of Behavioral Addictions*, 6, 103–109

Lee, C., Kim, H. & Hong, A. (2017). Ex-post evaluation of illegalizing juvenile online game after midnight: A case of shutdown policy in South Korea. *Telematics and Informatics*, 34, 1597–1606

Lee, D. & Schoenstedt, L.J. (2011). Comparison of Esports and traditional sports consumption motives. *ICHPER-SD Journal of Research*, 6, 39–44

Lewis, H. (2012). Why are we still so bad at talking about video games? *New Statesman*. https://www.newstatesman.com/culture/2012/11/why-are-we-still-so-bad-talking-about-video-games

Lieberman, J.D., Solomon, S., Greenberg, J. & McGregor, H.A. (1999). A hot new way to measure aggression: Hot sauce allocation. *Aggressive Behavior: Official Journal of the International Society for Research on Aggression*, 25, 331–348

Lillo, P. & Hodges, J.R. (2010). Cognition and behaviour in motor neurone disease. *Current Opinion in Neurology*, 23, 638–642

Lithfous, S., Dufour, A. & Després, O. (2013). Spatial navigation in normal aging and the prodromal stage of Alzheimer's disease: insights from imaging and behavioral studies. *Ageing Research Reviews*, 12, 201–213

Loguidice, B. (2015). The genesis of PC gaming: the PDP-1 and Spacewar! *PC Gamer*. https://www.pcgamer.com/uk/the-genesis-of-pc-gaming-the-pdp-1-and-spacewar/

Lowood, H. (2011). Memento mundi: Are virtual worlds history? In: *Digital Media: Technological and Social Challenges of the Interactive World*, M.A. Winget, W. Asprey eds. Scarecrow Press, pp. 3–25

MacDonald, K. (2018). Belgium is right to class video game loot boxes as child gambling. *Guardian*. https://www.theguardian.com/games/2018/apr/26/belgium-is-right-to-legislate-against-video-game-loot-boxes

Madary, M. & Metzinger, T.K. (2016). Real virtuality: a code of ethical conduct. Recommendations for good scientific practice and the consumers of VR-technology. *Frontiers in Robotics and AI*, 3, 3

Madigan, J. (2013). Why you don't burn out on *Candy Crush Saga*. http://www.psychologyofgames.com/2013/10/why-you-dont-burn-out-on-candy-crush-saga/

Marcus, A. (2011). Dutch university investigating psych researcher Stapel for data fraud. *Retraction Watch*. http://retractionwatch.com/2011/09/07/dutch-university-investigating-psych-researcher-stapel-for-data-fraud/

Marcus, A. (2012). Going Dutch: Stapel inquiry eyes credulous colleagues, institution, prompts national soul search. *Retraction Watch*. http://retractionwatch.com/2012/11/29/going-dutch-stapel-inquiry-eyes-credulous-colleagues-institution-prompts-national-soul-search/

Markey, P.M. (2015). Finding the middle ground in violent video game research: Lessons from Ferguson (2015). *Perspectives on Psychological Science*, 10, 667–670

Markey, P.M. & Ferguson, C.J. (2017a). Internet gaming addiction: Disorder or moral panic. *American Journal of Psychiatry*, 174, 195–6

Markey, P.M. & Ferguson, C.J. (2017b). *Moral Combat: Why the War on Violent Video Games is Wrong*. BenBella Books

Markey, P.M., Markey, C.N. & French, J.E. (2015). Violent video games and real-world violence: Rhetoric versus data. *Psychology of Popular Media Culture*, 4, 277–295

Marks, T. (2017). Overwatch league reveals minimum player salaries and benefits. *IGN*. https://uk.ign.com/articles/2017/07/27/overwatch-league-reveals-minimum-player-salaries-and-benefits

Marris, P. (1986). *Loss and Change*. Routledge

McDermott, C.J. & Shaw, P.J. (2008). Diagnosis and management of motor neurone disease. *BMJ*, 336, 658–662

McKenna, K. & Bargh, J. (2000). Plan 9 from cyberspace: the implications of the internet for personality and social psychology. *Personality and Social Psychology Review*, 4, 57–75

McKenna, K., Green, A. & Gleason, M. (2002). Relationship formation on the internet: what's the big attraction? *Journal of Social Issues*, 58, 9–31

McLeod, J.E. & Clarke, D.M. (2007). A review of psychosocial aspects of motor neurone disease. *Journal of the Neurological Sciences*, 258, 4–10

Mejia Uribe, F. (2018). Believing without evidence is always morally wrong. *Aeon*. https://aeon.co/ideas/believing-without-evidence-is-always-morally-wrong

Messner, S. (2016). Meet WoW's biggest hippie, a panda who reached max level by picking thousands of flowers. *PC Gamer*. https://www.pcgamer.com/uk/meet-wows-biggest-hippie-a-panda-who-reached-max-level-by-picking-thousands-of-flowers/

Milgram, S. (1963). Behavioral study of obedience. *Journal of Abnormal and Social Psychology*, 67, 371–378

Mills, K.L. (2016). Possible effects of internet use on cognitive development in adolescence. *Media and Communication*, 4, 4–12

Munafò, M.R., Nosek, B.A., Bishop, D.V., Button, K.S., Chambers, C.D., Du Sert, N.P., Simonsohn, U., Wagenmakers, E.J., Ware, J.J. & Ioannidis, J.P. (2017). A manifesto for reproducible science. *Nature Human Behaviour*, 1, 0021

National Youth Policy Institute. (2014). *Korea Children and Youth Panel Survey V: An Analysis on Daily Activities of the Children and the Youth*

Neuman, S.B. (1988). The displacement effect: Assessing the relation between television viewing and reading performance. *Reading Research Quarterly*, 23, 414–440

Neumann, M.M., Merchant, G. & Burnett, C., (2018). Young children and tablets: the views of parents and teachers. *Early Child Development and Care*, doi: 10.1080/03004430.2018.1550083

Neuroskeptic. (2015). How Diederik Stapel became a science fraud. http://blogs.discovermagazine.com/neuroskeptic/2015/01/20/how-diederik-stapel-became-fraud/

Newman, H. (2016). *Overwatch*: 9 Things you didn't know about director Jeff Kaplan. *Rolling Stone*. https://www.rollingstone.com/culture/culture-features/overwatch-9-things-you-didnt-know-about-director-jeff-kaplan-107522/

Newman, J. (2008). *Playing with Videogames*. Routledge

Newman, J. (2012). *Best Before: Videogames, Supersession and Obsolescence*. Routledge

Newman, J. (2016a). Mazes, monsters and multicursality. Mastering *Pac-Man* 1980–2016. *Cogent Arts & Humanities*, 3, 1190439

Newman, J. (2016b). Stampylongnose and the rise of the celebrity videogame player. *Celebrity Studies*, 7, 285–288

Newman, J. (2017). Glitching, codemining and procedural level creation in *Super Mario Bros*. In: M. Swalwell, A. Ndalianis,

H. Stuckey eds. *Fans and Videogames: Histories, Fandom, Archives*. Routledge, pp. 146–162

Newman, J. (2018). The Game Inspector: a case study in gameplay preservation. *Kinephanos: Journal of Media Studies and Popular Culture* (August), 120–148

Nickerson, R.S. (1998). Confirmation bias: a ubiquitous phenomenon in many guises. *Review of General Psychology*, 2, 175–220

Nielsen, R.K.L. & Kardefelt-Winther, D. (2018). Helping parents make sense of video game addiction. In: *Video game influences on aggression, cognition and attention*, C.J. Ferguson ed. Springer, pp. 59–69

Nintendo. (2018). *The Legend of Zelda: Breath of the Wild – Creating a Champion*. Dark Horse

Odgers, C.L. (2018). Smartphones are bad for some adolescents, not all. *Nature*, 554, 432–434

Open Science Collaboration. (2015). Estimating the reproducibility of psychological science. *Science*, 349, 943–951

Orben, A. (2017). Social media and suicide: A critical appraisal. *Medium*. https://medium.com/@OrbenAmy/social-media-and -suicide-a-critical-appraisal-f95e0bbd4660

Orben, A., Etchells, P. & Przybylski, A. (2018). Three problems with the debate around screen time. *Guardian*. https://www .theguardian.com/science/head-quarters/2018/aug/09/three -problems-with-the-debate-around-screen-time

Oskarsson, B., Horton, D.K. & Mitsumoto, H. (2015). Potential environmental factors in amyotrophic lateral sclerosis. *Neurologic Clinics*, 33, 877–888

Palus, S. (2015). Diederik Stapel now has 58 retractions. *Retraction Watch*. http://retractionwatch.com/2015/12/08/diederik-stapel -now-has-58-retractions/

Parkes, A., Sweeting, H., Wight, D. & Henderson, M. (2013). Do television and electronic games predict children's psychosocial adjustment? Longitudinal research using the UK Millennium Cohort Study. *Archives of Disease in Childhood*, 98, 341–348

Parkes, C.M. (2013). Elisabeth Kübler-Ross, on death and dying: A reappraisal. *Mortality*, 18, 94–97

Parkin, S. (2013). Shooters: How Video games fund arms manufacturers. *Eurogamer*. https://www.eurogamer.net/articles/2013-02-01-shooters-how-video-games-fund-arms-manufacturers

Parkin, S. (2015). *Death by Video Game: Tales of Obsession from the Virtual Frontline*. Serpent's Tail

Peel, N. (2014). Citizen Science: 'you don't need to be qualified to do this'. *Cancer Research UK blog*. https://scienceblog.cancerresearchuk.org/2014/10/03/citizen-science-you-dont-need-to-be-qualified-to-do-this/

Persky, S. & Blascovich, J. (2008). Immersive virtual video game play and presence: Influences on aggressive feelings and behavior. *Presence: Teleoperators and Virtual Environments*, 17, 57–72

Petter, O. (2018). Social media is giving children mentality of three-year-olds, warns researcher. *Independent*. https://www.independent.co.uk/life-style/social-media-dangers-children-mentality-three-years-old-susan-greenfield-a8479271.html

Players Guide To Electronic Science Fiction Games. (1982). *Electronic Games*, 1, 35–45

Pratchett, T. (1989). *Guards! Guards!* Transworld

Price, L. (2016). Playing games as addictive as heroin. *The Sun*. https://www.thesun.co.uk/archives/news/962643/playing-games-as-addictive-as-heroin/

Przybylski, A.K. (2014a). Who believes electronic games cause real world aggression? *Cyberpsychology, Behavior, and Social Networking*, 17, 228–234

Przybylski, A.K. (2014b). Electronic gaming and psychosocial adjustment. *Pediatrics*, 134, 716–722

Przybylski, A.K. (2019). Digital screen time and pediatric sleep: Evidence from a preregistered cohort study. *The Journal of Pediatrics*, 205, 218–223

Przybylski, A.K. & Weinstein, N. (2016). How we see electronic games. *PeerJ*, 4, e1931

Przybylski, A.K. & Weinstein, N. (2017a). A large-scale test of the goldilocks hypothesis: quantifying the relations between digital-screen use and the mental well-being of adolescents. *Psychological Science*, 28, 204–215

Przybylski, A.K. & Weinstein, N. (2017b). Digital screen time limits and young children's psychological well-being: Evidence from a population-based study. *Child Development*, doi: 10.1111/cdev.13007

Przybylski, A.K., Rigby, C.S. & Ryan, R.M. (2010). A motivational model of video game engagement. *Review of General Psychology*, 14, 154–166

Przybylski, A.K., Ryan, R.M. & Rigby, C.S. (2009). The motivating role of violence in video games. *Personality and Social Psychology Bulletin*, 35, 243–259

Purchese, R. (2013). 100 million people played *Call of Duty* since COD4. *Eurogamer*. https://www.eurogamer.net/articles/2013-08-13-100-million-people-played-call-of-duty-since-cod4

Quandt, T. (2017). Stepping back to advance: Why IGD needs an intensified debate instead of a consensus. *Journal of Behavioral Addictions*, 6, 121–123

Quandt, T., van Looy, J., Vogelgesang, J., Elson, M., Ivory, J., Mäyrä, F. & Consalvo, M. (2015). Digital games research: A survey study on an emerging field and its prevalent debates. *Journal of Communication*, 65, 975–996

Quoidbach, J. & Dunn, E. (2013). Give it up: A strategy for combating hedonic adaptation. *Social Psychological and Personality Science*, 4, 563–568

Rayson, S. (2017). The most shared Facebook content 2017. The top viral posts, videos and articles. https://buzzsumo.com/blog/the-most-shared-facebook-content-posts-videos/

Rigby, C.S. & Ryan, R.M. (2007). The Player Experience of Need Satisfaction (PENS) model. http://immersyve.com/white-paper-the-player-experience-of-need-satisfaction-pens-2007/

Riggs, B. (2017). The story of *D&D* part one: the birth, death and resurrection of *Dungeons & Dragons*. https://geekandsundry.com/the-story-of-dd-part-one-the-birth-death-and-resurrection-of-dungeons-dragons/

Ritchie, S.J., Wiseman, R. & French, C.C. (2012). Failing the future: Three unsuccessful attempts to replicate Bem's 'Retroactive Facilitation of Recall' Effect. *PLOS ONE*, 7, e33423

Rizzo, A., Difede, J., Rothbaum, B.O., Reger, G., Spitalnick, J., Cukor, J.

& McLay, R. (2010). Development and early evaluation of the Virtual Iraq/Afghanistan exposure therapy system for combat-related PTSD. *Annals of the New York Academy of Sciences*, 1208, 114–125

Rizzo, A.S. & Shilling, R. (2017). Clinical Virtual Reality tools to advance the prevention, assessment, and treatment of PTSD. *European Journal of Psychotraumatology*, 8, 1414560

Robbins, M.J. (2012). The elusive hypothesis of Baroness Greenfield. *Guardian*. https://www.theguardian.com/science/the-lay -scientist/2012/feb/27/1

Robbins, M.J. (2014). Mind Change: Susan Greenfield has a big idea, but what is it? *The Guardian*. https://www.theguardian.com/ science/the-lay-scientist/2014/oct/03/mind-change-susan -greenfield-has-a-big-idea-but-what-is-it

Ross, D.R., Finestone, D.H. & Lavin, G.K. (1982). *Space Invaders* obsession. *JAMA*, 248, 1177–1177

Rumpf, H.J., et al. (2018). Including gaming disorder in the ICD-11: The need to do so from a clinical and public health perspective: Commentary on: A weak scientific basis for gaming disorder: Let us err on the side of caution (van Rooij et al., 2018). *Journal of Behavioral Addictions*, 7, 556–561

Rutherford, A. (2016). It came from beyond the silver screen! Aliens in the movies. In: *Aliens: Science Asks: Is There Anyone Out There?* J. Al-Khalili ed. Profile Books

Ryan, R.M., Rigby, C.S. & Przybylski, A. (2006). The motivational pull of video games: A self-determination theory approach. *Motivation and Emotion*, 30, 344–360

Schink, J.C. (1991). Nintendo enuresis. *American Journal of Diseases of Children*, 145, 1094

Serino, S., Cipresso, P., Morganti, F. & Riva, G. (2014). The role of egocentric and allocentric abilities in Alzheimer's disease: A systematic review. *Ageing Research Reviews*, 16, 32–44

Simons, I. & Newman, J. (2018). *A History of Videogames*. Carlton Books Ltd

Smith, A. (2014a). The priesthood at play: Computer games in the 1950s. https://videogamehistorian.wordpress.com/2014/01/22/ the-priesthood-at-play-computer-games-in-the-1950s/

Smith, A. (2014b). Tennis anyone? https://videogamehistorian. wordpress.com/2014/01/28/tennis-anyone/

Smith, A. (2014c). One, two, three, four, I declare a space war. https://videogamehistorian.wordpress.com/2014/08/07/one -two-three-four-i-declare-a-space-war/

Smith, D. (2014). This is what *Candy Crush Saga* does to your brain. *Guardian*. https://www.theguardian.com/science/blog/2014/ apr/01/candy-crush-saga-app-brain

Smittenaar, P., et al. (2018). Harnessing citizen science through mobile phone technology to screen for immunohistochemical biomarkers in bladder cancer. *British Journal of Cancer*, 119, 220–229

Soechting, J.F. & Flanders, M. (1992). Moving in three-dimensional space: Frames of reference, vectors, and coordinate systems. *Annual Review of Neuroscience*, 15, 167–191

Solon, O. (2018). Former Facebook and Google workers launch campaign to fight tech addiction. *Guardian*. https://www .theguardian.com/technology/2018/feb/05/tech-addiction -former-facebook-google-employees-campaign

Stanton, R. (2015). *A Brief History of Video Games: From Atari to Virtual Reality*. Robinson

Stapel, D., translated by N.J. Brown. (2014). Faking science: A true story of academic fraud. https://errorstatistics.files.wordpress .com/2014/12/fakingscience-20141214.pdf

Stone, R.J. (2005). Serious gaming – virtual reality's saviour. In: *Proceedings of Virtual Systems and MultiMedia annual conference*, 773–786

Strasburger, V.C., Donnerstein, E. & Bushman, B.J. (2014). Why is it so hard to believe that media influence children and adolescents? *Pediatrics*, 133, 571–573

Stroebe, M., Schut, H. & Boerner, K. (2017). Cautioning health-care professionals: Bereaved persons are misguided through the stages of grief. *OMEGA – Journal of Death and Dying*, 74, 455–473

Stuart, K. (2017). Why diversity matters in the modern video games industry. *Guardian*. https://www.theguardian .com/technology/2017/jul/18/diversity-video-games-industry -playstation-xbox

Stuart, K. (2018). Atari founder Nolan Bushnell loses award after sexism outcry. *Guardian*. https://www.theguardian.com/games/2018/feb/01/nolan-bushnell-atari-pioneer-award-game-developers-conference-san-francisco

Swain, F. (2011). Susan Greenfield: Loving online is changing our brains. *New Scientist*. https://www.newscientist.com/article/mg21128236-400-susan-greenfield-living-online-is-changing-our-brains/

Tamborini, R. & Bowman, N.D. (2010). Presence in video games. *Immersed in media: Telepresence in everyday life*, C. Campanella Bracken, P.D. Skalski eds. Routledge, pp. 87–109

Tamborini, R., Eastin, M.S., Skalski, P. & Lachlan, K. (2004). Violent virtual video games and hostile thoughts. *Journal of Broadcasting and Electronic Media*, 48, 335–357

Tapjoy. (2016). The top personas of free-to-play mobile gamers – and how to treat them. *Medium*. https://medium.com/tapjoy/the-top-personas-of-free-to-play-mobile-gamers-and-how-to-treat-them-f36cb443e8c4

Taylor, A. (2015). The Turkish government's inexplicable call to ban *Minecraft*. *Washington Post*. https://www.washingtonpost.com/news/worldviews/wp/2015/03/10/the-turkish-governments-inexplicable-call-to-ban-minecraft

Taylor, S.P. (1967). Aggressive behavior and physiological arousal as a function of provocation and the tendency to inhibit aggression. *Journal of Personality*, 35, 297–310

Thier, D. (2018). *Overwatch* League's biggest problem is that it's all about *Overwatch*. *Forbes*. https://www.forbes.com/sites/davidthier/2018/02/15/overwatch-leagues-biggest-problem-is-that-its-all-about-overwatch/

Thompson, K.M. & Haninger, K. (2001). Violence in E-rated video games. *JAMA*, 286, 591–599

Troscianko, T., Meese, T.S. & Hinde, S. (2012). Perception while watching movies: Effects of physical screen size and scene type. *i-Perception*, 3, 414–425

Turing, A. (1948). Intelligent machinery. http://www.alanturing.net/turing_archive/archive/l/l32/l32.php

Turk, V. (2015). Inside Britain's new National Videogame Arcade. *Motherboard*. https://motherboard.vice.com/en_us/article/nzeynw/inside-britains-new-national-videogame-arcade

Twenge, J.M. (2017a). Have smartphones destroyed a generation? *The Atlantic*. https://www.theatlantic.com/magazine/archive/2017/09/has-the-smartphone-destroyed-a-generation/534198/

Twenge, J.M. (2017b). With teen mental health deteriorating over five years, there's a likely culprit. *The Conversation*. https://theconversation.com/with-teen-mental-health-deteriorating-over-five-years-theres-a-likely-culprit-86996

Twenge, J.M., Joiner, T.E., Rogers, M.L. & Martin, G.N., (2017). Increases in depressive symptoms, suicide-related outcomes, and suicide rates among US adolescents after 2010 and links to increased new media screen time. *Clinical Psychological Science*, 6, 3–17

Uston, K. (1982). *Mastering* Pac-Man. Signet

Van Rooij, A.J. & Kardefelt-Winther, D. (2017). Lost in the chaos: Flawed literature should not generate new disorders. *Journal of Behavioral Addictions*, 6, 128–132

Van Rooij, A.J., et al. (2018). A weak scientific basis for gaming disorder: Let us err on the side of caution. *Journal of Behavioral Addictions*, 7, 1–9

Volcic, R. & Kappers, A.M. (2008). Allocentric and egocentric reference frames in the processing of three-dimensional haptic space. *Experimental Brain Research*, 188, 199–213

Wagner, M.G. (2006). On the scientific relevance of eSports. In: *International conference on internet computing*, 437–442

Wason, P.C. (1960). On the failure to eliminate hypotheses in a conceptual task. *Quarterly Journal of Experimental Psychology*, 12, 129–40

Weinstein, N. & Przybylski, A.K. (2018). The impacts of motivational framing of technology restrictions on adolescent concealment: Evidence from a preregistered experimental study. *Computers in Human Behavior*, 90, 170–180

Weinstein, N., Przybylski, A.K. & Murayama, K. (2017). A prospective study of the motivational and health dynamics of Internet Gaming Disorder. *PeerJ*, 5, e3838

Wertham, F. (1954). *Seduction of the Innocent*. Rinehart & Company

West, G.L., Drisdelle, B.L., Konishi, K., Jackson, J., Jolicoeur, P. & Bohbot, V.D. (2015). Habitual action video game playing is associated with caudate nucleus-dependent navigational strategies. *Proceedings of the Royal Society B: Biological Sciences*, 282, 20142952

White, V. & Barbour, M. (2018). *Fortnite* game addiction led man into cocaine abuse and verge of losing job, family and home. *Mirror*. https://www.mirror.co.uk/news/uk-news/fortnite-game-addiction -led-man-12723697

Whitelocks, S. (2011). Computer games leave children with 'dementia', warns top neurologist. *Daily Mail*. https://www.dailymail.co.uk/ health/article-2049040/Computer-games-leave-children -dementia-warns-neurologist.html

Wilkinson, L. (2010). Reading, writing, and what Plato really thought. https://senseandreference.wordpress.com/2010/10/27/reading -writing-and-what-plato-really-thought/

Witkin, R.W. (2003). *Adorno on Popular Culture*. Routledge

Yarkoni, T. (2010). The capricious nature of p < .05, or why data peeking is evil. https://www.talyarkoni.org/blog/2010/05/06/ the-capricious-nature-of-p-05-or-why-data-peeking-is-evil/

Yee, N. (2006). Motivations for play in online games. *Cyberpsychology & Behavior*, 9, 772–775

Yong, E. (2012). Replication studies: Bad copy. *Nature*, 485, 298–300

Zajonc, R.B. (1968). Attitudinal effects of mere exposure. *Journal of Personality and Social Psychology*, 9, 1–27

Zeiler, M.D. (1968). Fixed and variable schedules of response-independent reinforcement. *Journal of the Experimental Analysis of Behavior*, 11, 405–414

Zendle, D. & Cairns, P. (2018). Video game loot boxes are linked to problem gambling: Results of a large-scale survey. *PLOS ONE*, 13, e0206767

Zendle, D., McCall, C., Barnett, H. & Cairns, P. (2018). Paying for loot boxes is linked to problem gambling, regardless of specific features like cash-out and pay-to-win: A preregistered investigation. *PsyArXiv*. doi: 10.31234/osf.io/6e74k

ABOUT THE AUTHOR

Dr Pete Etchells is a psychologist and science writer. He is a reader in psychology and science communication at Bath Spa University, and for four years he was the *Guardian*'s science blog network coordinator. He lives in Bristol, and occasionally Hyrule. This is his first book.